This book adds a strong dose of political ecology to conversations about global environmental governance. It provides an engaging collection of wide-ranging essays about the relationships among power, scale, and competing forms of knowledge, and features chapters from several of Europe's and America's most creative critical thinkers about environmental politics.

Ken Conca, Professor of Government and Politics, University of Maryland, USA

This book reveals how power circulates through some of our most promising efforts at environmental protection. By revealing the linkages between knowledge, space and place, it demonstrates that environmental governance is not simply a matter of organizing collective life to address specific problems but often involves reproducing the very obstacles we must overcome. Theoretically sophisticated, imaginatively conceived and provocative in its conclusions, this book offers a virtual roadmap for the critical school of environmental studies.

Paul Wapner, American University, USA

Environmental Governance

This edited collection makes a highly significant critical contribution to the field of environmental politics. It argues that the international-level, institutionalist approach to global environmental politics has run its course, employed solely by powerful actors in order to orchestrate and manipulate local communities within a continuing hegemonic system.

The outstanding international line-up of contributors to this volume explores the real advances that are being made in the areas where the local and global intersect, and how power fits into the equation. They explore the relationship between governance, power, and knowledge, using power as the main analytical tool.

The contributors adopt a variety of approaches and perspectives—some starting from the local level and shifting upward to the global, and some using a global perspective that narrows down to the local. Some chapters explore specific case studies and others employ a more conceptual framework—but all of them bring a new dimension to the relationship between power and knowledge in environmental governance. Power here is explored in all its guises—from relational to structural power.

An important and timely exploration of a topic at the forefront of global debate, *Environmental Governance* is essential reading for all students of global environmental politics, international political economy and international relations.

Gabriela Kütting is Associate Professor of Political Science and Global Affairs at Rutgers, The State University of New Jersey in Newark. Her research interests lie in the field of global environmental politics and she is the author of *Environment, Society and International Relations* (Routledge, 2000) and *Globalization and Environment: Greening Global Political Economy* (SUNY Press, 2004).

Ronnie D. Lipschutz is Professor of Politics and Co-Director of the Center for Global, International and Regional Studies at the University of California, Santa Cruz. His most recent books are *The Constitution of Imperium* (Paradigm, 2008) and *Globalization, Governmentality and Global Politics: Regulation for the Rest of Us?* (Routledge, 2005).

Environmental Governance

Power and knowledge in a local–global world

Edited by
Gabriela Kütting and Ronnie D. Lipschutz

LONDON AND NEW YORK

First published 2009
by Routledge
2 Park Square, Milton Park, Abingdon, Oxon OX14 4RN

Simultaneously published in the USA and Canada
by Routledge
270 Madison Avenue, New York, NY 10016

Routledge is an imprint of the Taylor & Francis Group, an informa business

© 2009 Editorial selection and matter Gabriela Kütting and Ronnie
Lipschutz; individual chapters the contributors

Typeset in Times New Roman by
Taylor & Francis Books
Printed and bound in Great Britain by
TJ International Ltd, Padstow, Cornwall

British Library Cataloguing in Publication Data
A catalogue record for this book is available from the British Library

Library of Congress Cataloging in Publication Data
   Environmental governance : power and knowledge in a local-global
world / edited by Gabriela Kütting & Ronnie D. Lipschutz.
       p. cm.
   1. Environmental policy. 2. Environmental policy–International
cooperation. 3. Environmental education. I. Kütting, Gabriela, 1967- II.
Lipschutz, Ronnie D.
   HC79.E5E57754 2009
333.7–dc22
2008041679

ISBN: 978-0-415-77712-4 (hbk)
ISBN: 978-0-415-77713-1 (pbk)
ISBN: 978-0-203-88010-4 (ebk)

Contents

Illustrations

Figures

Tables

Contributors

Ralf Brand, Lecturer, Manchester Architecture Research Centre, University of Manchester.

Ulrich Brand, Professor, Department of Political Science, University of Vienna.

Adam Fagan, Senior Lecturer, Department of Political Science, Queen Mary College, University of London.

Tim Forsyth, Reader, Institute of Development Studies, London School of Economics.

Michael Goldman, Professor, Department of Sociology and Institute for Global Studies, University of Minnesota.

Christoph Görg, Professor of Environmental Governance, University of Kassel and Head of the Unit of Environmental Policy, UFZ–Helmholtz Centre for Environmental Research, Leipzig.

Peter Jacques, Assistant Professor, Department of Political Science, University of Central Florida.

Andrew Karvonen, Walsingham Capper Research Assistant, Manchester Architecture Research Centre, University of Manchester.

Gabriela Kütting, Associate Professor, Department of Political Science and Division of Global Affairs, Rutgers the State University of New Jersey, Newark.

Ronnie D. Lipschutz, Professor of Politics, Department of Political Science, University of California Santa Cruz.

Karen Litfin, Associate Professor, Department of Political Science, Washington University.

Timothy W. Luke, Professor of Political Science, Virginia Tech.

Felix Rauschmayer, Senior Researcher, Department of Economics, UFZ–Helmholtz Centre for Environmental Research, Leipzig.

Acknowledgments

This book found its beginnings in a workshop on "Science, Knowledge Communities and Environmental Governance: The Global–Local Linkages" held at Rutgers Newark in May 2006 and funded by a Rutgers Academic Excellence Grant. We would like to thank the participants as well as the anonymous referees of the manuscript for their insightful comments. Mark Foley helped with the editing. We are particularly indebted to Wendy Godek, not only for her invaluable organizational skills at the workshop and during its preparation, but also for all her editing work on the manuscript.

Abbreviations and acronyms

ABS	Access and Benefit Sharing
BiH	Bosnia-Herzegovina
CBD	Convention on Biodiversity
CDM	Clean Development Mechanism
CEE	Central and Eastern Europe
CESD	Center for Environmentally Sustainable Development
CDE	capacity development for the environment
CIDA	Canada's foreign aid agency
CITES	Convention for International Trade in Endangered Species of Wild Fauna and Flora
CSE	Centre for Science and Environment
DEI	Directorate for European Integration
EGAT	Electrical Generating Authority of Thailand
ENGO	Environmental Nongovernmental Organization
ESS	Ecosystem Services
EU	European Union
FAO	Food and Agricultural Organization
GEN	Global Ecovillage Network
IFI	international financial institutions
IPCC	Intergovernmental Panel on Climate Change
IPE	International Political Economy
IPI	international political institutions
IPR	Intellectual Property Rights
IT-PGRFA	International Treaty on Plant Genetic Resources for Food and Agriculture
IUCN	World Conservation Union
LULUCF	Land Use, Land Use Change and Forestry
NAMA	Non-Agricultural Market Access Agenda
NGO	Nongovernmental Organization
MA	Millennium Ecosystem Assessment
MLC	Multi-Level Governance
OECD	Organization for Economic Cooperation and Development
OHR	Office of the High Representative

PRS	Poverty Reduction Strategies
PRSC	Poverty Reduction Support Credits
REC	Regional Environmental Center
SBSTAA	Subsidiary Body for Scientific, Technical and Technological Advice
TNC	Transnational Corporation
TPN	transnational policy network
TRIPS	Trade-Related Aspects of Intellectual Property Rights
UNDP	United Nations Development Program
UNFCC	United Nations Framework Convention on Climate Change
USAID	United States Agency for International Development
WBI	World Bank Institute
WCW	World Commission on Water for the 21st Century
WIPO	World Intellectual Property Organization
WRI	World Resources Institute
WRM	World Rainforest Movement
WSSD	World Summit on Sustainable Development
WTO	World Trade Organization
YRBL	Young Researchers of Banja Luka

1 Introduction

Who knew and when did they know it?

Gabriela Kütting and Ronnie D. Lipschutz

Ye shall know the truth, and the truth shall make you free

(Jesus, in John 8:32, KJV)

Scientia potentia est

(*Knowledge is power*, Francis Bacon, 1597)

Power/knowledge

(Michel Foucault, 1980)

Introduction

Before science was rational, it was metaphysical. The first modern scientists were alchemists, seeking Truths that would transform them and return humanity to a State of Grace. Those scientists—among them, Isaac Newton—sought the kind of "Truth" invoked by Jesus, not "truths" as they have since come to be understood and propagated by scientists and science. Only later, after the methods of alchemy were adapted to what we now call, in shorthand, the "scientific method," were the logics of rational cause and effect reified as the key to Universal Truth. As Francis Bacon in the sixteenth century, today we regard science and knowledge in instrumental terms, enabling a capacity not only to predict outcomes but also to cause them. Even after the post-modern turn, science possesses authority because it enables such capacities and calls then "power." And because science still seems Universal and True everywhere in the Cosmos, it appears to possess those powers once attributed to the alchemists' philosopher's stone: the ability to transform both the World and the Self.

Yet, as we shall suggest in this book, and following Michel Foucault, Bruno Latour, and others, knowledge cannot be regarded as either so simple or straightforward, even when it appears in the guise of scientific research. *What* we know, *how* we know it, and *where* we know it best are not merely the products of laboratories, fieldwork and computers. As Latour has shown, knowledge is *social* and, consequently, it cannot be abstracted from the context in which it is produced, accumulated, and deployed. Nor can it be detached from the *relations of power* that operate in those social contexts. Today, when the state of the global environment—especially with respect to climate change—is a focus of growing concern, debate and politics, the truths offered by science and scientists are being challenged in ways that seem irrational, if not downright nihilistic. *We know what must be done!* Why, then, don't we do it?

Let us, for a moment, consider climate change and the science that describes and accounts for it. The cumulation of *data* seems to point definitively in the direction of rising average global temperatures, with larger and smaller increases according to latitude, altitude, ocean currents, and other factors. Even the most sophisticated computer models and data sets cannot, yet, predict the specific effects of climate change on particular places and spaces, on valleys, meadows, communities, cities. At the same time, observations of rising temperatures, decreased rainfall, more intense storms, etc., in these particular places and spaces might, increasingly, appear to point to climate change as the culprit. Given the scientific method and its statistical requirements, however, most of the data are too anecdotal and too local to clearly determine cause and effect. The result is a crisis of inaction—too much information, not enough knowledge—exacerbated by the fear of risk: that we will act too soon, act in the wrong way, act at too much cost, act with too few benefits.

This is not a problem unique to research on climate change, environmental damage, or even social behavior. Our scientific methodology is flawed by what might be called "the uncertainty principle" (as opposed to the precautionary principle, and not to be confused with Heisenberg's). The uncertainty principle (UP) demands that valid inference depends on adequate statistics and minimal standard deviation from a norm. Thus, even if we "know what to do," as we do in the case of global climate change, we are inhibited from acting out of fear of unanticipated consequences (physical, social, economic) or appearing foolish. At the same time, we are warned that to act without a reliable sense of benefits is to act irrationally and to court high costs that we might never recover. This is the perhaps ironic lesson we take from Mancur Olson's *Logic of Collective Action* (1965). Hamstrung by the UP, the group cannot act together even as the individual cannot act alone.

This is the context in which knowledge in *space* and knowledge in *place* act at cross purposes. Knowledge in space is presumed to be universal, to encode that which applies equally in all places and at all times. Knowledge in place is assumed to be particularistic and contingent, and to have no relevance outside of the space in which it is acquired and applied. More to the point, as Timothy Luke argues in this volume,

> Place-based parameters for situating knowledge, spatializing community, and sizing contradiction concretely all too often are dismissed in favor of planetary-scale solutions conceptualized in abstract, place-effacing terms. Local knowledges, vernacular technics, and civic sciences as

environmental mediations, in turn, also are dismissed before the privileging of international knowledge formations, transnational technical networks, and national scientific societies.

It is not that "local knowledges" are invalid: bio-prospectors seek out place-based practices for clues about potential medicinal organisms, sometimes with extraordinary returns. The domination of space over place is ineluctably tied up with *power* as articulated in particular discourses of global management and governmentality. To quote Humpty Dumpty's response to Alice, "The question is ... which is to be master—that's all."[1]

Yet, Foucault reminds us that power is not a thing that can be accumulated or wielded; it produces us as subjects; it flows through the capillaries of social life, so to speak; it operates through discourses that serve to order social life that, in so doing, reproduce that life and discipline its tendencies toward unruliness and uncertainty. It is this last that is the fear of those who are master: risk is the lifeblood of capitalism, but too much disorder poses too much risk, more than even venture capitalists are willing to countenance. Too many demands for participation and inclusion, too many alternative "ways of doing things," too many challenges to the conventional wisdom— these all pose unacceptable risks to those who want to maximize returns but minimize losses (unless, of course, it is tax deductible).

To put the point another way, the uncertainties associated with science are paralleled and made worse by the uncertainties associated with social life. Science deals with physical "facts" whose invariance over time and space is central to prediction (and investment). Social life, by contrast, is the realm of habit and unanticipated consequences, of action and agency, of constraints that never constrain quite predictably enough. If place is where we act, space is invoked to render us politically docile. By the same token, if place is where we have power, that is where we must act to assert social power that flows beyond place and across space to other places.

Place, space and all that

This book is about knowledge and nature, place and space. In taking on these relationships, we make no claims to be the first to do so. Both editors of this volume have, in other works, interrogated those matters and others linked to them. What is different about this book is its inclusion of *power* as central to those relationships. The literature on environmental governance has mostly developed without reference to power, primarily as a result of its neoliberal-institutionalist focus. Where power *is* invoked, it is primarily through the lens of International Relations theory, for which it remains the main currency. As a general rule, the discourses on global governance (GG) and global environmental politics (GEP) fail to take account of inequalities in *social* power relations in environmental politics, whatever the level of analysis. Nor, with rare exceptions, do they treat the interplay between global and local as it is related to social power (for example, Breitmeier et al. 2006; Mitchell et al. 2006).[2]

There are several reasons for these lacunae. In essence, mainstream International Relations literature is based on the neoliberal-institutionalist assumption that multilateral institutions and their frameworks are the best way to address transboundary problems and it is, therefore, concerned with the "fine tuning" of global governance mechanisms and institutions. Thus, the study of both GG and GEP has been dominated by a somewhat revised and improved concept of what were once called "regime theoretical" approaches. Both GG and GEP are concerned primarily with relations between political actors and the institutional structures within which they operate. Scholars working in these two discourses regard institutions (aka "regimes") as the important social and political variable, both in terms of causing change and prescribing solutions (Young 2002: 3).[3] They are concerned with instrumentally solving environmental problems as political, institutional or policy issues. To put this point another way, GG and GEP are about what political science is about more generally: setting up institutional frameworks to solve problems facing sentient actors with standing (in both the legal and social sense). By contrast, we argue, environmental problems are different and, indeed, unique in social science analysis: Nature (our shorthand for "the environment") must be represented by interested parties rather than by itself (see Stone 1988; Latour 2004). Not only does this raise issues of "interest," it also makes nature vulnerable to compromises and frameworks that may be robust politically but ineffective ecologically.

The mainstream GG and GEP approaches are, however, being exposed to a growing number of challenges, some of which, such as the increasingly transnational nature of governance, have been taken up and incorporated into the GEP literature. But most of these challenges have led, instead, to alternative foci, such as the importance of consumption, structural issues surrounding global civil society outside of global governance, structural relations between nature and society, and the global role of environmental justice, to name some of the most important. Nevertheless, this work does not really communicate with the mainstream. At the same time, another group of scholars have been moving away from—or in some instances, were never close to—challenging the mainstream, focusing instead on alternative ways of protecting and restoring the environment at the global level. This approach may be focused on structural conditions, actors and agents, the relevance of the micro level to the macro, connections within the global political economy, or even normative (for example, global civil society studies, consumption issues, environmental justice). Again, there is a gap between the institutional and alternative ways of studying global environmental politics, and there seem not to be any significant attempts to analyze the interaction between the institutional and normative perspectives; that is, to create overlaps or dialogue.

Thus the research foci as well as the normative elements of GG and GEP are fundamentally different from the recent literature concerned with differential power relations because their research concerns are different. The first strives for politically successful solutions in a supposedly "power-neutral" paradigm while the other highlights inequalities that cannot be captured or addressed by institutionalists' analytical framework

Known unknowns and unknown unknowns—who knew?

This book argues that Global Environmental Governance (GEG) and its employment of environmental knowledge fundamentally constitute a top-down approach to problem-solving, employed by powerful actors in order to orchestrate and manipulate local communities within a continuing hegemonic system. We explore the relationship between governance, power and knowledge, using power as the main analytical tool from a variety of approaches, perspectives and case studies—some starting from the local level and shifting upward to the global, and some using a global perspective that narrows down to the local. Some contributors explore specific case studies while others employ a more conceptual framework—but all of them bring a new dimension to the relationship between power and knowledge in environmental governance. Power here is explored in all its guises—from relational to structural power.

But, as indicated above, this book is not only about power; rather it is concerned with the relationship between power and competing forms of knowledge: scientific and what, for lack of a better term, we call "indigenous" (aka local, experiential, social). Our concern with these relationships arises for several reasons. First, it seems evident that, without attention to the conditions and circumstances of everyday life and habitus, "top-down" approaches to environmental governance are unlikely to work as envisioned in the labs, think tanks, and conferences of decisionmakers and negotiators. Second, it is through the exercise of social power at the local level that strategies and practices best intersect with individual and group action and habitus in ways that might effect behavioral changes.

Consequently, and to a growing degree, knowledge practices and networks in environmental governance, especially as related to the way science and indigenous knowledge are practiced and socially organized, are being scrutinized as one of the cornerstones of global participatory politics, and recognized as vital to understanding the various levels at which global environmental politics intersects. Moreover, the *politics* of knowledge networks, power and environmental governance are fundamentally normative and their study falls into the domain of critical approaches, pushing boundaries from normative, conceptual and methodological perspectives. This puts the emphasis on structural issues underlying institutional frameworks.

Much of the GEG literature regards such local "epistemic communities" as benign, democratic, and participatory phenomena—although we ought to be careful in making such blanket assertions. Within this view, these "epicoms" have transcended traditional forms of state/interstate regulation and signal, perhaps, the beginning of a transnational era in which the power of both state and hegemonic economic actors are being challenged and undermined. Indeed, these knowledge networks are seen as elements in an emancipatory global civil society and often glorified as alternative forms of governance able to challenge both the power structures and the sclerosis of traditional state-centric forms of international policy-making and environmental diplomacy (Wapner 1996; Paterson 2000). Again, this is a proposition to be interrogated, rather than asserted.

Notwithstanding our caveats, there are two reasons why this new perspective is both necessary and desirable, stemming from problems associated with the mainstream focus on institutions. First, the mainstream focus captures a large part of *global* political economy and *global* political environment but misses the integrative, holistic level—in other words, the *political ecology* of the current environmental predicament. By widening this focus, a dramatically different picture of this predicament emerges and draws attention to different conceptualizations of the problem that are neglected in the institutional view.

Second, since the late 1980s, social movements and corporations have acquired rising status and recognition as important actors in both analysis of and practice in the international system, leading to a transformative shift in our views and understandings of international relations/politics. The growing shift to a global world view is also being matched by a desire to better understand global–local linkages. It is at this intersection, in particular, that this book makes its contributions.

Things to come

Theory and concepts

The first part of this book is concerned with a conceptual working through of the concepts of space, place, power and knowledge. The chapter by Tim Luke returns to Henri Lefebvre's *The Production Of Space* (1974/1991) to examine (a) how social practices underpin the generation of global spaces and local places, and (b) who is privileged in these social processes of perception and situation of knowledge. Environmental governance in its current discourse is about environmental management and not about attaining local ecological democracy globally. Environmental governance is seen to be a complex process that typically seeks to juggle the views and approaches presented, for example, by different forms of indigenous local knowledge, official bureaucratic knowledge, and professional-technical global (PTG) knowledge. The last of these, in particular, is still poorly situated in terms of actors' (and analysts'!) awareness of PTG knowledge as practice, and its mission as a power/knowledge regime. Luke rejects the so-called green state offered by Robyn Eckersley (2004) as having little to do with his ecological concepts and argues that "the challenge of globality and locality in environmental governance requires a return to 'local knowledge,' not bringing in the 'green state.'"

Next, Andrew Karvonen and Ralf Brand discuss the literature on ecological expertise. They identify four principal characteristics of expertise—ontological assumptions, epistemological approaches, power inequalities, and practical issues; employ their framework to test "traditional" experts' ability to deliver sustainable development; and demonstrate the experts' failures and gaps in their approach in terms of achieving desired goals. Karvonen and Brand then examine four alternatives to conventional forms of expertise: the outreach expert who communicates effectively to non-experts, the interdisciplinary expert who understands the overlaps of neighboring technical disciplines, the meta-expert who brokers the multiple claims of relevance between different forms of expertise, and the civic expert who engages in democratic discourse with non-experts and experts alike. Each of these, which can be described collectively as an "ecosystem of expertise," is required to manage the often-competing demands of sustainable development projects.

The last chapter in this section is by Peter Jacques, who traces the history of power, knowledge and governance with respect to the global ocean. Jacques traces and critiques the rise of world powers in constructing how societies and states understand, interact with and try to control and manage the sea. Before Europe's colonial expansion, coastal cultures saw the sea as a life-giving "Mother" or a kin-related creative force. In conceptual terms, it was Hugo Grotius, writing in the seventeenth century, who reconstructed the ocean as an open pool resource to be used by colonizing powers; it was those powers who provided the raw material for Grotius' theorizations. But his arguments were challenged by Britain, which sought to define the sea as a *mare clausum*, an enclosed space of national resources controlled by the colonial powers. Grotius then framed the colonial power as establishing a top-down legal and ontological knowledge base for the expansion of empire around the world, the results of which we still feel today.

Looking upwards

The book's second section uses the local as the starting point for framing of global–local linkages. The chapter by Christoph Görg and Felix Rauschmayer illustrates the general lack of awareness about how social scales are produced and which power relations are involved in recent discussions about multi-level environmental governance. They focus on the Millennium Ecosystem Assessment and show that, far from always being complementary and based on cooperation, analysis of and policy at different social scales can generate competition, conflict, and power struggles.

In the following chapter, Uli Brand examines the regulation of genetic resources based on the notion of the "internationalized state," as developed by Nicos Poulantzas. According to Brand, the internationalized state is at the center of environmental governance as well as a precondition for the complex processes and dynamics of the "post-Fordist" appropriation of nature. Brand illustrates this theoretical framework through the case of bio-diversity politics, in which this state is at the forefront of the hegemonic project of biodiversity management and the hierarchical division of nature. Indeed, he argues that, far from being marginalized, the modern state remains a powerful actor, even if in a role changed from that during the Fordist era.

Finally, in the last chapter in this section, Karen Litfin describes and analyzes the global ecovillage movement, tracing the scientific and philoso-phical outlines of an ontology of interbeing as its underlying philosophy. She investigates how the ecovillage movement gives expression to this ontology, and offers a preliminary evaluation of the movement's strengths and weaknesses as a contribution to global environmental governance.

Looking downwards

The book's third section begins with a global perspective. In his chapter, Michael Goldman analyzes the social relations between the World Bank as an institutional structure and particular communities where access to water access and its privatization are concerned. He suggests that, while the latter may be good for economic performance, privatization tends to increase rather than alleviate poverty. Further, Goldman questions the binary distinction assumed present in public–private partnerships, arguing that the boundaries between the two are almost always blurred. This raises normative questions about the analytical usefulness of making such a distinction and the implications for the study of how we conceptualize transnational power.

Adam Fagan also looks at multilateral institutions, but in the context of capacity-building in post-communist societies. He argues that capacity-building programs run by international agencies are based on two, possibly faulty assumptions: first, that democratic institutions have become entrenched in these societies and are functioning as desired; and, second, that a neces-sary level of organizational capacity and resource endowment are already present. The case of Bosnia, which he presents here, challenges both assump-tions. Fagan further criticizes the notion of capacity-building and its obfuscation by competing conceptualizations of capacity. According to Fagan, capacity-building is most notably not about building local political capacity to deal with particular problems or about equipping local NGOs with the capacity to represent their issues in wider forums. Instead, as it is imple-mented and practiced in these societies, capacity-building is about strengthening neoliberal-institutionalist models of governance and state substitution and, thus, legitimizing external governance.

In the final chapter of this section, Tim Forsyth applies critical analyses of environmental knowledge and discursive and deliberative governance to the study of land use and land cover policies and to approaches to forests under climate change policies. He takes issue with the view that epistemic communities provide neutral and vital assistance to policy-makers and argues that this view needs to be considered more critically. There needs to be more discussion about how we achieve this expertise, and the political implications of defining it closely. Moreover, there is a need to see "expertise" as more than simply the composition and objective of formal, technical bodies, but instead see expertise as knowledge claims that have somehow become stabilized (i.e. seen as natural) or considered socially legitimate.

Some preliminary conclusions

The main conclusion that we draw from these chapters, as well as the broader literature, is that both neoliberal-institutionalist views of environmental governance and civil society-focused accounts of social networks in global environmental governance largely neglect the unequal power relations, a function of tensions and inequities between spaces and places, uneven development characteristic of capitalism, as well as consequent inequalities in terms of poverty and environmental damages resulting from actions mediated through "space" to place. In the final and concluding chapter of this book, we examine these conundra more closely, asking whether and why more abstract "space-based" forms of knowledge must necessarily trump local "place-based" forms. Our arguments in that chapter take cognizance of the particular relationships between knowledge, power and accumulation, the last of which is usually characterized in terms of growth and prosperity rather than as transfers of various forms of capital through space. Knowledge, in this view, is not only powerful, it is also political, and it plays a central role in struggles among social forces in places and spaces (as in the case, for example, of bio-prospecting). Our goal in this last chapter is, therefore, not to offer definitive "solutions"—it is, we believe, both teleological and utopian to seek to end political conflict and struggle—but, rather, to suggest "processes" that might point agents toward knowledge-based strategies that foster effective forms of social power.

Notes

1 The exchange, from *Through the Looking Glass* (ch. 6), is:
  "When *I* use a word," Humpty Dumpty said, in rather a scornful tone, "it means just what I choose it to mean—neither more nor less."
  "The question is," said Alice, "whether you *can* make words mean so many different things."
  "The question is," said Humpty Dumpty, "which is to be master—that's all."
2 Note our distinction between the conventional understanding of power as articulated in neo-realism and neoliberalism, and the notion of *social power*, which brings in other dimensions. For more about this distinction, see Lipschutz and Conca (1993) and Barnett and Duval (2005).
3 For the most part, regime theories see institutions as dependent structures deployed by actors to address social problems or needs (Krasner 1983); we, by

contrast, regard them as enabling the construction of individuals and societies in a constitutive fashion.

References

Barnett, Michael and Raymond Duvall (2005). *Power in global governance* (Cambridge: Cambridge University Press).

Breitmeier, Helmut, Oran R. Young, and Michael Zürn (2006). *Analyzing international environmental regimes: from case study to database* (Cambridge, Mass.: MIT Press).

Eckersley, Robyn (2004). *The green state: rethinking democracy and sovereignty* (Cambridge, Mass.: MIT Press).

Krasner, Stephen, ed. (1983). *International regimes* (Ithaca, N.Y.: Cornell University Press).

Latour, Bruno (2004). *Politics of nature: how to bring the sciences into democracy* (Cambridge, Mass.: Harvard University Press; trans. Catherine Porter).

Lefebvre, Henri (1974/1991). *The production of space* (Oxford: Blackwell; trans. Donald Nicholson-Smith).

Lipschutz, Ronnie D. and Ken Conca, eds. (1993). *The state and social power in global environmental politics* (New York: Columbia University Press).

Mitchell, Ronald B., William C. Clark, David W. Cash, and Nancy M. Dickson, eds. (2006). *Global environmental assessments: information and influence* (Cambridge, Mass.: MIT Press).

Olson, Mancur (1965). *The logic of collective action: public goods and the theory of groups* (Cambridge, Mass.: Harvard University Press).

Paterson, Matthew (2000). *Understanding global environmental politics: domination, accumulation, resistance* (New York : St. Martin's Press).

Stone, Christoper D. (1988). *Should trees have standing? Toward legal rights for natural objects* (Palo Alto, Calif.: Tioga).

Wapner, Paul K. (1996). *Environmental activism and world civic politics* (Albany: State University of New York Press).

Young, Oran R. (2002). *The institutional dimensions of environmental change:fit, interplay, and scale* (Cambridge, Mass.: MIT Press).

Part I

Power, knowledge and environmental governance from a conceptual perspective

2 Situating knowledges, spatializing communities, sizing contradictions

The politics of globality, locality and green statism[1]

Timothy W. Luke

Introduction

A key contradiction resting at the core of everyday life is spatial. While one resides in a locality, the conditions of material existence are organized by market forces in such a way that one simultaneously inhabits many other sites beyond locality in regionality, nationality, and globality, which then are mystified further by the system of state sovereignty in the register of territoriality. Too often, environmental struggles, however, are reduced to apparently contradictory opposites, like globality vs. locality. With little consideration of what these binaries imply materially, operationally or spatially, environmental struggles often are displaced from all of the sites where they matter into other more occluded registers.

Jane Jacobs in *The Death and Life of Great American Cities* (1993/1961) pointed out the poverty of such simplicities as she noted how many clustered displacements are required to sustain urban ecologies. Every city as a locality actually coexists multispatially with its city regions, transplant regions, subsistence regions, clearance regions, supply regions, and abandoned regions, which are widely dispersed, incongruent, and yet still essential for each city. Hence, this brief discussion examines how science, knowledge communities, and environmental governance inadequately frame the global/local divide in simplistic discourses and practices tied to contemporary political theory, policy studies or ethical thought such that "the environment" is made ready to be subjected to "green statism" with little thought given to such multiple layers of spatiality.

Actually, there is very little awareness about how to size contradiction, spatialize community, or situate knowledge among environmental thinkers. Too many "environmental" discourses misapprehend, or even ignore, the spatial qualities of globality and locality, because they overlook "the dialectical relationship which exists within the triad of the perceived, the conceived, and lived" (Lefebvre 1991: 39) in spaces themselves. One analysis cannot correct this failing, but it might motivate others to begin a series of corrections. Globality and locality must, in fact, be appraised more materially, operationally, and spatially if consideration of their current ethical or political quandaries are to gain greater theoretical traction in often muddy discussions about "territoriality."

From the outset, it should be noted that the challenge of globality and locality as spatiality in environmental governance thus far mostly has failed to be met. Place-based parameters for situating knowledge, spatializing community, and sizing contradiction concretely all too often are dismissed in favor of planetary-scale solutions conceptualized in abstract place-effacing terms (Fischer 2000; Casey 1998; Luke 1996). Local knowledges, vernacular technics, and civic sciences as environmental mediations, in turn, also are dismissed before the privileging of international knowledge formations, transnational technical networks, and national scientific societies that embrace globality (Gottlieb 1993). Globalization has much to do with this, but one can imagine a globality rooted locality in ways that accommodate local, vernacular, and civic communities in the full richness of each and every particular place (Fischer 2000; Luke 1999a; Forester 1999). This revisitation of spatiality in the linkages of power/knowledge accounts for why these embedded, place-based approaches to environmental governance so rarely occur. And, in many ways, it suggests the prevailing discourses for environmental governance and green statism account for much of the shortfall (Cortner and Moote 1999; Darier 1999; Luke 1997). In fact, it would appear that most approaches to environmental governance seek "technocratic expertise" (Fischer 1990) for answers that always point toward a more governmentalized environment in an ecoglobalist register (Luke 2004). That is, these discussions essentially devolve into the routinized operations of "environmentality" (Luke 2005; 1999a; 1999b; 1997) as a power/knowledge formation as some seek to create new articulations of "green governance" (Torgerson 1999) or even a full-blown "green state" (Eckersley 2004).

Globalization as sizing contradictions

On the contradictions between "the global" vs. "the local," Beck distinguishes between three ideas—globalism, globality, and globalization—to appraise the global/local problematic. "Globalization," Beck (2000: 11) suggests, "denotes the *processes* through which sovereign national actors are crisscrossed and undermined by transnational actors with varying prospects for power, orientations, identities, and networks," so locality is left at the crisscrossed cuts of global forces scoring over national space. For Beck "globality" implies the more cultural, economic, and technical conditions of what is regarded as a world society. At the global and local level of spatial aggregation, many people have been living in a global society for quite some time. Indeed, globality is "the totality of social relationships which are not integrated into or determined (or determinable) by national-state politics" (Beck 2000: 10). Finally, "globalism" is what most marks the current conjuncture (French 2000; Luke 1995; Fukuyama 1992; Reich 1991; Ohmae 1990). Globalism enacts the precepts of an ascendant world-wide ideology, typically articulated and advanced by the world's more privileged and powerful managerial, professional-technical and intellectual classes (Hardt and Negri 2000). This ideology-in-action maintains,

> The world market eliminates or supplants political action—that is, the ideology of rule by the world market, the ideology of neoliberalism. It proceeds monocausally and economistically, reducing the multidimensionality of globalization to a single, economic dimension that is itself conceived in a linear fashion. If it mentions at all the other dimensions of globalization—ecology, culture, politics, civil society—it does so only by placing them under the sway of the world-market system.
>
> (Beck 2000: 9)

In this register, globalism motivates many to enact beliefs and practices that presume each state, society, and culture must be managed along the lines of a corporate capitalist enterprise. As Lefebvre notes with this globalist turn, "the debasement of civic life occurs in the everyday, facilitating the task of those who manage everyday life from above by means of institutions and services" (1981: 80).

Globally and locally, this stance also "involves a veritable imperialism of economics, where companies demand the basic conditions under which they can optimize their goals" (Beck 2000: 9). Absent the institutions of what would be a world government to guide today's world society, capitalist corporations have, in turn, the best possible conditions for continuous growth: "a globally *disorganized* capitalism is continually spreading out. For there is no hegemonic power and no international regime either economic or political" (Beck 2000: 13). Each firm therefore can act as if it were an element of a revolutionary vanguard for globalism by imagining that their goods and services, and those of other corporate entities, serve as an integral part of the world market's globalization, an explicit indicator of their business clients' globality, and a material marker, if only implicitly and for now, of the consumers' and suppliers' of any locality willingness to submit to globalism.

Globalist elites hold expectations for ever greater performance and rising profit which serve as the normative essence of today's globality. As Lyotard claims, this unending pursuit of capitalist rationalization "continues to take place without leading to the realization of any of these dreams of emancipation" (1984: 39). With so much less trust resting on non-economic narratives of truth, enlightenment or progress, Lyotard argues that the professional-technical expertise of the science and technology behind big business compels most publics and markets in each locality to accept globality as the sine qua non of "development." Once there, the local constructs of culture and exchange are displaced, falling almost entirely victim to the global sway of "another language game, in which the goal is no longer truth, but performativity—that is, the best possible input/output equation" (1984: 46) in the dust kicked up by crumbling territorial sovereignty.

Consequently, in each locality, the inhabitants soon realize globalism is truly what globality is about:

> the State and/or company must abandon the idealist and humanist narratives of legitimation in order to justify the new goal: in the discourse of today's financial backers of research, the only credible goal is power. Scientists, technicians, and instruments are purchased not to find truth, but to augment power.
>
> (Lyotard 1984: 46)

Accordingly, the logistics for today's rural/urban, global/local, and artificial/natural spaces often compound themselves with the political agendas of globalism.

Globalization as situating knowledge

Globalization, then, frequently is regarded as little more than a complex collection of changes that somehow add up to postnational, cross-border, transnational, or barrier-breaking change promoted by powerful and knowledgeable elites on a global and local level. Unconsciously spatial in his referents, Giddens, for example, asserts it is "the intensification of worldwide social relations which link distant localities in such a way that local happenings are shaped by events occurring many miles away and vice versa (1990: 64). Tabb claims globalization is "the process of reducing barriers between countries and encouraging closer economic, political, and social interaction" (2001: 1). Mittelman ties globalization to "an increase in interconnections, or interdependence, a rise of transnational flows, and an intensification of processes such that the world is, in some respects, becoming a single space" (2000: 5). While these definitions highlight how globalization blends culture, economics, politics, society, and technology together as new structural trends and individual practices, the central insight is how much one kind of spatiality itself is effaced, displaced, or neutralized to generate another type. Borders, nationality, boundaries, and international sovereignty, which are all linked with territorial spatiality, allegedly are regarded as phenomena that no longer matter as or, at least, matter as much as they once did.

The global is both wanted, and resisted, from above and below, but it arrives as abstract spatiality in empty functionality. As Virilio notes,

> In fact, there now exists a media nebula whose reality goes well beyond the frontiers of the ghettos, the limits of metropolitan agglomerations. The megalopolis is not Mexico City or Cairo or Calcutta, with their tens of millions of inhabitants, but this sudden temporal convergence that unites actors and televiewers from the remotest regions, the most disparate nations, the moment a significant event occurs here or there.
>
> (Virilio 2000: 69)

Globalism is presented as multiple forces streaking through empty frag-mented spaces from anywhere to serve those on the way ahead or far outside. It often also is felt, however, as the raw side of globality when those below, inside, and behind its destruction collapse under their loss of power, wealth and status as some of globalism's more mediated events of change.

Too many authorities, however, approach technology and culture in the mix of global and local through the mindsets of naive instrumentalism. That is, business organizations and big technical systems are simply tools, not unlike all other implements, and they merely are being used rationally by autonomous human agents to serve the consciously chosen instrumental ends of their users. It is assumed that global technical systems basically will be just like national, regional, or local systems except that their managers and clients, producers and consumers, officials and constituents simply will work at a larger scale, on faster time registers, and for more beneficiaries (Beck 1997; Appadurai 1996; Adas 1989). Even though we already know that national systems are not like regional or local ones, the naive instru-mentalism woven through many political analyses of globalization rehashes reality in this unproductive fashion. By remembering how sciences and technologies bring along their own "anonymous histories" (Giedion 1948) which reconfigure reality, shape space, temper time, and package perfor-mance, separate and apart from the conscious intention of their users, one must ask how political subjectivity might change amid global and local contradictions in much more fundamental ways.

Most importantly, "the global" of globalization is a polyfocal cluster of many different knowledge strategies—some corporate, some professional-technical, some geopolitical, some civic, some ideological, some ethnona-tional, some organizational—that create scores of new operational domains at many sites of transformation. In turn, "the local" also develops cultural discourses and practices beside, beyond, and beneath the scope of the global (Luke 2004). These emergent flexible geometries of indefinite boundaries, open architectures, and unfixed locations in globalities and localities constantly contradict the fixed geometries of definite boundaries, closed communities, and inflexible locations of nation-states as the spatial envelopes of "real life" (Agnew 1987).

In these formations, codes of exchange-based status rest upon owning, displaying, and using monetarily valorized objects, which are produced as commodities, in turn, by immense corporate collectives of human and non-human agents in accord with those same codes (Agger 1989). As their con-cursivities build, the codes provide a universal system of decipherable signs for clear unencumbered communication amidst the instability of global commerce, a regime of socialization for social relations in the vast expanses of world trade, and a means of individual and group valorization tied to what people own, how they use it, and where their enjoyment of possession and use occurs (Thrift 1996; Virilio 1995; Lefebvre 1981). Although these codes of meaning might offer nothing but an ever-changing flux of sign value, they carry material force as the contradictions between BMWs with Hondas, Rolexes with Timexes, or Hyatts with Holiday Inns all signal. Meanings are always "complicitous and always opaque," but they also are "the best means for the global social order to extend its immanent and permanent rule to all individuals" (Baudrillard 1996: 196). Through the spatialities spun up from globalization, the mediations of corporate globalist strategies are, all too often, continuously rendered "invisible, unthinkable, and unrepresentable" (Latour 1993: 34) by these complicities of commodification. In fact, the occlusion of who made what, where, when, and how creates an illusion of visible, thinkable, and representable relationships in global trade, world science or the latest technologies, but the real conditions of the commodity's creation and valorization frequently remain opaque in the flows of global exchange (Jacobs 1984).

Globalization as spatializing communities

To discuss "the environment" in global or local terms is to participate in the production of space as a social product. Here the thinking of Henri Lefebvre is invaluable. No national space will be left to be discovered, preserved, or safeguarded as sovereign territory if it can be seen only as a pre-existent externality that shall always remain untrammeled in human action. On the contrary, any social space, like our "environment," any "locality," or one's "community," always "manifests itself as the realization of a general practical schema" rooted in orders of homogeneity, fragmentation, and hierarchy that give rise "to multiple tactical operations directed towards an overall result" (Lefebvre 1981: 134). These problematic orderings result in historical appearances, conceptual frameworks or mental maps. As Lefebvre claims, few thinkers, and especially those working on the projects of environmental governance, ever admit fully,

> a representation of space—which is by no means innocent, since it involves and contains a strategy—is passed off as disinterested positive knowledge. It is projected objectively; it is affected materially, through practical means. There is thus no real space or authentic space, only spaces produced in accordance with certain schemas developed by some particular groups within the general framework of a society (that is to say, a mode of production).
>
> (Lefebvre 1981: 135)

Despite the well-meaning mystifications tying together the deliberative projects of collaborative governance, collective self-management or communal administration, Lefebvre's observations suggest those tactics soon become entangled in the stealthy globalist schematics of homogenized, fragmented, and hierarchical spatial practices. Consequently, as a complex social artifact, such social space, is made in accordance with an operating instrument in the hands of a group of experts, technocrats who are themselves representative of particular interests but at the same time of a mode of production, conceived not as a completed reality or an abstract totality, but as a set of possibilities in the process of being realized.

(Lefebvre 1981: 134)

At this juncture, it is imperative for any power/knowledge critique to investigate who sets the possibilities, what is the realm of the possible imagined to be, and how are they all to be realized?

Many accounts of locality, authenticity, or organicity still bear heavy traces of "the codes relating to space," even though those coded traceries could only be long-ago dissolved relics of others from their times. Still, these relics are strangely borne along in words, images, and metaphors. Lefebvre believes these codes can be eroded by epoch-making and era-breaking events, like those in the early 1900s:

The fact is that around 1910 a certain space was shattered. It was the space of common sense, of knowledge (*savoir*), of social practice, of political power, a space hitherto enshrined in everyday discourse, just as in abstract thought, as the environment of and channel for communications; the space, too, of classical perspective and geometry, developed from the Renaissance onwards on the basis of the Greek tradition (Euclid, logic) and bodied forth in Western art and philosophy, as in the form of the city and town. Such were the shocks and onslaughts suffered by this space that today it retains but a feeble pedagogical reality, and then only with great difficulty, within a conservative educational system. Euclidean and perspectivist space have disappeared as systems of reference, along with other former 'commonplaces' such as the town, history, paternity, the tonal system in music, traditional mortality, and so forth. This was truly a crucial moment. Naturally, 'common-sense' space, Euclidean space and perspectivist space did not disappear in a puff of smoke without leaving any trace in our consciousness, knowledge, or educational methods; they could no more have done so than elementary algebra and arithmetic, or grammar, or Newtonian physics.

(Lefebvre 1991: 25)

Granted their allegedly feeble reality, these commonalities still have weight because they will not disappear entirely in a puff of smoke, leaving no traces on our consciousnesses. This theoretical tracery remains, especially in our consciousness of Nature, knowledge of locality, and methods of global valorization. Spatiality, as a social product of sites, settings, and symbols, always is still charged with uncoded meanings no matter how integrated into operational systems they become; and, it is this place-based space of punctual being that must be recovered (Bachelard 1994).

To conduct an analysis of the environment, ecology, or Earth is to pre-occupy one's self with space and all the aspects, elements, and moments of social practice associated with it. Discursive appropriations of such spaces and their science, then, have particular implications inasmuch as this perspective on social practice is one in which:

1   it represents the political (in the case of the West, the "neocapitalist") use of knowledge. Remember that knowledge under this system is integrated in a more or less 'immediate' way into the forces of production, and in a 'mediate' way into the social relations of production;
2   it implies an ideology designed to conceal that use, along with the con-flicts intrinsic to the highly interested employment of a supposedly disin-terested knowledge. This ideology carries no flag, and for those who accept the practice of which it is a part it is indistinguishable from knowledge; and
3   it embodies at best a technological utopia, a sort of computer simulation of the future, or of the possible, within the framework of the real—the framework of the existing mode of production. The starting-point here is a knowledge which is at once integrated into, and integrative with respect to, the mode of production. The technological utopia in question is a common feature not just of many science-fiction novels, but also of all kinds of projects concerned with space, be they those of architecture, urbanism, or social planning.(Lefebvre 1991: 8–9)

Each of these qualities can be found in many blueprints for environmental governance, and their effects, which are only partly explicit, are troubling. That green politics can be rooted implicitly in designs for a high-technology utopia, some reactionary dream-based ideology, or even today's existing capitalist political economy is an unsettling fact. This conflicted reality must be acknowledged, but not necessarily accepted as inevitable (Briden and Downing 2002; Luke 1996).

The moral force animating many visions of environmental politics is found in Nature, even though it is concealed in too many oblique ways amid a diverse array of discourses, developments, and disciplines. In spite of their supporters' fixations upon Nature's alleged originality, Lefebvre observes, "everyone wants to protect and save nature; nobody wants to stand in the way of an attempt to retrieve its authenticity. Yet at the same time everything conspires to harm it" (1991: 30–31). Nature here is both the pre-categorical stuff of reality and the emergent overlays of spatiality. Its spaces are social pro-ducts, and all that conspires to acclaim their authenticity, or heedlessly harm them, are displaced by the illusions of Nature's opacity and transparency.

Indeed, spatiality—understood as both social production and a social product—can be assayed in its fullest particularity only by indicating "the extent that it ceases to be indistinguishable from mental space (as defined by the philosophers and mathematicians) on the one hand, and physical space (as defined by practico-sensory activity and the perception of 'nature') on the other" (Lefebvre 1991: 27). While it is a social product, space is never just a collection of sites, an aggregation of sense data, an emptiness packed with things, or a formless veil draped over phenomena, events, or places. Its production as a social artifact unfolds instead through all these spatial qualities as "a double illusion, each side of which refers back to the other, reinforces the other, and hides the other," creating simultaneously "the illusion of transparency" and "the illusion of opacity" (Lefebvre 1991: 27).

Many works rooted in rational analysis transpire within the illusion of transparency in which "space appears as luminous, as intelligible, as giving action free rein," even as the illusion of opacity veils most analyses of the environment "chiefly because of its appeal to naturalness, to substantiality" (Lefebvre 1991: 27, 31). Devotees for spatial transparency treat what occurs in space as conveying

> a miraculous quality to thought, which becomes incarnate by means of a design (in both senses of the word). The design serves as a mediator—itself of great fidelity—between mental activity (invention) and social activity (realization); and when it is deployed in space the illusion of transparency goes hand in hand with a view of space as innocent, as free of traps or secret places. Anything hidden or dissimulated—and hence dangerous—is antagonistic to transparency, under whose reign everything can be taken in by a single glance from that mental eye which illuminates whenever it contemplates.
>
> (Lefebvre 1991: 28)

At the same time, the illusion of opacity is planted in strong epistemic conventions about realist essences "from which the proper and adequate word for each thing or 'object' may be picked," and thus "substantiality, naturalness, and spatial opacity nurtures its own mythology" (Lefebvre 1991: 30). The allegedly strict realism of expert social analysis, therefore, thus tacitly conjures up both its substantive foci and its transparent frames for their coincident exploration in spatial investigations. Ironically, "each illusion embodies and nourishes the other ... the rational is thus naturalized, while nature cloaks itself in nostalgias which supplant rationality" (Lefebvre 1991: 30).

The manifest, or occasionally latent, flaw in such environmental analysis is its common promotion of some "basic sophistry where by the philosophico-epistemological notion of space is fetishized and the mental realm comes to envelop the social and physical ones" (Lefebvre 1991: 5). Practical concrete mediations between these two realms are still always needed. That one cannot move back-and-forth between the mental and social at will, however, is a conceptual constraint that rarely is heeded. Common sense, pragmatic imperatives, or legal conventions then just conflate the two.

The challenge of environmental governance

Environmental governance in many ways marks another instance of how "received representations and commonly used words are insidious vehicles for a morality, an ethics and an aesthetics that are not declared to be such," and, quite clearly, the best example of this twist under neoliberalism is "the substitution of the 'user,' figure of everyday life, for the political figure of the 'citizen'" (Lefebvre 1981: 71). As Nature becomes in these frames an ecological commons, planetary infrastructures or biodiversity assets, the citizen thus—despite Aldo Leopold's pleas otherwise—is demoted to being a mere inhabitant, and "the inhabitant is reduced to a user, restricted to demanding the efficient operation of public services" (Lefebvre 1981: 79).

Cultivating the correct green consciousness among these many "users," in turn, now seems to be the mission of environmental studies, ecophilosophy or even environmental political theory, which prefigure the construction of some sort of "green state." Harmonizing those user demands with terrestrial utility services is a critically important task that biophysical science, many knowledge communities, and environmental governance also prepare themselves to provide (Berkes et al. 2000; Evernden 1992). In contemporary transnational capitalism, "everyone knows how to live." Yet, as other domains of disciplinary discourse illustrate,

> They know it thanks to a knowledge that does not originate with them, which they have assimilated, and which they apply to their own individual cases, managing their personal affairs—their everyday lives—in accordance with the models developed and diffused for them.
>
> (Lefebvre 1981: 81)

Green citizenship, ecotopianism, or environmental agency is no exception to this pattern, because they all struggle to find the right knowledge essential for these would-be environmental governance designers to propound a "rational ecology" (Dryzek 1987). Indeed, users are shaped to serve as critical receptacles of a particular culture, or "a mixture of ideology, representations and positive knowledge. The enormous culture industry supplies specific products, commodities to which users have a "right," so that the output of this industrial sector no longer has the appearance of commodities but, rather, of objects valorized by them and destined exclusively for use (Lefebvre 1981: 80). Use here is clearly a mystification, but so too is the role of the knowledge communities and sciences needed by the cultivation of green states and green citizens to suit environmental governance (Nowotny et al. 2001; Sklair 2001; Torgerson 1999).

An unawareness of these tendencies in environmental political thought and practice can be found almost anywhere. To typify the problem here for environmental governance, however, one can turn to *The Green State: Rethinking Democracy and Sovereignty* (Eckersley 2004). Eckersley's proposed new "critical political ecology" has been celebrated for outlining one effort to expand what is regarded as political project that "expands the boundaries of the moral community to include the natural environment in which the human community is embedded" (2004: back cover). While spatial terms are constantly deployed in the work, her analysis essentially ignores the complexity and materiality of spatiality itself. The book's index, for example, does even not tag "globality" or "locality" as key points of reference.

The spatial aporias in her analysis can be mapped by examining the index, which omits "borders," "boundaries," "space," "spatiality," and even "territory" as vital items of interest to readers seeking key referents in their studies about the environmental governance of Nature. "Community" is cited as "Community, Taylor on, 105" to note how Charles Taylor agrees "community is a structural precondition of human selfhood and moral agency." Here again, however, "structure," "function," "materiality" also are not marked in the index for special attention; but, even more amazingly, "biodiversity," "ecology," "ecosystem," "environment," "life," and "planet" also are omitted as items of discursive distinction by Eckersley in her challenging blueprint for environmental governance. Much is indexed on "globalization," "sovereignty," "democracy," and even "ecological" this and that. Yet, even Nature itself appears only as "Nature, representation of, 120–26, 131," but that brief discussion only slogs through how Steven Vogel, Jürgen Habermas, and Robert Goodin have imagined how human beings might "speak on behalf of" nonhuman beings in Nature to include them in the human community that is embedded in Nature. Unfortunately, "embeddedness," and whatever this means in Eckersley's analysis, also is merely a spectral presence; it too is not indexed as a topic for any focused consideration.

That a treatise on "the green state" meant to reposition humanity and Nature with regard to popular democracy and state sovereignty basically should be so blind to issues of spatiality, as they are all rooted in globality and locality, is troubling (Luke 1994; Tuan 2006/1981). Yet, this work, like so many others in contemporary political theory, is hobbled by a classical unawareness with definite Aristotlean origins. Aristotle divides reason into three types: *theoria, techne,* and *phronesis.* For him, *theoria* certainly is and *techne* maybe would examine space. However, the polis as a project is tied much more to the practices of citizenship rather than spatialities for material existence. The relative invisibility of *theoria* or *techne,* as worthy concerns in ethico-political discourse fixated on *phronesis,* are problematic quirks in discussions of issues rooted in ethics and politics. As a result, most serious efforts at defining the juridico-legal characteristics of a *green* state all dither away. Whether it is Eckersley, Dryzek (2006), or Torgerson (1999), green statists and deliberative democrats grope around to delimit the prime conditions of deliberative democracy for the green statism, while ignoring, for most intents and purposes, the materiality of Nature, the spatiality of embeddedness in the environment, and the socio-ecological *techne* required for a green *phronesis* to be viable.

Hence, Eckersley's exploration of the green state is completely hobbled with most of the same ethico-political worries that one might drag up to discuss a red (socialist) state, white (conservative), purple (aristocratic), or black (fascist) state. The "environment" as site, system, setting or structure appears only as an epiphenomenal or, at best, an ephemeral aspect of this political effort to describe a green (ecological) state. Even though Eckersley believes her project "is not to dodge but rather to confront the moral and epistemological challenges associated with the attempt to represent nature for its own sake" (2004: 121), this immaterial, aspatial, and untechnical mode of confrontation essentially effaces Nature to incorporate it into "the moral community" floating in abstract theoretical space of an anthropomorphic ecocentrisim where some reliable humans can assume a moral trusteeship over its interests (Eckersley 2004: 121).

In these respects, Eckersley's green statism typifies how Lefebvre understands "global space" becomes established "in the abstract as a void waiting to be, as a medium waiting to be colonized" (1991: 125). Of course, Eckersley's rightful anger over the industrial degradation of Nature tacitly acknowledges how the voids of global space are colonized. Lefebvre anticipates Eckersley's critique, but he also warns against such projects for designing a self-empowering green state charged with governance of "the environment." The abstract voids of globality and locality in global spaces, as Lefebvre asserts (1991: 125), are answered "later by the social practice of capitalism" and "this space would come to be filled by commercial images, signs and objects. This development would in turn result in the advent of the pseudo-concept of the environment (which begs the question: the environment of whom or of what?)"

Eckersley's visions of the green state, therefore, perfectly exemplify a politics presaged in Lefebvre's sense of abstract space, especially how its content always appears abstract, even though it can be grasped only by means of certain practices for dealing with it. In this respect,

> *Abstract* space can only be grasped *abstractly* by a thought that is prepared to *separate* logic from the dialectic, to *reduce* contradictions to a false coherence, and to *confuse* the residua of that reduction (for example, logic and social practice). Viewed as an instrument—and not merely as social appearance—abstract space is first of all the locus of nature, the tool that would dominate it and that therefore envisages its (ultimate) destruction. This same space corresponds to the broadening of that (social) practice which gives rise to ever vaster and denser networks on the surface of the earth, as also above and below it.
>
> (Lefebvre 1991: 307)

Philosophizing abstractly about the green state, Eckersley slips into an instrumentalized sense of spatiality and presumes to forestall its destruction by advancing, albeit in a deliberate green democratic fashion, the proliferation of the vast and dense networks that constitute the worlds of commodities degrading the Nature they rest within (Torgerson 1999).

This strategic space is where the disputatious mimesis of forms for "ecological democracy" also might agitate for the advent of "the green state." All space is social practice, and the social practices of this unusually "groundless" ecological democracy treat the Earth with,

> ... as an ideology in action—an empty space, a space that is primordial, a container ready to receive fragmentary contents, a neutral medium into which disjointed things, people and habitats might be introduced. In other words: incoherence under the banner of coherence, a cohesion grounded in scission and disjointedness, fluctuation and the emphemeral masquerading as stability, conflictual relationships embedded within an appearance of logic and operating effectively in combination ... It is here that desire and needs are uncoupled, then crudely cobbled back together. And this is the space where the middle classes have taken up residence and expanded—neutral, or seemingly so, on account of their social and political position midway between the bourgeoisie and the working class. Not that this space 'expresses' them in any sense; it is simply the space assigned them by the grand plan: these classes find what they seek—namely, a mirror of their 'reality', tranquillizing ideas, and the image of a social world in which they have their own specially labeled, guaranteed place. The truth is, however, that this space manipulates them, along with their unclear aspirations and their all-too-clear needs.
>
> (Lefebvre 1991: 308–9)

Unfortunately, as one situates this knowledge, the green statist strain of ecological democracy discourse believes in the utility behind this homogenization and fragmentation of abstract space even as it bemoans their existence.

Once in the grip of the hierarchization that such complexity implies, the green state could just deploy a model of sectoral command-and-control to manage the ecosystems under its purview. Indeed, for ecological democrats and green statists,

> This homogenizing and fractured space is broken down in highly complex fashion into models of sectors. These models are presented as the product of objective analyses, described as "systemic", which, on a supposedly empirical basis, identify systems of subsystems, partial "logics", and so on. To name a few at random: the transportation system; the urban network; the tertiary sector; the school system; the work world with its attendant labour market, organizations and institutions; and the money market with its banking-system. Thus, step by step, society in its entirety is reduced to an endless parade of systems and subsystems, and any social object whatsoever can pass for a coherent entity. Such assumptions are taken for established fact, and it is on this foundation that those who make them (ideologues, whether technocrats foundation or specialists, convinced of their own freedom from ideology) proceed to build, isolating one parameter or another, one group of variables or another.
>
> (Lefebvre 1991: 311)

Out of such sliced-and-diced abstract space, Eckersley pushes for the acceptance of her green public sphere in which green democratic actors allegedly could

> both deepen and extend democracy in ways that are more sensitive to the highly pluralized context of today's societies confronting complex ecological problems in an increasingly borderless world. However, the project of building the green state can never be finalized rather, it is a dynamic and ongoing process of extending citizenship rights and securing inclusive forms of political community.
>
> (2004: 16)

Because pollution crosses borders, Eckersley asserts ecological democracy must have transboundary dimensions. With little material attention given to "ambit claims" as spatial problematics, she instead turns to a norms-based risks/rewards notion of disemplaced "affectedness" to orient the transnational green democratic state rather than civic republican ideals or liberal cosmopolitan constraints. Since "state responsibility for environmental harm could develop" some principles to more "effectively protect ecosystems and environmental victims" (2004: 16), Eckersley's hierarchical vision of risk/reward calculi homogenizes globality and locality in vast folds of abstract space. Transboundary environmental problems to her pose the opportunity to operate for some apparent environmental good on a transboundary/supraterrritorial basis without much hesitation. In folding such abstracted space, she struggles to show "how 'affectedness' may come into play in the development of supplementary structures of rule that create transboundary rights of ecological citizenship," and that "this supplementary structure of rule should be developed by multilateral negotiations" (2004: 16–17) allegedly in pursuit of the ecocentric good.

Before this endless parade of systems, and social objects, like "affectedness" or "moral community," "the environmental" here does become a coherent pacified entity ready to be rediscovered beyond territoriality or taken as an established fact for its "governance" on a planetary scale. Eckersley's panoply of transnational "moderating forces" illustrates how loosely

> the logical consistency and practical coherence of a particular system will be asserted with no prior evaluation—even thought the most cursory analysis would inevitably destroy the premise. The claim is that specific mechanisms are being identified in this way, which partakes of a "real" aspect of reality, and that these mechanisms will be clearly discernible once they, and some particular facet of the "real", have been isolated. In actuality, all we have here is a tautology masquerading as science and an ideology masquerading as a specialized discipline. The success of all such "model-building," "simulation" and systemic analysis reposes upon an unstated postulate—that of a space underlying both the isolation of variables and the construction of systems. This space

validates the models in question precisely because the models make the space functional.

(Lefebvre 1991: 311–12)

Disemplaced locally and globally by world wide webs of exchange, communities of knowledgeable and less knowledgeable people who might face imminent ecocide or crimes against Nature, as Eckersley claims, must yield to the functionalities of this abstract ecocentric space. While it is putatively aspatial, immaterial, and nonoperational, the ecological democracy of green states requires a certain spatiality, materiality and operationality to succeed. Otherwise, it remains a quite fictive project. And, yet, such thinking is naively advanced as having some theoretical discipline required for green statists to oversee the everyday life of ecological democrats seeking ecologically responsible statehood (Fischer 2000; McNeill 2000).

Nonetheless, "daily life is where 'we' must live; it is what has to be transformed" (Lefebvre 1981: 66). The limits of ecological sustainability as well as those of political domination through technical expertise and property ownership in everyday environments are spatialized structures with material quiddity. Here, for citizens,

> as they encounter more obstacles, barriers and blockages than ever in modernity, how is it that so many people have not realized that they were coming up against the boundaries of daily life, boundaries that are invisible, yet cannot be crossed because of the strength of daily life? They come up against these boundaries like insects against a window pane.
>
> (Lefebvre 1981: 66)

Unless and until the homogeneity, fragmentation, and hierarchy that connect these transparent panes of containment are broken apart, the cruel trap of combining a pretense of discursive transparency with constraints of disciplinary totality in a green state will capture many in conflicted dreams about enforcing democratic accountability for certain forms of ecological irresponsibility.

In an era of neoliberal economy and professional-technical managerialism, one should not assume "the social structures of international anarchy, global capitalism, and the liberal democratic state are necessarily anti-ecological and mutually reinforcing, or that they foreclose the possibility of any progressive transformation of states as governance structures" (Eckersley 2004: 14). While none of these formations are necessarily anti-ecological, they still are quite often contingently, materially, and operationally anti-ecological with regard to their social production of spatial sites, material settings, and practical structures. If they were not, the environmental movement undoubtedly would not need to exist.

Greater democratic accountability, however, is not a sure-fire panacea. Of course, decades of environmental resistance have promoted "moderating forces," including:

1   The rise of environmental multilateralism, including environmental treaties, declarations, and international environmental standards.
2   The emergence of sustainable development and "ecological modernization" as competitive strategies of corporations *and* states.
3   The emergence of environmental advocacy within civil society and of new democratic discursive designs within the administrative state, including community "right to know" legislation, community environmental monitoring and reporting, third-party litigation rights, environmental and technology impact assessment, statutory advisory committees, citizens' juries, consensus conferences, and public inquiries.(Eckersley 2004: 15)

Eckersley never makes clear why relying upon these clustered apparatuses for greater democratic accountability will truly create a green accountable democracy for Nature and Society. Even if these three developments do function in mutually reinforcing ways, the material inertia of spatial practices are such that "a possible trajectory of development that moves away from 'organized ecological irresponsibility' (to adapt Ulrich Beck's phrase) to more ecologically responsible modes of state governance" (Eckersley 2004: 15) could very well be derailed. Change instead might follow this trajectory down to an unintended impact area of "irresponsible ecological organization" as the calculi of consent in environmental multilateralism, sustainable development, and environmental advocacy instead produce institutional impasse, governmental gridlock, and accountability angst.

Eckersley does not fret over such contradictions, because she tacitly senses only abstract space in transboundary spillover effects from environmental emergences actually justifying what she calls "ecological intervention" (2007: 293–316). While preferring local ecological defense to global ecological intervention, the green state must be locked and loaded in case it is called upon—usually via multilateral collaboration after meeting three very thin or contestable tests of legitimacy, legality, and morality—to hit the beach in ecohumanitarian interventions. Of course, such actions would be meant "to prevent ecocide and crimes against nature involving human rights violations" (2007: 312), since those pretexts have the most pull in globalist discourse. More astounding, however, is how she waives the writ of emergency authority over the green state for "the most challenging case of all—the military rescue of nonhuman species—conflicts with deeply entrenched international legal and political norms concerning state territorial rights" (2007: 312). Floating in the abstract space of green statism, she is certain "the legal norms of territory have, appropriately, started to fray to the point where extending the idea of 'the responsibility to protect' to include biological diversity is no longer unthinkable" (Eckersley 2007: 312). In other words, the green state must stand ready to pay any price, bear any burden, meet any hardship, and oppose any foe to assure the survival and success of ecocentrism.

Still, the collective choice conundrum will be ever-present, and just as confounding when it is "green" as when it is non-green. Indeed, the general good will assumed by many to be a solid background condition in today's environmental movement rarely is there. The contradictions of collective choice shall prove even more pernicious as such good will is discovered to be one of the movement's most limited, and perhaps quite nonrenewable, resources. At the end of the day, green states still remain states, and ecological democracy only insures a new cadre of people—who will make various rulings in civil society, multilateral institutions, citizens' juries, community monitoring, or advisory committees—shall do their work more effectively after wrapping their green vision for the state itself around all of their machinations.

Such celebrations of adaptive, collaborative, or deliberative forms of democratic governance imply that the opening for new freedoms can be found and enjoyed. As Lefebvre warns, these exercises, however, could only cloak control in new communitarian ethics or fresh collective self-management ideologies. Such tactics tacitly concede "it is self-evident that the state alone cannot ensure control over an entire society … In reality, what we have is a state controlling daily life because it helps to create it. And it even *moulds* it. It fashions it" (Lefebvre 1981: 126). Inviting publics to organize, manage, and direct themselves at a time they are unwilling or unable to pay for state experts or public officials to act for them implicitly allows expert and official directives to fashion their own collaborative controls in a manner that extends the control of everyday life by recreating it anew in, around, and through the commodity form. Resistances against the commodity continue; but, at the same time, "the essential thing today is the state, which increasingly elevates itself above its own conditions in the world of commodities which simultaneously supports the world in general and tends to shatter each particular state, dissolving it into the global" (Lefebvre 1981: 125).

The environment in these discursive work-ups for ecological democracy, whether it is the built, unbuilt, or yet-to-be-built environment, clearly acquires and retains the characteristics of a commodity. As Lukács (1971) suggests, the commodity's most beguiling capabilities include reducing producers and production to products. Whether as goods or services, each commodified object and event contains, but conceals, the constellation of conflicted social relations that enable its creation as relations of abstract spatiality. Globalization's commodifying powers at the global and local levels then let spatiality, materiality, and operationality to spin into these twin turns of conceptual containment and concealment as "the environment" becomes a another settled site for expert governance.

Spatiality as coupled global/local systems

As technoscientific maneuvers of green statism aim to reshape the Earth into a set of terrestrial infrastructures, they require some management to leverage its once opaque machinic regularities as a new political economy that has been rendered transparent. This machinic nature, then, acquires via analysis its own unique spatiality. On one level, its spatiality is flexible with regard to the settings of its localities, stabilities, or properties. Here the multiple point-based manifolds of spatiality appear as mediations of practices in place and in process. As De Certeau asserts, this sort of space exists when,

> one takes into consideration vectors of direction, velocities, and time variables. Thus space is composed of intersections of mobile elements. It is in a sense activated by the ensemble of movements deployed within it. Space occurs as the effect produced by the operations that orient it, situate it, temporalize it, and make it function in a polyvalent unity of conflictual programs or contractual proximate.
>
> (De Certeau 1988: 117)

Both "biocomplexity" and "sociocomplexity" fold together as the material economies of human and nonhuman systems needed to abstractly situate, temporalize, and functionalize ensembles of moving ideas, goods, organisms, and energies. A good example is Eckersley's "transboundary spillover effects."

On yet another level, abstract global spatiality finalizes the globalist city discussed in Lefebvre's "urban revolution" (2003: 1–22) through which the rational organization of space struggles to synchronize human activities with those of other humans and non-humans into the polyfocal "now-wheres," "now-whens," "now-whats," and "now-whos" of conceived spatiality as lived-in spaces. In these locales, stable interconnected properties, practices, and populations instantiate "place" or "an instantaneous configuration of positions" (De Certeau 1988: 117) that imply well-policed stability. For Lefebvre these embedded cycles of emplacement are fields of "the urban," infiltrating globally into what once was social and natural, countrified and citified, peasant and proletarian with differential, disjunctive, and discontinuous complexities.

In attempts to gauge such spatiality, that blindness induced by calls of crisis at structural sutures in time or theoretical twists in history often occlude what is at hand. Hence, Lefebvre maintains "the urban (urban space, urban landscape) remains unseen" (2003: 29), because human cognition and perception are trained to be incapable of bringing it into sight. Snagged by the detritus of industry, modernity simply piles up as postmodernity; yet, there is much more at work beyond the "blinding" (assumptions we accept dogmatically) and the "blinded" (the misunderstood) that now are "complementary aspects of our blindness" (Lefebvre 2003: 32). Green states will try to overcome such blindness by grinding new spatial optics to detect disruptive snarls in the world wide webs of social exchanges, but those lenses will always have serious distortions.

To postulate that Nature exists as some threatened cluster of settings, and that it can be defined, and then managed within zones of the green state, as environmentality discourses assert, implicitly concedes that "the urban revolution" fully has taken hold—deruralizing, deindustrializing, deterritorializing, and perhaps even dehumanizing what was raw nature in the production of human settlements as civilization. Instead of what once was believed to be Nature's harmonies, ensembles of machinic systems coexist in chaotic, turbulent, complex strings of self-organizing stability, knitting together a planet-wide community that Lefebvre labeled "the urban" in 1970. What once seemed only like "a horizon, an illuminating virtuality" (Lefebvre 2003: 17) a generation ago, is now fully recognizable. And, many models for the green state illustrate this shift. While virtual, the urban remains abstract, but it is still also a focus of collective materiality and social action. Consequently, the critical project arises alongside the urban revolution's reconstitution of all environments and their inhabitants:

> Theoretical knowledge can and must reveal the terrain, the foundation on which it resides: an ongoing social practice, an urban practice in the process of formation. It is an aspect of the critical phase that this practice is currently veiled and disjointed, that it possesses only fragments of a reality and a science that are still in the future. It is our job to demonstrate that such an approach has an outcome, that there are solutions to the current problematic.
>
> (Lefebvre 2003: 17)

Nearly a generation later, then, the pretense of ecological democrats building a green state as multilateral/transnational institutions essentially acknowledges a planetary society now exists along with the "global city" that constitutes it (Briden and Downing 2002).

The contemporary identification of "the environment" as a focal engagement for science and government, which is worth spending the vast sums of money upon, transforms it into a legitimate pursuit for knowledge communities to study. As Lefebvre asserts,

> Can the concept of an object (of a science) withstand close examination? Apparently more precise and more rigorous than the concept of a "domain" or "field," it nonetheless brings with it significant complications. For the object presents itself, or is presented, as *real* prior to any examination. It is said that there is no science without an object, no object without a science ... The concept of a scientific object, although convenient and easy, is deliberately simplistic and may conceal another intention: a strategy of fragmentation designed to promote a unitary and synthetic, and therefore authoritarian, model. An object is isolating even if conceived as a system that is dissimulated beneath the apparently "objective" nature of the scientific object. The sought-for-system constitutes its object by constituting itself. The constituted object then legitimates the system ... In other words, the "real" sociological object is an image and an ideology.
>
> (Lefebvre 2003: 56–57)

The state's and market's grudging endorsement of "the environment" as a policy priority for green governance exemplifies all of these tendencies. Its object is unstable, elusive, and ideological. Something exists at the interface of Nature and Society, but global spatiality becomes real in these terms only with certain preferred styles of examination, like the images of endangered environments and the ideologies of green statists. By postulating the analytical constructs of global spatiality, the environment becomes another twist in scientists' and technologists' articulation of "time-space," or, if you prefer, the inscription of "time in space," becomes an object of knowledge" (Lefebvre 2003: 73).

Once again, however, the positivistic pretense and interventionist impulse behind scientific power and knowledge is quite problematic (Fischer 1990; Jasanoff 1990). This entire pose draws its abstract ideology into the inscriptions of "time in space," because

> space is only a medium, environment and means, instrument and intermediary ... The relation between time and space that confers absolute priority to space is in fact a social relationship inherent in a society in which a certain form of rationality governing duration predominates. This reduces, and can even destroy, temporality. Ideology and science are merged.
>
> (Lefebvre 2003: 73–74)

Lefebvre's famous "triad of the perceived, the conceived, and the lived" (1991: 30) must be kept in mind, and the local knowledges, embedded ecologies, and thick understandings of "directly *lived*" representational spaces should anchor this radical recollection. The extreme poverty of most environmental philosophizing by green statists about environmental governance matches Lefebvre's fears about losing sight of "the lived." That is,

> the perceived-conceived-lived triad (in spatial terms: spatial practice, representations of space, representational spaces) loses all force if it is treated as an abstract model. If it cannot grasp the concrete (as distinct from "the immediate"), then its import is severely limited, amounting to no more than that of one ideological mediation among others.
>
> (Lefebvre 1991: 40)

Green statists' efforts to work around the spatial unfortunately forget that model construction is never free from criticism, and that best use of models comes comparing their tentative results to what is agreed to be real. Mistaking the model for the mechanisms in the green state is to confuse the map with the terrain. As Lefebvre argues, models are always provisional, and no method guarantees "absolute 'scientificity'," because,

> Even mathematics and linguistics are unable to guarantee a perfectly and definitively rigorous methodology. Although there are models, none

of them can be realized completely satisfactorily, none of them can be generalized, or transferred, or exported, or imported outside the sector within which they were constructed without exercising considerable precaution. The methodology of models is said to continue and refine the methodology of concepts. There are specific concepts, characteristic of each partial science, but none of them can completely determine an object by tracing its contours, by grasping it. The effective realization of an object involves considerable risk; even if the analyst constructs objects, these are provisional and reductive. Consequently, there are many models that do not constitute a coherent and completed whole.

(Lefebvre 2003: 66)

There is a finalism in the "sought-for-system" of ecological democracy emerging from abstract science as the "searched-for-system-now-found" as the green state.

The green statist imaginary of environmental governance, therefore, must be questioned severely at this juncture. Viewed as "Life" placed in "the Cosmos," or considered as sites where the forces of technoscientific production are in constant contention with resistances of everyday life, the Earth—or the spatiality of all terrestrial ecologies on this life-sustaining planet—continues to unfold its known and unknown qualities to science. As De Certeau concedes, the locality of place remains little more that a palimpsest:

Scientific analysis knows only its most recent text; and even then the latter is for science no more that the result of its epistemological decisions, its criteria and its goals. Why should it then be surprising that operations conceived in relation to this reconstitution have a "fictive" character and owe their (provisional?) success less to their perspicacity than to their power of breaking down the complexion of these interrelations between disparate forces and times.

(De Certeau 1988: 202)

The project of global ecological citizenship qua the imperatives of green statism clearly marks the latest efforts to expand "the empire of the evident in functionalist technocracy" (De Certeau 1988: 203). What is lost is the richness of grounded place-based knowing, as this preliminary overview has sought to demonstrate with regard to the reimagination of planetary places, processes, and practices at the interface of industrial and biophysical ecologies as the setting for a green public sphere, a green state, and the environmental governance brought to their interactions.

To close, but not to conclude, the challenge of globality and locality in environmental governance will require some sort of a return to thick "local knowledge," and not bringing in the thin "green state." Materiality and operationality work in the register of lived space as well as conceived space. To understand aspatiality for what some label a green public sphere, one can begin with Wendell Berry, Jane Jacobs, or Vandana Shiva. Pushing and pulling deliberative democratic discourse into the environment for the green state is a fascinating disciplinary diversion, but Murray Bookchin, Wendell Berry, Paul Goodman, or Harry C. Boyte have had far more to say here than Dryzek (2006) about ecological democracy. Regarding the green state, Eckersley's pious hopes could turn quite sharply into Ophuls' pernicious ecoauthoritarian imperatives with very little difficulty unless lived space is put on par with conceived space. One must emplace local knowledge in all of its environments, and do so without privileging positive epistemic communities' operationalism.

When any representations of space, which can be explicit or implicit, exalt "conceptualized space," or "the space of scientists, planners, urbanists, technocratic subdividers and social engineers," then one finds them pushing to "identify what is lived and what is perceived with what is conceived" (Lefebvre 1991: 38). Since they presume to express the power/knowledge behind what is conceived, technocratic subdividers and social engineers, like too many proponents of the green state, ecological public spheres or environmental civil society, exemplify Lefebvre's fears about an eclipse of "the lived" in their presumption of scientific authority, community knowledge, or environmental governance through their expert conceptual works-up of representational space. Indeed, ideology and knowledge can barely be divided as representation "supplants the concept of ideology and becomes a serviceable (operational) tool for the analysis of spaces" (Lefebvre 1991: 45).

Caution, then, is called for. Too much of today's environmental governance discourse reads like draft directives for empowering "environmental governors." In turn, such green governors' faith in their own sense of good science, their expert community knowledge, and their global fears of crisis would erase the lived, the local, and the living. In a quest to allow such green professional-technical experts great sway, if not formal authority, to realize the green state, the Earth would see Empire coming as environmentality (Luke 2004) rather than many diverse campaigns to attain local ecological democracy globally.

Note

1 Passages in this chapter draw from Luke, "A Harsh and Hostile Land: Edward Abbey's Politics and the Great American Desert," *Telos*, 141 (Winter 2007): 5–28; and Luke, "Ideology and Globalization: From Globalism and Environmentalism to Ecoglobalism," *Rethinking Globalism*, Manfred Steger (ed.), Lanham, MD: Rowman and Littlefield, 2004: 67–77.

References

Adas, M. (1989) *Machines as the Measure of Men: Science, Technology, and Ideologies of Western Dominance*, Ithaca, NY: Cornell University Press.
Agger, B. (1989) *Fast Capitalism*, Urbana: University of Illinois Press.

Agnew, J. (1987) *Place and Politics: The Geographical Mediation of State and Society*, Boston, MA: Allen and Unwin.

Appadurai, A. (1996) *Modernity at Large: Cultural Dimensions of Globalization*, Minneapolis: University of Minnesota Press.

Bachelard, G. (1994) *The Poetics of Space*, reprint ed., Boston, MA: Beacon Press.

Baudrillard, J. (1996) *The System of Objects*, London: Verso.

Beck, U. (2000) *What is Globalization?* Oxford: Blackwell.

——(1997) *The Reinvention of Politics*, Oxford: Polity Press.

Berkes, F., Folke, C., and Colding, J. (eds.) (2000) *Linking Social and Ecological Systems: Management Practices and Social Mechanisms for Building Resilience*, Cambridge: Cambridge University Press.

Briden, J. C. and Downing, T. E. (2002) *Managing the Earth: The Lineacre Lectures 2001*, Oxford: Oxford University Press.

Casey, E. (1998) *The Fate of Place: A Philosophical History*, Berkeley: University of California Press.

Cortner, H. J. and Moote, M. A. (1999) *The Politics of Ecosystem Management*, Washington, DC: Island Press.

Darier, E. (1999) *Discourses of the Environment*, Oxford: Blackwell.

De Certeau, M. (1988) *The Practice of Everyday Life*, Berkeley: University of California Press.

Dryzek, J. (2006) *Deliberative Global Politics: Discourse and Democracy in a Divided World*, Cambridge: Polity.

——(1987) *Rational Ecology: Environment and Political Economy*, London: Blackwell.

Eckersley, R. (2007) "Ecological Intervention: Prospects and Limits," *Ethics and International Affairs*, 21(3), 293–316.

—— (2004) *The Green State: Rethinking Democracy and Sovereignty*, Cambridge, MA: MIT Press.

Eder, K. (1996) *The Social Construction of Nature: A Sociology of Ecological Enlightenment*, London: Sage.

Evernden, N. (1992) *The Social Creation of Nature*, Baltimore, MD: Johns Hopkins University Press.

Fischer, F. (2000) *Citizens, Experts, and the Environment: The Politics of Local Knowledge*, Durham, NC: Duke University Press.

——(1990) *Technocracy and the Politics of Expertise*, London: Sage.

Forester, J. (1999) *The Deliberative Practitioner: Encouraging Participatory Planning Processes*, Cambridge, MA: MIT Press.

French, H. F. (2000) *Vanishing Borders: Protecting the Planet in the Age of Globalization*, New York: Norton.

Fukuyama, F. (1992) *The End of History and the Last Man*, New York: Free Press.

Giddens, A. (1990) *The Consequences of Modernity*, Stanford, CA: Stanford University Press.

Giedion, S. (1948) *Mechanization Takes Command: A Contribution to Anonymous History*, New York: Norton.

Gottlieb, R. (1993) *Forcing the Spring: The Transformation of the American Environmental Movement*, Washington, DC: Island Press.

Hardt, M. and Negri, T. (2000) *Empire*, Cambridge, MA: Harvard University Press.

Jacobs, J. (1993/1961) *The Death and Life of Great American Cities*, New York: Vintage.

——(1984) *Cities and the Wealth of Nations*, New York: Random House.

Jasanoff, S. (1990) *The Fifth Branch: Science Advisers as Policymakers*, Cambridge, MA: Harvard University Press.

Latour, B. (1993) *We Have Never Been Modern*, London: Harvester Wheatsheaf.

Lefebvre, H. (2003) *The Urban Revolution*, Minneapolis: University of Minnesota Press.

——(1991) *The Production of Space*, Oxford: Blackwell.

——(1981) *The Critique of Everyday Life, Vol. 3: From Modernity Towards a Metaphilosophy of Daily Life*, London: Verso.

Lukács, G. (1971) *History and Class Consciousness*, Cambridge, MA: MIT Press.

Luke, T. W. (2005) "Environmentalism as Globalization from Above and Below: Can World Watchers Truly Represent the Earth?" *Confronting Globalization: Humanity, Justice and the Renewal of Politics*, P. Hayden and C. El-Ojeili (eds.), New York: Palgrave Macmillan: 154–71.

——(2004) "Ideology and Globalization: From Globalism and Environmentalism to Ecoglobalism," *Rethinking Globalism*, Manfred Steger (ed.), Lanham, MD: Rowman and Littlefield, 67–77.

——(1999a) "Training Eco-Managerialists: Academic Environmental Studies as a Power/Knowledge Formation," *Living with Nature: Environmental Discourse as Cultural Politics*, F. Fischer and M. Hajer (eds.), Oxford: Oxford University Press, 103–20.

——(1999b) "Environmentality as Green Governmentality," *Discourses of the Environment*, Eric Darier (ed.), Oxford: Blackwell, 121–51.

—— (1997) *Ecocritique: Contesting the Politics of Nature, Economy and Culture*, Minneapolis: University of Minnesota Press.

—— (1996) "Identity, Meaning, and Globalization: Space-Time Compression and the Political Economy of Everyday Life," *Detraditionalization: Critical Reflections on Authority and Identity*, S. Lash, P. Heelas, and P. Morris (eds.), Oxford: Blackwell, 109–33.

——(1995) "New World Order or Neo-World Orders: Power, Politics and Ideology in Informationalizing Glocalities," *Global Modernities*, M. Featherstone, S. Lash, and R. Robertson (eds.), London: Sage, 91–107.

——(1994) "Placing Powers, Siting Spaces: The Politics of Global and Local in the New World Order," *Environment and Planning A: Society and Space*, 12: 613–28.

Lyotard, J.-F. (1991) *The Inhuman: Reflections on Time*, Stanford, CA: Stanford University Press.

——(1984) *The Postmodern Condition*, Minneapolis: University of Minnesota Press.

McNeill, J. R. (2000) *Something New Under the Sun: An Environmental History of the Twentieth-Century World*, New York: Norton.

Mittleman, J. (2000) *The Globalization Syndrome*, Princeton, NJ: Princeton University Press.

Nowotny, H., Scott, P., and Gibbons, M. (2001) *ReThinking Science: Knowledge and the Public in an Age of Uncertainty*, Cambridge: Polity Press.

Ohmae, K. (1990) *The Borderless World: Power and Strategy in an Interlocked Economy*, New York: Harper and Row.

Reich, R. (1991) *The Work of Nations: Preparing Ourselves for 21st Century Capitalism*, New York: Knopf.

Sklair, L. (2001) *The Transnational Capitalist Class*, Oxford: Blackwell.

Tabb, W. (2001) *The Amoral Elephant: Globalization and the Struggle for Social Justice in the Twenty-First Century*, New York: Monthly Review Press.

Thrift, N. (1996) *Spatial Formations*, London: Sage.

Torgerson, D. (1999) *The Promise of Green Politics: Environmentalism and the Public Sphere*, Durham, NC: Duke University Press.

Tuan, Y.-F. (2006/1981) *Space and Place: The Perspective of Experience*, Minneapolis: University of Minnesota Press.

Virilio, P. (2000) *The Landscape of Events*, Cambridge, MA: MIT Press.

——(1995) *The Art of the Motor*, Minneapolis: University of Minnesota Press.

3 Technical expertise, sustainability, and the politics of specialized knowledge[1]

Andrew Karvonen and Ralf Brand

The dominant role of technology in contemporary societies requires the public to rely on individuals with specialized knowledge to invent, design, manufacture and maintain increasingly complex artifacts and networks. As Stilgoe et al. (2006: 16) note, "Our everyday lives are played out through a series of technological and expert relationships." In spite of the increasing reliance on technologies and technical expertise, there has been an erosion of trust between the public and technical experts since the 1970s as contemporary environmental, social, and economic problems have revealed the limitations and unintended consequences of scientific and technological development. Thus, the role of technical experts in contemporary society is in flux. The emphasis in recent decades on creating more sustainable modes of life has only increased the tensions between scientific and technological development, environmental impacts, social conditions, and specialized knowledge.

In this chapter, we draw on work from the fields of environmental sociology (Hajer 1995; Dryzek 1997; Hannigan 2006), political science and policy analysis (Fischer 1990; 2000; 2006; Irwin 1995; Bäckstrand 2003; 2004; Stilgoe et al. 2006), and Science and Technology Studies (Sclove 1992; 1995; Moore 2001; 2007; Brand 2005a) to explore the relationship between experts and non-experts in environmental and sustainable decision-making. These authors have examined how specialized knowledge of technical experts and the informal knowledge of non-experts has been expressed in environmental politics, policy debates, urban development, and other venues.[2] Of particular interest is how experts from different disciplines interact with one another and the public they are ostensibly chartered to serve.

We begin with an overview of the ascendancy of the technical expert in contemporary society and a summary of the critiques of expertise. We then provide a brief discussion of sustainability, with particular emphasis on how it differs from previous conceptualizations of environmental problems, and question how traditional models of expertise fit within this new paradigm. Finally, we present four models of expertise that have been applied since the 1980s to create more sustainable modes of human life and conclude with a discussion of the implications that sustainability has for technical experts in the future.

The rise of the technical expert

The beginnings of technocracy—or perhaps more accurately termed "expertocracy"—can be traced to the Enlightenment when individuals began to acquire or were granted the power to shape and direct societies through scientific and technological development. Their efforts produced large complex systems including gas, electric, water, sewage, and transit networks, making technical experts particularly influential in public policy and city building activities (Seely 1996). We might say that experts served as the "human face" of technological networks, symbolizing the founding tenets of modernity including efficiency, stability, functionality, objectivity, and perhaps most importantly, progress (Hickman 1992).[3]

The rise of the technical expert in modern societies resulted in a privileged status for those with specialized knowledge. For example, vernacular German includes proverbs expounding the superiority of the engineer, such as *dem Ingeniör ist nichts zu schwör* (no task is too difficult for the engineer), with the engineer serving as a prominent symbol of national identity. The slogan "Made in Germany" was conceived after World War II to tie the nation's future to earlier technical achievements of genius inventors such as Werner von Siemens. In the US, a similar trend occurred at the turn of the twentieth century as the cowboy was replaced by the engineer as the symbol of American culture (Hickman 1992). Thayer describes the importance of the expert to the collective American psyche as follows:

> We have never lost the myth that technological innovation and invention is America's rightful spiritual territory ... Clearly Americans place greater social value upon those people whose occupations involve scientific discovery and technological development than on those who deal with social issues or problems. Starting salaries for engineers are roughly twice those of social workers or teachers.
>
> (Thayer 1994: 32)

Today, the most conspicuous technical experts in developed countries include natural scientists and engineers whose specialized knowledge is based on the formal study of a scientific or technical discipline. We can also include other disciplines under the banner of technical expertise, including architects, planners, lawyers, and policy experts. In this chapter, we focus specifically on technical experts in urban contexts—urban planners and designers, civil and environmental engineers, architects and landscape architects—but intend for the discussion to address all forms of expertise that explicitly address scientific and technical issues.

In all of these cases, the social power of the technical expert is derived from a combination of professional status (e.g. engineers and architects), adherence to the scientific method (natural scientists), or simply the mastery of a specialized field of knowledge through formal training (urban planners).

The technical expert is differentiated from non-experts by the possession of a "core set" of specialized knowledge as well as an elevated position in society, with non-experts deferring to the expert's superior judgment. As Selinger and Crease (2006a: 230) point out, "The phenomenon of expertise ... is ultimately and inextricably tied to its social utility."

While the pursuit of expertise has the social effect of elevating the individual to semi-god status, it comes at the expense of a narrowed perception through specialization.[4] Experts are celebrated for their microscopic, specialized analysis of problems rather than emphasizing a macroscopic, holistic perspective. As such, it would be antithetical to be considered a "holistic expert." Cliff Hague, former president of the UK's Royal Town Planning Institute, remarks in this context that:

> Twentieth century higher education and research has been dominated by analysis. Ever more sophisticated ways have been found to break experience down into its constituent parts. New disciplines have been built by reducing scope while deepening, and making more particular, the knowledge and methodologies.
>
> (Hague 1997: 4)

Critiques of expertise

This sacrifice of breadth for depth seems the logical price to pay for the acquisition of expert knowledge. Such a strategy facilitates the division of labor among different disciplines, a pragmatic approach to dealing with the increasingly complex technical artifacts and systems that comprise contemporary societies. However, the specialized worldview of the technical expert has not gone unchallenged. At the most basic level, the limited perspective of the expert is problematic because of the inability to "see the forest for the trees." As Lane and McDonald (2005: 724) argue, "technical knowledge simultaneously sharpens our focus and obscures our vision." But specialized knowledge has deeper problems beyond its atomistic worldview, four of which we discuss briefly in the following paragraphs.

First, ontological and epistemological critiques of expertise challenge the commonly held assumptions about knowledge generation practices. The ontological assumption of traditional forms of expertise is that of a knowable and unequivocally re-presentable world "out there," the basis of positivist philosophy. Harding (2000: 129) describes this stance as the dream of "one world, one and only one possible true account of it, and one unique science that can capture that one truth most accurately reflecting nature's own order." It follows that there is a universal knowledge free from the shackles of context, its validity and applicability independent of both time and space. In this perspective, knowledge overcomes immanence and rises to the realm of transcendence. Thus, the positivist approach to problem solving, environmental or otherwise, is through the application of universal knowledge. Adherents of universal knowledge tend to adhere to a teleological notion of progress and believe in ultimate solutions that can be discovered by following the "proper path of science" (Moore 2001). Naturally, positivists tend to ignore post-modern and post-structural scholars who argue that science is plural rather than unitary (Harding 2000). Critics of positivism dismiss foundational claims that are universal and ahistorical because they allegedly reduce the world to isolated, discrete and meaningless pieces. Instead, they forward a holistic, pluralistic imagination (Schlosberg 1999; Guy and Moore 2007).

A second critique of expertise is that it relies on a positivist worldview that couples the universality of scientific and technical knowledge with the notion that this knowledge is value-free and neutral. Technical experts tend to be portrayed as objective actors in policy-making activities, transcending partisan interests and "speaking truth to power" (Fischer 2006; Stilgoe et al. 2006). However, the existence of multiple forms of formal knowledge, and the inherent political character of this knowledge, is readily apparent in environmental conflicts.

The institutional bias toward expert knowledge has been countered by the emergence of counter-experts, individuals who can dispute technical experts on their own terms (Yearley 2000). Arguably the most famous of environmental counter-experts is Rachel Carson, whose writings were highly influential during the founding of contemporary environmental movements. In *Silent Spring*, Carson (1962) relied on a network of researchers and scientific evidence rather than moral arguments to make the case against the indiscriminate use of pesticides in the US (Lytle 2007). Her approach of "fighting science with science" helped to spawn the emergence of counter-expertise in environmental conflicts where a high degree of uncertainty and the presence of conflicting values are both common and unavoidable.

Since the 1960s, environmental NGOs have become increasingly adept at employing counter-experts to muddy the scientific waters through the introduction of competing interpretations of a particular scientific or technical issue. Outside of scientific debates, other technical experts can also serve as counter-experts, as in the case of Jane Jacobs (1961) intervening in master planning efforts in the 1960s. This is not to say that counter-experts are equals to experts but rather that they challenge their authority using equivalent methods and language. For example, competing expert knowledges are frequently marshaled by property developers and nongovernmental organizations (NGOs) to deliberate over the implications of environmental impact assessments.

The rise of counter-experts is a response to the inclination for technical experts to frame technical problems through the eyes of their elite employers (Fischer 2000). Foreman (1998: 60) argues that technical experts in government and corporations become the "perceived handmaidens in science and technology" and can even work at odds with the public they are ostensibly chartered to serve. In this context, Fischer notes that the emergence of the counter-expert in contemporary environmental disputes:

redirects our attention ... to the limits of our knowledge ... [and] uncertainties [that] have shaken the public's faith in the experts. After having long trusted experts generally, citizens are confronted with the task of choosing which experts to believe and trust.

(Fischer 2000: 61)

A third critique of technical expertise points to the existence of experiential, local, or tacit knowledge arising from personal experience and exploration outside the confines of educational institutions and without strict adherence to the scientific method.[5] Thus, multiple forms of *formal* knowledge are joined by multiple forms of *informal* knowledge. Scott (1999: 320) differentiates between formal and informal knowledge using the classical notions of *techne* and *metis* where the former involves "impersonal, often quantitative precision and a concern with explanation and verification," while the latter refers to indigenous knowledge, meaning, experience, and practical results. This distinction is particularly apparent when comparing Western science to other forms of knowledge, with the former being abstract, reductionist, and oriented toward the separation of humans from non-humans (Lane and McDonald 2005). Stakeholders who lack formal knowledge are often portrayed as being "incapable of grasping the technical nuance and methodological complexity of science" (Kleinman 2000: 139). In this regard, Turner (2001: 123) observes that, "expertise is treated as a kind of possession which privileges its possessors with powers that the people cannot successfully control, and cannot acquire or share in."

The recognition of different forms of knowledge by post-positivists highlights the tension between democratic forms of governance and technical expertise. When discussing scientific and technical problems, holders of experiential, local, or tacit knowledge are generally not granted a seat at the decision-making table due to an institutional bias toward formal knowledge. As such, the possession of technical expertise has significant political implications by marginalizing those who do not subscribe to a positivist worldview and the primacy of expert opinion. The centrality of the technical expert in political systems is commonly referred to as *technocracy*, where technical experts rule by virtue of their specialized knowledge and position in the dominant political and economic institutions. Here, expert knowledge is applied to the task of governance and promotes technical solutions to political problems, with the technical expert assumed to be above partisan politics and an irrational general public (Fischer 1990).

Fourth and finally, there are important practical issues that cannot be resolved through the application of technical expertise. For example, Ulrich Beck (1992) argues that the question of whether we should use nuclear energy can never be answered with an objective "yes" or "no" because issues of risk and risk perception require "soft" and culturally specific responses. Values and politics are embedded in sociotechnical developments and no "Pareto optimum" calculation can ever offset a collective preference for caution. This is clearly the case with contemporary scientific disputes over climate change, genetically modified organisms, human cloning, nano-technology, and the like. A technocratic response to these conflicts is to portray critics of scientific and technical solutions as irrational and the mis-sion of technical experts often becomes one of educating objectors to the "facts" of a particular problem or even ignoring their pleas. However, the idea that solving "wicked problems" by uncovering all of the facts is not only delusional; it can lead to an impasse in decision-making due to the lack of data (the common problem of "paralysis by analysis").

Clearly, the contemporary model of technical expertise has numerous problems related to epistemological and ontological issues, objectivity, poli-tical power, and practical matters, as summarized above. The deficiencies of the positivist worldview become even more apparent when we consider the notion of sustainability in the following section.

Sustainability as a challenge to the primacy of the technical expert

Sustainability has multiple meanings and interpretations, although most advocates would probably agree that it involves a holistic approach to sol-ving complex, interrelated, and multi-dimensional problems. Dryzek (1997: 126) argues that the main accomplishment of sustainability has been "to combine systematically a number of issues that have often been treated in isolation, or at least as competitors." Thus, the principal advantage of sus-tainability is that it takes a pluralistic and inclusive view of problem solving, as opposed to conventional problem solving that limits its focus to particular elements while overlooking unintended consequences as well as the proverbial "big picture."

The conceptual comprehensiveness of the sustainability agenda is, for better or worse, a result of its multidisciplinary genealogy. One of the earliest examples of this holistic form of thinking can be traced to English and German forest management practices in the seventeenth century, as articu-lated by John Evelyn and Hans Carl von Carlowitz. They argued that one should not harvest more wood than a particular forest yields, instead advo-cating for a form of steady-state resource extraction. In the nineteenth century, urban social reformers such as Edwin Chadwick extended the degradation of environmental conditions beyond economic management by recognizing the link between the poor health conditions of the British working class and urban sanitary conditions. The contemporary notion of sustainability has its roots in these early modern practices that recognize the interrelated quality of seemingly independent problems.

The most widely cited definition of sustainability is attributed to the so-called Brundtland Commission, and states that sustainable development "is devel-opment that meets the needs of the present without compromising the ability of future generations to meet their own needs" (WCED 1987: 43). This broad definition of the concept has proven difficult to translate into practice, and many scholars have developed heuristic models to elucidate the application of sustainability. Perhaps the most famous of these is the *Three E* model that describes sustainability as the triad of *E*conomic viability, *E*nvironmental protection, and social *E*quity.[6] The model is intended to highlight the challenge of simultaneously accommodating a multiplicity of competing demands. In other words, the openness of the sustainability concept to various claims and concerns comes at the price of compromise. Campbell (1996) highlights a crucial implication of this model by identifying the inherent conflicts between each pair of "Es" and the pressing need for strategies to resolve these tensions. From this perspective, sustainability issues involve the management of conflict through a "restless, dialectical process" of open discussion and negotiation (Healey 2004: 95).

Recognizing the importance of negotiation between competing interests reveals sustainability as an inherently political endeavor. Prugh et al. (2000: 7) note that "sustainability is provisional; it is subject to multiple conceptions and continuous revision, the very stuff of politics." Sustainability is also context specific, or as Guy and Moore (2005: 1) argue, it is "more a matter of local interpretation than of the setting of objective or universal goals." Identifying the most suitable political system to facilitate successful resolution of conflicts and the amicable exchange of interpretations then becomes a pressing concern for sustainability advocates (Moore and Brand 2003; Moore 2007). Clearly, then, the conventional model of technical expertise that purports to be objective, apolitical, and value-free is not an ideal fit for political interpretations of sustainability.

Despite the inherent politics of the sustainability charter, the Western world has generally addressed this challenge by relying heavily on technical expertise (see Tate et al. 1998). Technical experts have been tapped to develop more efficient and effective technologies to avoid stakeholder conflicts and unintended consequences, a prime example being the development of renewable energy strategies to replace fossil fuels. This is the underlying message of ecological modernization advocates in Northern Europe and their green business counterparts in North America who argue that industrial society's harmful aspects can be expunged through the application of improved technologies (for example, see Hawken et al. 1999; McDonough and Braungart 2002). The attractiveness of ecological modernization stems from its implicit assumption that environmental and social problems can be overcome without leaving the path of modernization (Hannigan 2006). Thus, sustainability becomes a technocratic endeavor, one that retains power in the hands of the political and economic elites, strengthening the compact between technical experts and their elite employers. As Dryzek (1997: 147) concludes, "in its most limited sense, ecological modernization looks like a discourse for engineers and accountants."

Bäckstrand (2004: 707) is equally critical of ecological modernization because it exacerbates "the dichotomous divide between nature and society, social and scientific knowledge, expert and non-expert knowledge ... hence, ecological modernization does not rely on a new conception of science." However, she adds that more radical forms of ecological modernization are possible. Strong, bottom-up notions of ecological democracy that champion public deliberation communication and participation by civil society can serve as an antidote to the technological fix approach of weak or top-down ecological modernization approaches. Bäckstrand and other critics of ecological modernization do not call for the wholesale abandonment of technical expertise, but rather contend that technology can be directed by society as a whole rather than imposed from above by powerful elites. Such bottom-up approaches emphasize the creation of political communities to deliberate on conflicts and to transform them via equitable and lasting solutions.

Finding common ground between technical experts and sustainability

Those who advocate for the deliberative, bottom-up model of sustainability will likely agree that conventional notions of expertise are not an optimal fit with notions of sustainability. In other words, we should be careful when employing the term *sustainable expert* because of the inherent conflicts between specialized and holistic worldviews as well as the related political issues. Does this mean that there is no such thing as expertise in sustainability? Do we need to abandon specialized knowledge and adopt a holistic worldview that takes into account multiple viewpoints? Is there reason to believe that the technical expert may gradually become an endangered species, as Dreyfus and Dreyfus (1986) fear? We argue that while the fit between technical expertise and sustainability is not ideal, it is far from a hopeless endeavor. Rather than abandoning specialized knowledge outright, we see possibilities for renovating technical expertise to align with the goals of sustainability. In the following paragraphs, we identify four types of expertise that have been employed since the 1980s to reorient holders of specialized knowledge toward more sustainable goals. We label these approaches the *outreach expert*, the *multidisciplinary expert*, the *meta-expert*, and the *civic expert*. Each makes unique and helpful contributions to the renovation of conventional forms of expertise.

The outreach expert

One response to the eroding credibility of technical experts has been a call for a more informed and scientifically literate public. This movement, first taken up in the 1980s, focuses on issues of risk and uncertainty in science and technology, and is frequently referred to as "the public understanding of science." The intent has been to improve communication of scientific and technical knowledge to affected citizenry and in turn, to educate the public about the importance of this knowledge (Wynne 1996; Turner 2001). Jamison (2005) argues that "using science and technology appropriately means, for one thing, that we know how to talk about it and that we have what might be called a collectively shared understanding of the relevant science or technology, that is, that we are scientifically literate." Clearly, this is an appealing and desirable model; it would be difficult to argue against a more educated public, particularly with respect to important issues of science and technology.

One way that scientists and technical experts have imparted their knowledge to the public has been through Science Shops that have proliferated in the United Kingdom, the Netherlands, and other Northern European countries (see Irwin 1995).[7] The concept has also been adopted by several universities in these countries, and we describe these activities collectively as the *outreach model*. We define outreach as "the activity of an organization in making contact and fostering relations with people unconnected with it, [especially] for the purpose of support or education and for increasing awareness of the organization's aims or message" (OED 2007). The model implies that scientific and technical organizations (and universities in particular) should serve as repositories of wisdom, reaching out to those who are implicated in the application of specialized knowledge.

In some circumstances, the dissemination of specialized knowledge can be useful for at least partially resolving the tensions between experts and non-experts. It has the potential to level the knowledge playing field to some degree and open up debate over technical and scientific problems by disseminating shared language and understanding of the problems. As such, it can be an effective strategy for rebuilding trust between the techno-scientific community and the general public. However, this model has significant shortcomings. First, it does little to address existing power differentials between experts and non-experts, and instead falls back on the conventional "sage on the stage" model of modern scientific and technological development. It has a tendency to reinforce paternalistic, positivist notions of expertise where knowledge elites retain a core set of knowledge that they impart to an ignorant public. This approach can be seen as token reform of technical expertise because its sole emphasis is to bring the public up to speed while leaving expert practice unchanged. Furthermore, it implies that the public, through its ignorance of science and technology, is largely to blame for scientific and technical failures, further exacerbating the lack of trust between experts and non-experts. Finally, it continues to adhere to the "truth to power" model of expertise with respect to the public; it talks to the public but does not listen (Stilgoe et al. 2006). Thus, we conclude that the outreach expert model is a necessary but insufficient form of technical expertise.

The multidisciplinary expert

A second option for accommodating and aligning technical expertise with the discursive and political nature of sustainability is to increase the permeability between existing disciplinary boundaries. The notion of "disciplinary silos" is familiar to anyone who has worked in a university setting where scholars in different departments pursue similar problems in parallel rather than collaboratively, due to ingrained disciplinary habits and restrictive institutional and disciplinary norms and structures (Fischer 2006). The pursuit of sustainability research agendas has the potential to transcend these norms and structures by recognizing the overlaps between related disciplines and by initiating collaborative work. The aim here is not to abandon specialized knowledge but rather to improve experts' understanding of their role with respect to other technical disciplines, particularly where commonalities or overlaps exist.

Multidisciplinary expertise can, of course, reside in the individual. For example, the groundbreaking work of physician John Snow in mid-nineteenth-century London to address the problem of cholera is a famous example of an individual employing multidisciplinary expertise. Snow transgressed the disciplinary boundaries of medicine, chemistry, demography, sociology, and cartography to debunk the widely embraced miasma theory as the primary cause of urban disease transmission (see Johnson 2006). Likewise, the father of landscape architecture and urban planning, Frederick Law Olmsted, was a multidisciplinary expert who incorporated issues of functionality, aesthetics, and social needs in his parks and urban designs. He acknowledged the connections between social and environmental problems, although the political and cultural dimensions of his projects tended to be less successful than his engineering and landscape design elements (Spirn 1996).

While multidisciplinarity can be an individual endeavor, we are more interested here in partnerships that are formed by experts from two or more disciplines to address problems of sustainability. The formation of multi-disciplinary teams is a common practice in sustainability, as exhibited in the partnership of architect William McDonough and chemist Michael Braungart (McDonough and Braungart 2002) or the collaboration between business entrepreneur Paul Hawken, physicist Amory Lovins, and management consultant Hunter Lovins (Hawken et al. 1999). Collaboration leads to the identification of commonalities and the formation of a new core set related to but independent of the core sets of each individual. Thus, multi-disciplinary expertise reinforces the legitimacy and power of expert knowledge through an alliance between two or more core sets of technical expertise.

An example of the benefits of multidisciplinary cooperation is illustrated by activities in the Belgian city of Hasselt in the mid-to-late 1990s. Located 70 kilometers east of Brussels, Hasselt was plagued by severe traffic-related problems. Engineers proposed a conventional technical solution of building a third ring-road around the city to divert automobile traffic from the historic center. Those trusting in the virtue of individuals argued that the transportation problems could be solved through campaigns to change citizen behavior by encouraging walking, cycling, and public transport. However, the city council chose to ignore both the proposed technological fix and the behavioral fix solution and instead, embarked on a multi-pronged approach to encourage non-automobile forms of transportation. The driving lanes in the inner city were narrowed and hundreds of trees were planted to create a more pleasant and walkable city center environment. Facilities for bicyclists (bicycle lanes, storage sheds, and showers) were introduced along with bicycle pool programs where adults could volunteer to accompany children to school. Another program was established to provide bonuses to employees who cycled to work. Public transport services were increased eightfold and included new bus routes with five-minute intervals and heated rooms for waiting passengers.

As a whole, the multifaceted planning solution undertaken in Hasselt involved a partnership of public policy, urban design, and engineering experts that created a combination of "hard" infrastructure strategies and "soft" social solutions to form a multifaceted transportation strategy at several levels. One of the co-designers of these solutions contended that the technical experts initially "made the mistake of only looking at the 'engineering' side of it," and went on to argue that the success of the project "is all about a combination of measures, definitely not only by engineers: engineering, mentality, environment, city building, social issues, communication" (Moerkerk 2002).

There are, of course, a number of formidable barriers to overcome in the pursuit of multidisciplinary research agendas including but not limited to jargon, epistemological assumptions, funding protocols, and the portioning of reputational credit arising from joint projects. For example, the politics of "units of assessment" (UoA) as promulgated by the UK Research Assessment Exercise is an example of an institutional structure that creates disincentives to collaborate across disciplinary boundaries. The work of every UK academic researcher has to be allocated to one of the sixty-seven subject-based UoAs, and critics argue that this mechanism poses problems for the practice of multidisciplinary research—although the responsible organization denies that this is the case (HERO 2002).

Similar to the previous model of the outreach expert, the multidisciplinary expert has merit but again fails to question the idea of a core set of specialized knowledge being retained by technical experts. Sustainable problem solving remains in the elitist province of the alma mater and does not challenge the boundary between experts and non-experts. Also, the multidisciplinary expert continues to promote technocratic approaches over the inclusion of tacit and experiential forms of knowledge.

The meta-expert

Taken to its extreme, the preceding notion of the multidisciplinary expert begins to resemble an entirely new class of expert that we label here the *meta-expert*. The role of the meta-expert goes beyond disciplinary collaboration and is dedicated to juggling the sundries of multiple specialized knowledges and, in effect, acting as a broker of technical expertise. Meta-experts are generalists with a clear understanding of what specific disciplines can and cannot contribute to problems of sustainability. They do not subscribe to a core set of knowledge but rather have the license to "pick cherries"—they are unabashed "eclecticists" who have the skill to translate across different clusters of expertise. As such, meta-experts act as interdisciplinary brokers, developing specific solutions through the synergy of multiple core sets of knowledge.

An example of meta-expertise is evident in sustainable building practices that have emerged in North America and Northern Europe in the past decade. In sustainable building projects, the building owner or developer hires a sustainable building consultant to facilitate brainstorming sessions or charrettes with project team members and identify synergies between different building strategies. For instance, the meta-expert might recognize the multiple benefits of designing the project with a green or vegetated roof (insulating properties, increased roof life, stormwater runoff, aesthetics, etc.) and then coordinate the strategy by facilitating discussion and design between the various project team members (architect, mechanical engineer, structural engineer, landscape architect, and civil engineer). The sustainable building expert recognizes that sustainability strategies are multi-valent and have numerous intended and unintended implications for the project as a whole. In the above example, the green building consultant might recognize how the green roof strategy could interfere with other project goals such as rainwater harvesting, a daylighting approach that relies on roof skylights, or cost limitations. By identifying these conflicts in advance, the meta-expert can initiate dialogue among the team members to decide on the optimal strategies to pursue.[8]

Meta-experts adhere to the ontological assumption that sustainability is neither a problem of simplicity nor a problem of disorganized complexity but rather a problem of "organized complexity" (Jacobs 1961). Under the first model, cause-and-effect chains can be fully explained, and thus, solved by formulaic management rules. Under the second model, these chains are too complex to be fully described and can be tackled only with stochastic evaluations of previous interventions. The third model as followed by meta-experts recognizes that patterns can be understood but not by a sole individual. As such, technical expertise consists of "situated knowledges" and solving problems requires the pooling of knowledges to develop a shared asset base. The purpose of the meta-expert is to identify potential linkages and facilitate their co-discovery by mediating between different technical experts.[9] Unlike the multidisciplinary expert who retains a core set of specialized knowledge, the meta-expert coordinates many core sets to devise a meta set of knowledge. Cliff Hague (1997: 4) argues that planners are reasonably well equipped to play the role of the meta expert because "town planning ... has [always] prioritized synthesis over analysis. Planners have been magpies across the disciplines, picking relevance where they found it." One could also imagine public policy experts, sociologists, anthropologists and geographers being particularly well positioned for such roles.

The civic expert

The previous three models of expertise have advantages over traditional models of expertise because they improve non-expert understanding of scientific and technical knowledge (the outreach expert model) or increase communication and collaboration between experts (the multidisciplinary expert and meta-expert models). However, none of these models systematically challenges the privileged status of expert knowledge or attempts to engage in a substantive manner with non-experts. In other words, they do not challenge the technocratic mode of decision-making and fail to require that technical experts also *listen* to the so-called non-experts. Brand (2005b: 19) describes these seemingly ordinary individuals as the "ultimate experts in user behavior" because they literally create everyday conditions.

John Dewey advocated for new forms of collaboration between experts and the public as early as the 1920s, arguing that, "The man who wears the shoe knows best that it pinches and where it pinches, even if the expert shoemaker is the best judge of how the trouble is to be remedied" (Dewey 1927/1954: 207). The attitude towards experts as first suggested by Dewey, William James, and other American Pragmatists, has more recently been forwarded by advocates of civic environmentalism such as DeWitt John (1994) and William Shutkin (2000). Here, a number of informal expertises (experiential, local, tacit, and indigenous) are also perceived to be valid. The acknowledgement of a plurality of expert knowledge challenges what Bruno Latour (1987) refers to as "science-as-institution" by admitting other actors to scientific and technical decision-making processes. This is not a direct assault on the conventional technical expert but rather a call to enrich science and technological decision-making by embracing a wider range of expert opinion (Stilgoe et al. 2006).

To accommodate ideas of tacit or experiential knowledge, and to facilitate two-way communication between experts and non-experts, we introduce a fourth category of expertise, the *civic expert*. Civic expertise revolves around participatory models of specialized knowledge and highlights the social contingency of technological endeavors by eliciting critical reflection on social circumstances and needs, and allows for the transparent and accountable recognition of non-focal technological consequences (Sclove 1992; Bäckstrand 2004). For example, new models of scientific debate that have emerged in Northern Europe in the last decade over genetically modified foods and nanotechnology represent a softening in the stance of experts and a new relationship with the public that replaces passive acceptance for interested partnership (Stilgoe et al. 2006). From this perspective, the top-down authority of the expert involved in technocratic forms of politics is replaced by democratic politics where experts and non-experts function as collaborators or partners in problem solving. This arrangement does not guarantee an equitable distribution of power between stakeholders but at the very least, allows for the possibility that non-expert voices can be heard.

A number of promising techniques have been developed to advance the notion of civic science and expertise, including constructive technology assessment, strategic niche management, citizen panels, and the *L'Eprouvette* initiative at the University of Lausanne.[10] The intent of these approaches is to open policy-making procedures to actors other than technical experts by including citizen voices in scientific and technological debates (see Rip et al. 1995). Schot and Rip (1997) refer to these processes as "second-order learning" that involve critical reflection upon the assumptions that underpin the pursuit of factual and technical first-order learning. The involvement of citizens in technical decision-making broadens expertise by not only asking the question of "how" but also of "why".[11] These notions of civic expertise have been adopted by a wide variety of STS scholars including Arie Rip, Richard Sclove, Sheila Jasanoff, Brian Wynne, and Steve Fuller, among others.

Civic expertise is not only a policy model but can be project-oriented and hands-on. An example of civic expertise in architectural practice is the emergence of design/build practices since the 1990s that involve service learning and project-based education. The most widely known design/build program in the US is the Rural Studio at Auburn University in Alabama, founded by Samuel Mockbee and Dennis K. Ruth in 1992. This approach has spread to several other architecture schools, notably the University of Virginia, the University of Washington, and the University of Texas at Austin. The purpose of design/build is to increase the public role of the architect through advocacy and engagement with under-served communities. Design/build programs combine community outreach, formal education, and architectural design and production through a one- or two-semester engagement in a small building project such as a house or community center. The technical expert (architecture professor) acts as the moderator between the experts-to-be (architecture students) and community members, resulting in "a mutual exchange between the designer and the client, and in the best cases, a mutual benefit to both. Through a participatory process these benefits are defined, clearly understood by all, and mutually sought" (Bell 2004: 13). Architectural design thus becomes a democratic process of negotiation between all interested parties.

The idea here is that public engagement in scientific and technological development needs to move upstream, rejecting the "end-of-pipe" model where the public is reactive to the consequences of science and technology and instead, makes transparent the assumptions, values, and visions that drive science in the first place (Wilsdon and Willis 2004). Proponents of civic expertise argue that this mode is not antithetical to science and technological development. Indeed, the spirit of science is skeptical, exploratory, and uncertain, with the practices of peer review, publication, and argument being a foundational practice in the scientific and technical communities, if only to a select group within the community. Advocates of civic science argue that new questions about scientific and technological development are not a threat but rather an opportunity to develop better scientific and technological solutions. As such, experts should be "on tap, not on top" (Stilgoe et al. 2006).

Nowotny et al. (1999) argue that it is only through participatory, discursive, and multifaceted approaches that science can become socially robust and accountable. The civic expertise model is the point where practical considerations about the feasibility, acceptability, and efficacy of technological interventions for sustainability converge with the normative call for the democratization of technology (see Sclove 1995; Fischer 2000). Civic expertise is a significant departure from conventional technical expertise, relying on the notion that "the rules for [the] *production* of scientific [and technical] knowledge will have to change in order to enact civic science" (Bäckstrand 2003: 34, emphasis added). This approach is related to Mode 2 Science as proposed by Gibbons et al. (1994) by involving non-experts through transdisciplinary practices such as citizen juries and consensus conferences.

Similar to the meta-expert model, an existing group of technical experts is aligned toward a civic mode of expertise. Forester describes the role of participatory planners as follows:

> In cities and regions, neighborhoods and towns, planners typically have to shuttle back and forth between public agency staff and privately interested parties, between neighborhood and corporate representatives, between elected officials and civil service bureaucrats. They do not just shuttle back and forth though. Trying to listen carefully and argue persuasively they do much more. They work to encourage practical public deliberation—public listening, learning and beginning to act on innovative agreements too—as they move project and policy proposals forward to viable implementation or decisive rejection.
>
> (Forester 1999: 143)

The civic expert model moves beyond the ecological modernization version of sustainable development and frames knowledge generation as a socially distributed phenomenon that includes experts and non-experts alike. The goal of the expert is not to generate reliable knowledge validated by disciplinary peers but to develop robust knowledge from socially distributed expertise (Nowotny et al. 1999; Bäckstrand 2004). Robust knowledge emphasizes the processes of knowledge generation rather than the end product of these processes (Nowotny 2003). The ultimate benefit of the civic expertise model and the increased input of non-experts is the potential for improved decision-making via "the intelligence of democracy" (Lindblom and Woodhouse 1993). Searching for agreement among multiple stakeholders allows for the acknowledgement of the polyvalent nature of science and technology and enlists stakeholders in the process of characterizing and considering a technology's social implications (Sclove 1992).

As a whole, the practice of discursive technological development suggested by the civic expertise model is the most ambitious proposal outlined here. However, it faces specific and particularly significant barriers, including entrenched power relations, as well as a lack of familiarity and experience with deliberative practices among all involved parties, experts and non-experts alike. Likewise, there is a significant epistemological difference in that knowledge emerges from deliberation rather than being imparted by the technical expert to non-experts. It should be no surprise that these more democratic forms of technological development have emerged in political cultures such as Denmark and the Netherlands where citizen participation in political decision-making processes is encouraged and commonplace. However, participatory technological policy-making continues to be an exception to the rule even in these countries, highlighting the formidable challenges to expanding scientific and technological debates to include the general public.

Towards an ecosystem of expertise

Table 3.1 provides a summary of the four models of expertise described above. The models can be differentiated by their epistemological and disciplinary assumptions, their attitudes toward other experts and the public, and how they envision the flow of technical knowledge. We have argued elsewhere that these models as a whole comprise an *ecosystem of expertise*

Table 3.1 Four models of expertise to address sustainability

	Outreach expert	*Multidisciplinary expert*	*Meta-expert*	*Civic expert*
Cliché role	"The educator"	"The good neighbor"	"The broker"	"The democrat"
Epistemological assumptions	Core set of scientific principles	Overlap of disciplinary core sets	Cherry-picking and synergism of core sets	Emergent from discourse
Disciplinary assumption	Mono-disciplinary	Multidisciplinary	Interdisciplinary	Transdisciplinary
Attitude toward other experts	Competitors	Potential collaborators	Necessary collaborators	One of many sources of knowledge
Attitude toward the public	Receivers of expert wisdom	Not considered	Not considered	Partner in generating solutions
Knowledge flow	Top-down	Lateral	Lateral and discursive	Multi-directional and discursive
Role of power	Competition between disciplines for the exclusive claim to truth	Defined by overlaps between disciplines	Emergent from collaboration between disciplines	Shared and contested between experts and non-experts
Example	Science Shops	Hasselt transportation	Sustainable building consultant	Design/build programs

where different niches are filled by different interpretations of what it means to be an expert in sustainability issues (Brand and Karvonen 2007).

There are clearly merits to each approach and a general conclusion we forward is that, at this early stage in the development, it is not important to determine which model is most effective. In other words, each of these models should be welcomed because it challenges traditional roles of the technical expert in different ways. Each model encourages holders of specialized knowledge to consider their multiple roles as experts, citizens, and participants in democratic politics, to assess their individual strengths and weaknesses, and determine how to orient their work and allegiance toward one or more of these models. For example, those of us who are better at collaborating with other experts should do so while those of us who are better at communicating with the public might choose the Outreach Expert model or the more aggressive Civic Expert model. We recognize that such a pluralist attitude toward expertise is an idealized perspective whose implementation will face numerous hurdles in terms of institutional incentives, vested interests, power gradients, and so on. We describe these modes of expertise in the hope of arousing debate among practitioners and theorists of sustainability as an invitation to strategize on methods to overcome these barriers.

However, an important question that lurks in the background of this framework is the motivation for technical experts to change their attitudes and orientations toward other disciplines and the public. Why should experts sacrifice their relatively privileged social position? Three points come to mind that may make these models more appealing. First, the models of expertise presented above can potentially help to reverse the erosion of trust between experts and the general public. Sustainability problem solving can be seen as a way to bridge the gulf between those with specialized knowledge and those who are implicated in the application of this knowledge.

Second, the quest for more sustainable solutions can appeal to the problem solving disposition shared by most, if not all, technical experts. The promise of more socially acceptable and, in essence, more effective solutions is worth the work required in renovating existing scientific and technical approaches to problem solving.

And finally, there is an ethical dimension to expertise. With professionals such as architects and engineers, ethics is embodied in their commitment to serve society and thus, new models of expertise offer a way to fulfill their social contract. For non-professionals, an ethical argument cannot rely on the professional's social contract but can appeal to the citizen within the technical expert. We leave these normative dimensions of expertise for future study but recognize that this is perhaps the most formidable barrier to adopting these models.

In conclusion, we venture two challenges to all technical experts. First, it is important to maintain a bird's-eye view of the system and resist the temptation of adopting old or new claims of exclusivity. There are advantages to all of the different niches that these emerging models of expertise offer, and the goal of experts should be to appreciate these different niches and seek strategic collaborations and new modes of practice. Second, a formidable barrier to the further development of these modes of expertise is the institutional barriers that inhibit multidisciplinary, interdisciplinary, and transdisciplinary collaboration. There is a need to lobby for the dissolution or at least lowering of these barriers if sustainable approaches to scientific and technological development are to become widespread. The former is an individual challenge, the latter a political one.

Notes

1 This chapter is a revised version of an article that was published in *Sustainability: Science, Practice, and Policy* (see Brand and Karvonen 2007).
2 Another emerging discourse on expertise has been introduced by philosophers of science. Harry Collins and Robert Evans call this discourse "Studies of Expertise and Experience" and emphasize a core set of knowledge held by experts (see Collins and Evans 2002; 2007; and Selinger and Crease 2006a). This is a markedly different interpretation of expertise when compared to STS scholars who question the legitimacy of knowledge claims made by technical experts (for an extended critique of Collins and Evans, see the June 2003 issue of *Social Studies of Science*).
3 For a helpful discussion of progress as it relates to scientific and technological development, see Marx 1999.
4 With respect to specialization, it is often joked that experts know more and more about less and less until they know everything about nothing (Stilgoe et al. 2006).
5 Those with tacit knowledge have been referred to as "lay experts" but we avoid this term due to its internal inconsistency (see Collins and Evans 2002; Stilgoe et al. 2006).
6 This model is also referred to as the Three P model (people, prosperity, and planet) or the Triple Bottom Line.
7 The US has no equivalent model of Science Shops, although the National Science Foundation attempted to support similar activities through its "Science for Citizens Program" in the late 1970s (Fischer 2006).
8 The meta-expert approach to sustainable building has been codified in programs such as the US Green Building Council's Leadership in Energy and Environmental Design (LEED) and the Building Research Establishment's Environmental Assessment Method (BREEAM) (see www.usgbc.org and www.breeam.org).
9 Biologist E. O. Wilson (1998) describes the synthesis of knowledge using the term "consilience" and advocates for finding common ground for explanation between humanities and sciences. We are encouraged by his call to bridge disciplines although we disagree with the inherent positivist assumptions in his argument.
10 See Labo, "L'Eprouvette" at www.unil.ch/interface/.
11 Habermas (1973) makes a distinction between *Verfügungswissen* and *Orientierungswissen*; the former refers to the knowledge related to how to do stuff (the general domain of natural scientists and engineers) while the latter refers to knowledge about whether or why to do stuff (typically the realm of social scientists).

References

Bäckstrand, K. (2003) "Civic Science for Sustainability: Reframing the Role of Experts, Policy-Makers and Citizens in Environmental Governance," *Global Environmental Politics* 3: 24–41.

————(2004) "Scientisation vs. Civic Expertise in Environmental Governance: Eco-feminist, Eco-modern and Post-modern Responses," *Environmental Politics* 13: 695–714.

Beck, U. (1992) *Risk Society: Towards a New Modernity*, Newbury Park, CA: Sage Publications.

Bell, B. (2004) *Good Deeds, Good Design: Community Service through Architecture*, New York: Princeton Architectural Press.

Brand, R. (2005a) *Synchronizing Science and Technology with Human Behaviour*, London: Earthscan.

————(2005b) "Urban Infrastructures and Sustainable Social Practices," *Journal of Urban Technology* 12: 1–25.

Brand, R. and Karvonen, A. (2007) "The Ecosystem of Expertise: Complementary Knowledges for Sustainable Development," *Sustainability: Science, Practice, and Policy* 3: 21–31.

Campbell, S. (1996) "Green Cities, Growing Cities, Just Cities?: Urban Planning and the Contradictions of Sustainable Development," *Journal of the American Planning Association* 62: 296–312.

Carson, R. (1962) *Silent Spring*, Boston, MA: Houghton Mifflin.

Collins, H. and Evans, R. (2002) "The Third Wave of Science Studies: Studies of Expertise and Experience," *Social Studies of Science* 32: 235–96.

————(2007) *Expertise: A New Analysis*, Chicago: University of Chicago Press.

Dewey, J. (1927/1954) *The Public and Its Problems*, Athens, OH: Swallow Press.

Dreyfus, H. L. and Dreyfus, S. E. (1986) *Mind Over Machine: The Power of Human Intuition and Expertise in the Era of the Computer*, New York: Free Press.

Dryzek, J. S. (1997) *The Politics of the Earth: Environmental Discourses*, New York: Oxford University Press.

Fischer, F. (1990) *Technocracy and the Politics of Expertise*, Newbury Park, CA: Sage Publications.

————(2000) *Citizens, Experts, and the Environment: The Politics of Local Knowledge*, Durham, NC: Duke University Press.

————(2006) "Environmental Expertise and Civic Ecology: Linking the University and its Metropolitan Community," in A. C. Nelson, B. L. Allen, and D. L. Trauger (eds.) *Toward a Resilient Metropolis: The Role of State and Land Grant Universities in the 21st Century*, Alexandria, VA: Metropolitan Institute at Virginia Tech.

Foreman, C. H., Jr. (1998) "Blended Rationality and Democracy: An Elusive Synthesis for Environmental Policy Reform," *Science Communication* 20: 56–61.

Forester, J. (1999) *The Deliberative Practitioner: Encouraging Participatory Planning Processes*, Cambridge, MA: MIT Press.

Gibbons, M., Limoges, C., Nowotny, H., Schwartzman, S., Scott, P., and Trow, M. (1994) *The New Production of Knowledge: The Dynamics of Science and Research in Contemporary Societies*, London: Sage Publications.

Guy, S. and Moore, S. A. (2005) "Introduction: The Paradoxes of Sustainable Architecture," in S. Guy and S. A. Moore (eds.) *Sustainable Architectures: Cultures and Natures in Europe and North America*, New York: Spon Press.

————(2007) "Sustainable Architecture and the Pluralist Imagination," *Journal of Architectural Education* 60: 15–23.

Habermas, J. (1973) *Erkenntnis und Interesse*, Frankfurt: Suhrkamp.

Hague, C. (1997) "Foreword," in M. Higgins and F. Simpson (eds.) *Work-Based Learning Within Planning Education*, London: University of Westminster Press.

Hajer, M. A. (1995) *The Politics of Environmental Discourse: Ecological Modernization and the Policy Process*, Oxford: Clarendon Press.

Hannigan, J. (2006) *Environmental Sociology: A Social Constructionist Perspective*, 2nd ed., New York: Routledge.

Harding, S. (2000) "Should Philosophies of Science Encode Democratic Ideals?," in D. L. Kleinman (ed.) *Science, Technology, and Democracy*, Albany: State University of New York Press.

Hawken, P., Lovins, A., and Lovins, L. H. (1999) *Natural Capitalism: Creating the Next Industrial Revolution*, Boston, MA: Little, Brown and Co.

Healey, P. (2004) "Creativity and Urban Governance," *Policy Studies* 25: 87–102.

HERO (Higher Education and Research Opportunities in the United Kingdom) (2002) "Briefing Note 14: Interdisciplinary Research and the RAE," Online. Available at http://admin.hero.ac.uk/sites/hero/rae/Pubs/briefing/note14.htm (accessed August 3, 2006).

Hickman, L. A. (1992) "Populism and the Cult of the Expert," in L. Winner (ed.) *Democracy in a Technological Society*, Dordrecht, the Netherlands: Kluwer Academic Publishers.

Higgins, M. and Simpson, F. (1997) *Work-based Learning Within Planning Education: A Good Practice Guide*, London: University of Westminster Press for the Discipline Network in Town Planning.

Irwin, A. (1995) *Citizen Science: A Study of People, Expertise and Sustainable Development*, New York: Routledge.

Jacobs, J. (1961) *The Death and Life of Great American Cities*, New York: Random House.

Jamison, A. (2005) "On Nanotechnology and Society," *EASST Review* 24: 3–5, Online. Available at www.easst.net/review/sept2005/jamison (accessed February 1, 2008).

John, D. (1994) *Civic Environmentalism: Alternatives to Regulation in States and Communities*, Washington, DC: CQ Press.

Johnson, S. (2006) *The Ghost Map: The Story of London's Most Terrifying Epidemic—and How it Changed Science, Cities, and the Modern World*, New York: Riverhead Books.

Kleinman, D. L. (2000) "Democratizations of Science and Technology," in D. L. Kleinman (ed.) *Science, Technology, and Democracy*, Albany: State University of New York Press.

Lane, M. B. and McDonald, G. (2005) "Community-based Environmental Planning: Operational Dilemmas, Planning Principles and Possible Remedies," *Journal of Environmental Planning and Management* 48: 709–31.

Latour, B. (1987) *Science in Action: How to Follow Scientists and Engineers Through Society*, Philadelphia, PA: Open University Press.

Lindblom, C. E. and Woodhouse, E. J. (1993) *The Policy-Making Process*, 3rd ed., Englewood Cliffs, NJ: Prentice Hall.

Lytle, M. H. (2007) *The Gentle Subversive: Rachel Carson, Silent Spring, and the Rise of the Environmental Movement*, New York: Oxford University Press.

Marx, L. (1999) "Environmental Degradation and the Ambiguous Social Role of Science and Technology," in J. K. Conway, K. Keniston, and L. Marx (eds.) *Earth, Air, Fire, Water: Humanistic Studies of the Environment*, Amherst, MA: University of Massachusetts Press.

McDonough, W. and Braungart, M. (2002) *Cradle to Cradle: Remaking the Way We Make Things*, New York: Northpoint Press.

Menand, L. (2001) *The Metaphysical Club*, New York: Farrar, Straus, and Giroux.

Moerkerk, G. (2002) Personal communication, July 16.

Moore, S. A. (2001) *Technology and Place: Sustainable Architecture and the Blueprint Farm*, Austin, TX: University of Texas Press.

——(2007) *Alternative Routes to the Sustainable City: Austin, Curitiba, and Frankfurt*, Lanham, MD: Lexington Books.

Moore, S. A. and Brand, R. (2003) "The Banks of Frankfurt and the Sustainable City," *Journal of Architecture* 8: 3–24.

Nowotny, H. (2003) "Democratising Expertise and Socially Robust Knowledge," *Science and Public Policy* 30: 151–56.

Nowotny, H., Scott, P., and Gibbons, M. (1999) *Re-thinking Science: Knowledge and the Public in an Age of Uncertainty*, Malden, MA: Blackwell.

OED (Oxford English Dictionary Online) (2007) Definition of 'outreach'. Online. Available at http://dictionary.oed.com (accessed February 1, 2008).

Prugh, T., Costanza, R., and Daly, H. (2000) *The Local Politics of Global Sustainability*, Washington, DC: Island Press.

Rip, A., Misa, T. J., and Schot, J. (eds.) (1995) *Managing Technology in Society: The Approach of Constructive Technology Assessment*, New York: St. Martin's Press.

Schlosberg, D. (1999) *Environmental Justice and the New Pluralism*, New York: Oxford University Press.

Schot, J. and Rip, A. (1997) "The Past and Future of Constructive Technology Assessment," *Technological Forecasting and Social Change* 54: 251–68.

Sclove, R. (1992) "The Nuts and Bolts of Democracy: Democratic Theory and Technological Design," in L. Winner (ed.) *Democracy in a Technological Society*, Dordrecht, the Netherlands: Kluwer Academic Publishers.

——(1995) *Democracy and Technology*, New York: Guilford Press.

Scott, J. C. (1999) *Seeing Like a State: How Certain Schemes to Improve the Human Condition Have Failed*, New Haven, CT: Yale University Press.

Seely, B. E. (1996) "State Engineers as Policymakers: Apolitical Experts in a Federalist System," in J. R. Rogers, D. Kennon, R. T. Jaske, and F. E. Griggs, Jr. (eds.) *Civil Engineering History: Engineers Make History*, New York: ASCE.

Selinger, E. and Crease, R. P. (2006a) "Dreyfus on Expertise: The Limits of Phenomenological Analysis," in E. Selinger and R. P. Crease (eds.) *The Philosophy of Expertise*, New York: Columbia University Press.

——(2006b) "Introduction," in E. Selinger and R. P. Crease (eds.) *The Philosophy of Expertise*, New York: Columbia University Press.

Shutkin, W. A. (2000) *The Land That Could Be: Environmentalism and Democracy in the Twenty-First Century*, Cambridge, MA: MIT Press.

Spirn, A. W. (1996) "Constructing Nature: The Legacy of Frederick Law Olmsted," in W. Cronon (ed.) *Uncommon Ground: Rethinking the Human Place in Nature*, New York: Norton.

Stilgoe, J., Irwin, A., and Jones, K. (2006) *The Received Wisdom: Opening Up Expert Advice*, London: Demos.

Tate, J., Mulugetta, Y., Sharland, R., and Hills, P. (1998) "Sustainability: The Technocratic Challenge," *Town Planning Review* 69: 65–86.

Thayer, R. L., Jr. (1994) *Gray World, Green Heart: Technology, Nature, and the Sustainable Landscape*, New York: John Wiley.

Turner, S. (2001) "What is the Problem with Experts?," *Social Studies of Science* 31: 123–49.

Wilsdon, J., and Willis, R. (2004) *See-through Science: Why Public Engagement Needs to Move Upstream*, London: Demos.

Wilson, E. O. (1998) *Consilience: The Unity of Knowledge*, New York: Knopf.

World Commission on Environment and Development (WCED) (1987) *Our Common Future*, New York: Oxford University Press.

Wynne, B. (1996) "May the Sheep Safely Graze? A Reflexive View of the Expert–Lay Knowledge Divide," in S. Lash, B. Szerszynski, and B. Wynne (eds.) *Risk, Environment and Modernity: Towards a New Ecology*, Thousand Oaks, CA: Sage Publications.

Yearley, S. (2000) "Making Systematic Sense of Public Discontents with Expert Knowledge: Two Analytical Approaches and a Case Study," *Public Understanding of Science* 9: 105–22.

4 The power and death of the sea

Peter Jacques

The Earth as common once as Light and Aer,
They then by Art did measure, bound and
Snare.

> (Ovid, *Metamorphoses*, quoted from John Selden's *Mare Clausum* [1652])

People inhabit coastal spaces with particularity, but particularities of human social-marine histories and inhabitation confront a buttress of modernism that seeks to homogenize and normalize marine space, peoples, and non-human life for accumulation. I will argue that the proposition of "ontology" is basic to power, and I will draw on histories of ocean politics to construct an illustrative case. "Onto" refers to being, and the word connotes the essence of being. The power that is ultimately the focus in this essay is the power to re-make "being," particularly of Others, as a way to dominate and order people and non-human nature. Simply, to order being, is to order how we live in the world.

People not only inhabit a space but they inhabit notions of being that relate to that space that operate as a sense of purpose and inform social action. I will present the case that the modernist notions of "ocean" have been based on exclusion, where the ocean and its inhabitants (including coastal peoples) are instrumentalized for use by a privileged caste of elites in a well-worn path found in ocean politics. But, dominant social minorities do not just magically appear. They are constituted and erected purposefully, and in order to maintain their dominance must maintain the hierarchies of power (Enloe 1996).

In this case, European imperial powers used their own natural capital (e.g. forests) and social capital (e.g. engineering) to create large ships and weapons to burst out of their ecological space to conquer other people and use "overseas" ecological space for their own metabolism. At the base of this process is a justificatory presumption of being "civilized" and superior, but the prelude to this move is a cognitive and ethical transition that instrumentalizes non-human nature into a mechanism to be used without limit (Merchant 1980). Merchant identifies this moment in European history as the "death of nature," and to the extent that such logic is thrust upon the ocean by Grotius and Selden (described below), the "age of reason" rains death upon the ocean in symbol first, then biological cataclysm seen through fundamental changes to the communities of life since.

This ideational power for wanton use provides the social justification to collect trees and make ships and guns and use them against Others who were deemed inferior, savage and who were seen as retained in the mythical state of nature. As such, ideational force creates material force that then reinforces the ideational origins and the Western ontology of mechanistic exclusion of people from nature, like the ocean, creating a master ontological narrative about how to live with the sea and those anchored to the sea.

This means that the two aspects, our social imagination of what is possible and "good" in the world are inter-related with the material space we inhabit with others, both human and non-human. Consequently, ontologies tie into material wealth and power, but ontologies also are a form of power in themselves as way to manipulate and control meaning, purpose, and normalization of specific disposal of the ocean and the life therein. In dominating meaning, other meanings are silenced, and the multitudes of ontologies are simplified and impoverished; thus, as dominant meaning for use pervades our approach to the World Ocean, we concomitantly simplify and reduce the communities of life as well. Indeed, Sponsel (2000) indicates that contemporary homogenization of people and culture in South- and East Asia is linked to and occurring at the same time as the homogenization and simplification of non-human ecology in the same region.

In disposing of the multitudes of particular ocean-ontologies around the world, the modern colonial period was able to normalize the disposal of not only fish and whales, but of people "overseas." Val Plumwood, for example, notes that a utilitarian anthropocentrism has empowered the West and helps explain its current hegemony:

> Rationalist constructions of human-centredness and their associated ethical and epistemic exclusions and illusions have in the modern age helped western culture and the economic rationality of capitalism achieve its position of dominance, *by maximizing the class of other beings that are available as "resources" for exploitation without constraint.*
>
> (Plumwood 2002: 100, emphasis added)

Plumwood argues that the "rationalist" conceit—that to be a person (human nature) is to embody the economistic idea demanding that decisions are "good" when they pay-out to radically excluded and hyper-alienated individuals encouraged to disregard the long term, the social, and the living as in *homo economicus*—promotes a profound displacement of self. As a result, "western cultural traditions in which anthropocentrism is deeply rooted, develop conceptions of themselves as belonging to a superior sphere apart, and this disempowers social, ecological, and relational *being* as an option" (at 99). Such ontological illusions have led us to disembed ourselves as ecological beings who live in ecological space with limits and needs of its own. As such, social privilege justifies wanton use of the oceans through the exclusion of those that depend on and live in the same, including marine life, causing worldwide marine crises and the empowerment of this very process. Thus, catching sharks—ancient creatures who predate humans by millions of years—and slicing off their fins and dumping their bleeding bodies into the water for them to die is allowable only insomuch as we do not recognize the validity of the sharks to their own life. To frame such practice as immoral, especially in policy arenas or scientific consideration, is disparaged as emotional, irrational, and sentimental. The fact that such disparagement is powerful indicates one mechanism of how the dominant instrumental ontology maintains its power over other ways of living in the world.

This chapter will examine how ocean ontologies have been reduced to a homogenized order with a singular, master purpose of instrumental radical exclusion. Here I follow Plumwood in that radical exclusion is the displacement of humans from ecology. I will illustrate how this power undergirds the disposal of marine life, peoples who are overseas from core power centers, and marine space like beaches and mangroves to generate oceans of crisis. Further, marking out the ocean as a tool for immediate or intermediate accumulation is a precondition for the rise of colonialism and contemporary global control of human and non-human nature for global capitalism. In order for this to be accomplished, other non-instrumental notions of being with the ocean must be silenced, and dominant ethics is blinded to all but the fetishes of maximum sustained yields of fish, shipping routes, and pollution dilution.

Positioning ocean ontologies

What other meanings have been produced in social-marine settings? We might wonder what has become of the Sea Mother, roiling, birthing, raising, and taking the lives of fragile creatures as the progenitor of a living world? Many of the "old coastal cultures" of the world appear to have dwelled with the notion that the ocean—alive, breathing, acting, and filled with intention—was an agent which humans had to negotiate with, not one that had to obey *them*, or which humans could themselves order with impunity. These ideas of a sea-with-a-will-of-its-own were interconnected to material lives that occupied an ocean–land complex of space that was critical to coastal lives. The ocean itself was viewed as powerful because it conditioned so many dimensions of life. It was powerful because of its immeasurable girth, depth, and space that was a part of the house that coastal people lived in with other non-human residents. The ocean was an agent, a home, a source of energy, a space for traversing, and reference or anchor to a multi-dimensional world.

Some aspects of this view still carry over into contemporary Western science. For example, the ocean is understood as the birthplace of life on earth, where all life evolved and emerged from. Sylvia Earle writes in the foreword of Prager and Earle's *The Oceans*:

The ocean has sustained us and shaped our existence on Earth since life emerged from the ancient sea. Today nearly three-quarters of the planet are covered by the oceans, 97 percent of the Earth's water lies in the sea, and within it lies 97 percent of the planet's living space. Air-sea interactions dictate climate and weather, and ocean currents regulate the Earth's global thermometer. Spreading of the underlying seafloor creates mountains, deep undersea trenches, and active hydrothermal vents that abound with strange marine organisms. The ocean teams with life millions of years in the making, from the tiniest of microscopic bacteria to the largest of living creatures, the blue whale. And, from the ocean's bounty of small floating plants, our atmosphere is thankfully enriched with oxygen and depleted of carbon dioxide. In short, without the ocean there would be no Earth or life as we know it, for ours is a life-giving, water-blessed planet.

(Prager and Earle 2000: ix)

Thus, in addition to being the amniotic fluid of the world, the ocean holds the momentum of stored solar energy like no other source on earth, it is the largest habitat and ecological space on earth, and is the home to some of the most astounding life in the world (think maybe of the manta ray, saw fish, hammerhead shark, blue whale, or sea dragons) alongside some of the tiniest algae and plankton that support all of the above either through immediate or intermediate webs.

Whereas some coastal cultures in the Indian Ocean from 500 BC to 1500 AD held the ocean as a void to be crossed for trading (Steinberg 2001), many coastal cultures integrated the sea with the land as one unified and complex space. Knowledge about the nature of surprise, grace, and severity of the ocean's unpredictable changes allowed coastal communities' ability to adapt and live with the ocean over millennia. On the other hand, modernism assumes that the ocean can be strictly governed through the power of science and technology, such as with fish stocks, and this has replaced humility among other virtues. Consequently, modern fishery management has failed in many ways where coastal communities had succeeded, such as through approaching fish with a sense of chaos and complexity (Acheson and Wilson 1996) that likely engenders less rapacious social action. Make no mistake— traditional cultures still brought extinction down upon the sea (Jackson et al. 2001), but for the most part, these communities were able to maintain marine ecosystems to permit subsistence survival—in some cases for 40,000 years—which is nigh the birth of modern humanity itself.

Today, world politics is wrapped in the power of the sea, but nations wear this power in a much different way than the old coastal cultures. The character of this power is as different as means are to ends, where the sea was of and in itself a powerful force with many dimensions as they were held in the minds of varied peoples, but today these dimensions have been impoverished, at the same time that life in the sea itself has been impoverished. Let us look at a few of the ontologies that have been suppressed.

Ontologies of the sea

Indigenous people of the South Pacific have commonly thought of the ocean as a global and universally interconnected and unified space which can be used but must be protected in a way to sustain life that depends on it (Jackson 1993). Fijian traditional cultures uses the word *vanua* for a "named area of land and sea seen as an integrated whole with its human occupants" (Berkes et al. 1998: 411). Similar notions of a bounded locality that weaves the land, sea, and people together are found in the Solomon Island idea of *puava*, and the Yap idea of *tabinau*. Berkes et al. write that:

> The common point in each is that the term refers to an intimate association of a group of people with land, reef, and lagoon and all that grows on or in them. It is the "personal ecosystem" of a specific group of people. In the Solomons, for example, a puava is a defined, named territory consisting of land and sea, and it includes all areas and resources associated with a *butubutu* or descent group.
>
> (Berkes et al. 1998: 412)

Not only do these ideas provide a sense of different ontological positions of the sea, but these cultural ideas provide ethical mechanisms that integrate people with the ocean. This idea of land–(reef)–sea continuity is shared by the Torres Strait Islanders at Erub, who express this idea in *gedira gur*, "the sea that belongs to the land," with *ged* meaning "home place," which deeply ties the individual islander to a specific location of land and sea (Scott and Mulrennan 1999).

These positions integrate the ocean and coast and the people who live there with a responsibility to a host of values that place material production as one value among several. For example, indigenous Caribbean people saw the ocean as a primal and creative force. The Taino (Arawak) viewed the birth of the ocean (*bagua*) and its dependent organisms as the first act of creation (Oliver 1997). Perhaps the Taino saw themselves at the center of creation because they were in the center of the ocean, a view which came with "the awesome responsibility of making it work for all generations to come" (Oliver 1997). Likewise, Johannes is well known for showing that, in the Pacific, all conservation measures in the West were first practiced there well before modern industrial nations thought them necessary or interesting: "Almost every basic fisheries conservation measure devised in the West was in use in the tropical Pacific centuries ago" (Johannes 1978: 352).

The above characteristics I have sketched out are likely crude and insufficient simplifications of ancient[1] maritime beliefs, but what is clear is that there was a multitude of *non*-commodified ocean ontologies. In the Pacific Northwest, the intrinsic value of sea and land are drawn together through salmon, a species that lives in the ocean but is born and dies inland, providing relatively predictable food sources, threading land and ocean and people together in vital, ancient forms (see Ames 1994). In Egypt, the "self-created

Supreme Being," Nun, was the primeval ocean from which other gods and the world emerged (James 1969). In Inca cosmology, Viracocha, "foam of the sea" and Mama-Cocha, "Sea Mother" or "Mother of All Water," are nurturing symbols (Isbell 1985) that found the idea for many Peruvians that their very physiological structure mirrors the water-laced Incan cosmology (Bastien 1985). Like the Pacific cultures who integrated the land and sea, the Incas appear to have seen lakes, rivers, and other water as manifestations of the ocean, upon which the land rested (Reinhard 1985). Here, earth, freshwater, sea and human body are interconnected and governed by and make up identity. Such ways of living with the ocean are not likely to legitimize unrestrained appropriation of marine life or home.

In sum, the beliefs of some old coastal cultures—and even the mountain-centered culture of Peru and the Inca—saw the ocean in a multitude of ways: alive; having its own order and purpose that may or may not be separate from human purpose; inhabited by a creative force; as the recipient or source of creative energies; as a space bridging and separating home and other; as a source of material production; as an anchor for integrated spaces that are tied to social identity; and, even ideas integrating and weaving cosmology, the ocean, and physiology.

These cultures, living for millennia on the beaches of the world, saw themselves tied together in an integrated and unreduced physical and subjectively embodied space of land–sea–sky. In the South Pacific, the specificity of affiliation was distinct to the cay linked to specific stars (Scott and Mulrennan 1999); and the Incan ideas of ocean space connect to a particular vital lake. In each of these cases, the ocean not only provides material, it is interconnected with how people placed themselves, their being, into the world. It was not a possession to be rationally appropriated, or a simple water column with instrumental resources in it, and nor was it a simple avenue to other instrumental resources of other peoples, but something much more ontologically pressing and more demanding of humility in the face of such vital complexity. It appears likely that these notions of being were not separate from the places where coastal peoples found themselves, but co-evolved together as these cultures worked with and used their coastal homes. For example, each of these ontologies indicates that the coastal peoples must live with and adapt to the conditions of particular ecologies, and none of these ontologies indicate a right to wanton use of other ecologies. Living in or across multiple ecologies (see Luke, this volume), and taking from other people in those respective other spaces is not represented in any of these coastal ideas; and, these ocean ontologies—varied though they are—are non-instrumental and inclusive, where people are embedded in marine ecology instead of radically excluded from it.

Yet, the multitudes of gods of the ocean were not left unmolested, and neither were the people who dreamt of them. José Oliver laments:

> The Tainos are no longer amongst us; their genes have been diluted among the new Old World populations. Their culture—as an integrated

holistic system, as a mode of interacting with the natural and supernatural surroundings—is for all practical purposes gone as well.

(Oliver 1997: 152)

There is a connection between the death of the Tainos and the loss of a living, integrating marine-centered world. This connection comes from the ability to define the essence of marine worlds to serve layers of modern political order. I will now begin to discuss the contributions of Grotius and John Selden as *compatible* in their positions about the purpose of the ocean and the power that came to order the world from this meaning, instead of the usual presentations of these writers as contradictory.

Enter globalism

On May 14, 1493, Pope Alexander VI decreed by papal bull that Spain and Portugal should share the world. On June 7, 1494 in the Spanish village of Tordesillas, the Kings and Queens of Spain and Portugal happily consented:

In the name of God Almighty, Father, Son, and Holy Ghost, three truly separate and distinct persons and only one divine essence. ... Thereupon it was declared by the above-mentioned representatives of the aforesaid King and Queen of Castile, Leon, Aragon, Sicily, Granada, etc., and of the aforesaid King of Portugal and the Algarves, etc.: [I.] That, whereas a certain controversy exists between the said lords, their constituents, as to what lands, of all those discovered in the ocean sea up to the present day, the date of this treaty, pertain to each one of the said parts respectively; therefore, for the sake of peace and concord, and for the preservation of the relationship and love of the said King of Portugal for the said King and Queen of Castile, Aragon, etc., it being the pleasure of their Highnesses, they, their said representatives, acting in their name and by virtue of their powers herein described, covenanted and *agreed that a boundary or straight line be determined and drawn north and south, from pole to pole, on the said ocean sea, from the Arctic to the Antarctic pole.* ... And all lands, both islands and mainlands, found and discovered already, or to be found and discovered hereafter, by the said King of Portugal and by his vessels on this side of the said line and bound determined as above, toward the east, in either north or south latitude, on the eastern side of the said bound provided the said bound is not crossed, shall belong to, and remain in the possession of, and pertain forever to, the said King of Portugal and his successors. And all other lands, both islands and mainlands, found or to be found hereafter, discovered or to be discovered hereafter, which have been discovered or shall be discovered by the said King and Queen of Castile, Aragon, etc., and by their vessels, on the western side of the said bound, determined as above, after having passed the said bound toward the west, in either its north or south latitude, shall belong to, and remain in the possession of, and pertain forever to, the said King and Queen of Castile, Leon, etc., and to their successors.

(1494, online at the Avalon Project of Yale Law School)

Amicably, it was settled who got what side of the world—the Spanish claimed the Pacific Ocean and the Gulf of Mexico and Portugal claimed the Atlantic south of Morocco and the Indian Ocean. This may be the first applied European use of "global" in terms of the ocean, as the parties literally divided up the world's oceanic basins, and from this point on, the idea of European ocean law put the whole world in its cup and globalism was born.

Thus, having used their fleets to expand, subdue, and trade, the Portugese found themselves in the Straits of Malacca in 1602. The Portuguese did not want anyone to step in on "their" side of the world, so they moved to exclude other countries, and the Dutch state-firm, The Dutch East India Company, politely disagreed, whereby Captain Heemskerk of the Company captured the Portuguese *Catherine*. He then took the ship and crew back to Amsterdam and sold the lot.[2] The famed and brilliant Dutch jurist, Hugo de Groot, or Grotius, was retained by the Dutch East India Company to defend this capture and disposal, whereby he personally argued for the state-firm and wrote a legal brief that would grip the world for over 300 years. *Mare Liberum* was first published in 1609 and "remained hegemonic … until the end of the nineteenth century" (Connery 2001: 179). Chapter III in *Mare Liberum* casts the papal bull as an illicit donation of property not owned by the pope, and while the Spanish were willing to say they were launching war on indigenous peoples for rejections of the "True Faith," Grotius cleanly rejects this occupation based on religious doctrine as robbery and injustice (Grotius 1916: see chapter IV).

Colonialism had been launched from Spanish ships of course in 1492, two years prior to the above treaty but, before 1492, Spain had almost no territory outside its own borders apart from the Canary Islands. Thus, Spanish colonialism expanded during the sixteenth century using the ideational legitimation of Roman Catholicism and natural law to justify its expansion and accumulation (MacLachlan 1991) of space, people, and resources from "overseas"; and these exploits then were used to fund further exploits. Gold from the island of Hispaniola, for example, funded further colonial penetration into the "New World."

Importantly, Grotius argued that it had been well known since Plutarch "that the civilizing of barbarians had been made the pretext for aggression, which is to say that a greedy longing for the property of another often hides itself behind such a pretext" (Grotius 1916: 14). I have noted with others elsewhere that European imperial powers expanded outward pretending to do a service claiming and "civilizing" "savage" peoples and attempting to "save" their souls and advance human "progress," but that behind this rhetoric of beneficence was the goal of dispossessing indigenous-held land to accumulate more wealth and power for empires soon to become core states in the world capitalist system (Jacques et al. 2003). While Grotius clearly rejects the idea of taking land from others *simply* because they are "infidels," the very first words in *Mare Liberum* clarify to whom Grotius is appealing: "To the Rulers and to the Free and Independent Nations of Christendom" (Grotius 1916: 1).

Grotius is often named the "father of international law," and legal concepts between European nations were pretty vacant until Grotius developed his own notions. Grotius based his thinking on "natural law," or universalistic conditions which all humanity is subject to, principally based in European ideas of religion, reason, public authority of nations, and property. He describes this type of thinking:

> He [the Christian god] had drawn up certain laws not graven on tablets of bronze or stone but written in the minds and the hearts of every individual, where even the unwilling and the refractory must read them ... Now since no man can be ignorant of these facts unless he ceases to be a man, and since races blind to all truth except what they receive from the light of nature, have recognized their [natural laws] force, what, O Christian Kings and Nations ought you to think, and what ought you to do?
>
> (Grotius 1916: 2)

The argument here is to the Christian kings, whom he says should let the Dutch East India Company do what they wish on the seas in order to trade, but he couches the state-firm's activities as a matter of natural law, where:

> There is not one of you who does not openly proclaim that every man is entitled to manage and dispose of his own property; there is not one of you who does not insist that all citizens have equal and indiscriminate right to use rivers and public places; not one of you who does not defend with all his might the freedom to travel and of trade.
>
> (Grotius 1916: 3)

Apparently, as universal as natural law is, it still only extends to men who have property, and permits "citizens" to use public resources "indiscriminately." Remembering that citizenship is a state-based concept, and that nation-states grew as a specific European institution gaining ground at this very time, it is clear that "citizens" can only refer (for Grotius) to elites in Europe. Grotius (1916: 3) notes also that for anyone preventing the use of these rights, "the King of the universe has laid upon you the command to take cognizance of the trespass of all other men, and to punish them ... "

Grotius then turns his argument of natural law to the oceans, and frames the European-colonial imagination about the ocean as a space that is common to "all *nations*," and which cannot be enclosed, owned or dominated because it is a highway where "innocent passage" must be allowed:

I shall base my argument on the following most specific and unimpeachable axiom of the Law of Nations, called a primary rule or first principle, the spirit of which is self-evident and immutable, to wit: Every *nation* is free to travel to every other nation, and to trade with it.

(Grotius 1916: 7, emphasis added)

Why are nations free to use the ocean in particular? Grotius notes that in ancient times, nature provided that all things were held in common, but over time—he notes gradually—nature came to become occupied by use, and this converted that element of nature eventually to individual private property. Conversely and consequently, "that which can not be occupied, or which never has been occupied, cannot be property" (Grotius 1916: 27). Grotius notes through Thucydides, that land which cannot be assigned to any one nation is undefined and undetermined by border, and "All things which can be used without loss to any one else come under this [common property, *res communis*] category" (1916: 27).

the sea is common to all, because it is so limitless that it cannot become a possession of any one, and *because it is adapted for the use* of all, whether we consider it from the point of view of navigation or of fisheries.

(Grotius 1916: 28, emphasis added)

The persuasiveness and elegance of Grotius' words to the European elite provided the conceptual and ontological conversion to a modern artifact or token. *This is the first modern power of the sea*, where Grotius appropriates the meanings and relationships of all peoples (as a matter of "natural law") toward the entire World Ocean and institutionalizes instrumentalism as infallible divine will. The space of the ocean is no longer alive here, but literally empty and even unoccupied.[3] The power to convert the sea from ends to means then changes the relationship of the ocean to people. Who could argue that humans should not dispose of the ocean as they wished if it was immutable natural law to do so with such an empty and vacuous, yet (paradoxically) infinitely resourceful space? Therefore, it is evident that Grotius assumed that the ocean, including its fisheries, are without limit, and that there should be no limit on the indiscriminate use of the ocean. Also, while sovereigns may tax their own fishers, they may not justly limit in any way the fishing of any other country as a matter of what would later become called "extraterritoriality," or outside the jurisdiction of that sovereign.

Grotius contends that all people cannot help but agree that the entire ocean is free for the use of all nations to dispose of as they wish. This clearly sets out the oceans—and he includes the littoral zone of beaches and the shoreline as well—as open pool resources and highways of passage for trade with no rules for access or use.[4] Consequently, *Mare Liberum* is justified as the force behind so-called "tragedies of the commons" where there are no rules and individuals raid a limited resource to its demise at the expense of the larger community using the resource (see NRC 2002 for a summary of this expansive literature). However, Alcock (2002) has argued that the raiding of fisheries did not end even after 90–95 percent of this open pool resource had been closed through Exclusive Economic Zones that extend out 200 miles from a coastal nation, set out in the United Nations Convention on the Law of the Sea. This indicates that it is not the open pool resource regime rules driving the raiding. Rather, I argue it was the meaning set out and naturalized as unquestionable by *Mare Liberum* that the World Ocean's ontological purpose was to support a modernized enterprise for instrumental use in the ocean and "overseas."

Indeed, Grotius believes that the natural law of the universe indicates that both the non-human natural world and the state were created by the Christian god, and anyone who denies natural law, particularly of trade, innocent passage, property, indiscriminate use of the commons, and private property *forfeits their humanity*, and may be punished, presumably through martial power and dispossession of land through the Euro-Christian state. Being in the world is dominated, then, by this hegemonic form.

Grotian logic was not immediately accepted by all, as we shall see—but Grotius' ontology of the ocean was never seriously questioned in the core since its inception in mainstream international forums. Here the main objections are brought by the British jurist, John Selden. However, below he explains his ontological view of the marine world, clearly quoting Seneca:

> The Sea stands without motion, as it were som[e] dull heap of matter that Nature could not bring to perfection.
>
> (Selden 1972: 127)

Thus there is no disagreement that the World Ocean is a non-dynamic store to be instrumentally and fully exploited. Selden, who was dedicated to the British king, did specifically (1) contend that oceans *can* be occupied and therefore owned; and (2) specifically defended the domination of oceans around the British Isles as the integrated whole of British sovereignty and control. Eventually, though, Selden's argument was discarded, and even the British adopted the Grotian principles (see Introductory Note of Grotius 1916). Nevertheless, it is of interest to visit this rebuttal. Of course, one element in both is a parochial representation of nationalism by both Grotius and Selden, who are each arguing for their own empire and how these empires can and will use the ocean for their own purpose.

Importantly, Selden first lays out his terms. He clarifies that "sea" refers to

> the whole sea, as well as the main ocean or out-land seas, as those which are within-land, such as the Mediterranean, Adreatick, Aegean or Levant, British, and Baltick seas, or any other of that kinde, which differ no otherwise form the main, then as Homogenous or Similary parts of the same bodie do from the whole.
>
> (Selden 1972: 12)

Of "law" he believes that prescriptions "concern either mankinde in general, that is all nations; or not at all. That which relate's to the generalitie of mankinde, or *all Nations*, is either *Natural* or *Divine*" (Selden 1972: 12).[5] However, while the "laws of nature are immutable," not all law is "obligatorie [natural]," as some is "permissive" or changeable depending on human need. Thus, the idea of colonial and instrumental use of the ocean is not in dispute, but is accepted as a starting point since Tordesillas. What is, however, in dispute are the limits the European nations would place on themselves in using the ocean for imperio-corporate purposes. Selden (1972: 19–20) argues first by biblical decree that, in the same way as Adam, "Noah and his Sons did afterward and so became Lord of the whole World," and that the Bible says the ocean can be possessed just like the land as there are references to maritime borders. Selden then notes several historical societies, like the Creten and Roman peoples who controlled passage on the ocean, pointing out that this is indeed possible in practice and legal custom.

More importantly, Selden later argues that inasmuch as you can stop someone from crossing your field with their sheep, you can practically block passage on the ocean. This is legal because the laws of commerce are not natural for Selden, but derived by agreement and custom—they are socially determined, not divinely determined. He opposed Grotius' proposition that the ocean was unbounded (it is bounded by islands, inlets and coasts) and unchanged by one person's use, particularly when pearls and coral and fisheries are considered: "The Sea (I suppose) is not more inexhaustible than the whole world ... and therefore the Dominion of the Sea is not to be opposed upon this accompt [account]" (Selden 1972: 143).

In sum, Selden argued that the sea could be enclosed by nations who could rightfully own it as Noah commanded the land granted in presumptive biblical title, much like the Treaty of Tordesillas, and it is possible to keep others out as one keeps those out of your backyard. While Selden is far less poetic in his argument, history seems to bear out some of Selden's assumptions over Grotius—the ocean is limited, and in some ways can be plied by military and bureacratic force to restrict access; and, with the onset of the exclusive economic zone, has been substantially legally enclosed.

If we think of modernism as a force for accumulation, we can see the modern ocean's purpose and meaning written by Grotius *and* Selden. Luke helps us understand this more fully:

> The creative destruction of capitalism has all too often been displaced, mystified, or confused with vague terms like "modernity," "progress," or "technological-industrial development" ... *modernity has much more to do with the advent of market rationality, commodified social relations, private property, and global capitalist interests.*
>
> (Luke 2006: 131, emphasis added)

From this perspective, we can see that both Grotius and Selden were erasing multiplicities of meaning and being which were embedded into social–marine relationships found around the world while imposing a monolith of modernism. For Grotius, the ocean is principally an intermediary for accumulation, and for Selden it is an immediate source. The Grotian ocean precipitates both the wanton immediate use of the oceans and the intermediate use of the oceans to usurp ecologies "overseas" presumed to be *terra nullius* (empty, uninhabited land). The fact that these erased multiplicities may appear "backward" or the re-telling of these notions may appear "romanticized" indicates just how much modernity has mystified not only its own processes, but its very preconditions.

Connery (2006: 499) writes that there is such an extensive Western antagonism to the sea that was not found elsewhere in the world, seen through Western biblical and mythological triumph over the sea until it is defeated and eliminated, that it serves as an elemental antithesis—or "object of elemental rage." This, he notes, feeds into metaphors that make the ocean "meaningless materiality," like that pointed out by Steinberg, where a 1990 Meryl Lynch two-page ad shows the ocean with the caption, "for us, this doesn't exist" implying a *mare nullius*. It is easy to also read both the Grotian and Seldenian ocean as one that is filled with meaningless materiality to be superseded; and, if this is the birth of "the international" then it is based on nullifying non-instrumental materiality for vulgar accumulation. International relations, then, is a study in irony.

We might argue that both perspectives did eventually take hold, with Grotian law grasping the first chokehold on the oceans with free seas, then *mare clausum* national enclosures to 200 miles taking the second. In either case, the ocean is cast as commodity for global capitalist interests, epitomized through interests in accumulating wealth through overfishing, mining, enclosing of common pool mangroves for private shrimp ponds, global trade in seafood, and transportation of nearly all commodities. As Steinberg (2001) writes, the social construction of the ocean has changed from "Davy Jones' Locker to the Foot Locker" (referring to the preternatural life-taking power of the ocean being transformed into a highway for commodity flows, where in one example, the cargo of shoes are lost at sea), and that it is insufficient to refer to the usual supposed dichotomy of Grotius vs. Selden.

Of power

The power to dominate ways of being in the world has repercussions for the generation of all other types of power, from material use of force to agenda-setting, because it normalizes one way of living in the world over others.

At first, we see that the ocean was imbued with multiplicities and particular meanings through a great variety of cultures around the world. Many imbued the ocean with its own power and agency, as in indigenous coastal cultures, which limited what these cultures saw as legitimate uses of their own power and effort in the sea. Some of these cultures saw a multitude of spaces and identities as ontologically integrated with the rest of the world, and constitutive.

Then, by "Art" as Ovid presciently describes, transformations of control spread over the Earth at the same time that European jurisprudence not only constituted the ocean as a tool for accumulation, but erased other ontological priorities and particularities, as a way to preclude other non-instrumental uses. Without this step, the rest would likely not have followed. If the ocean were the Christian god, it is difficult to imagine Grotius saying it could be used indiscriminately, and that anyone interfering with this use could be punished via war. Thus, the first modern power of the sea is to erase other notions and meanings with its own design. This design is made in a specific historical time of imperial nation-building that grows into diffuse, globalized commodified relations of contemporary corporate-led global capitalism that still sees the ocean as a tool for immediate (oil, fish) accumulation and intermediate accumulation through container ships, trawlers, and oil tankers.

The Spanish saw fit to use the ocean to conquer and destroy people like the Taino as an opportunity to build up the proto-Spanish state, pretending to "civilize" indigenous peoples through dispossession. While Grotius rejects this pretense, the ocean is still a passage for imperio-corporate trade and profit which he believes is ordained in *immutable* natural law. Selden sees the ocean as limited and able to be dominated and controlled like any other "dull heap," which also creates ideational pathways for trade and conquest. Grotius' and Selden's arguments have often been counterposed, but their ontological assumptions and projects are the same, and both assume that the ocean belongs to and can be disposed of as their empires see fit.

Ultimately, *Mare Liberum* was persuasive among the colonial set, imagining the World Ocean into the ultimate abstraction—limitless, vast, and free for all to use indiscriminately. This is exactly the kind of abstraction of space that Connery, via Edward Casey, notes was a "hegemonic category of thought" that emerged during the seventeenth century (remember *Mare Liberum* was published in 1604) for the purposes of nation-building. Here the ocean, as Connery describes it, becomes mere distance, "something to be superseded" (Connery 2006: 497). In superseding the dead "dull heap" of ocean, nations with imperial fleets can connect to other places to annihilate other people, as in the Taino, and loot its shores. *Mare Liberum* normalizes the oceans for just this type of enterprise, Grotius willing or not. This is seen historically in the Spanish search for gold, but also in the intercontinental sugar–cotton–slave triangle of domination operated by the British, among others, that took slaves from Africa, enslaved them in the Caribbean and the colonial and post-colonial United States, and shipped their cotton and sugar to Europe for manufacturing (Jacques 2006). Steinberg points out that *mare liberum* was much less absolute *until* the British imposed end to slavery—but modernity's ontology of the ocean was necessary for the beginning of the intercontinental slave trade that rested upon the imperial bursting outward from the European continent.

Natural law here is important to the construction of power also, because it normalizes a specific ontology as infallible. Thus, I have argued that it was not that Grotius made the ocean open for all to use that set up matrices of world power *and* marine crises, but rather it was what he made it open *for* that became so disastrous. Even after the open pool regime is closed, the purpose remains the same—instrumental enterprise—and closing *mare liberum* fails to change the essential place that the World Ocean holds in the minds of technocratic elite of the modern nation-state. During modernity, such violence is unaccountable to the living spaces of the World Ocean whether as the source of life, a home, an organism, an integrated part in the universe that creates identity, or other purpose, because what had been "as *common* once as light and air" had been bound in *logos* that precludes non-instrumental ontologies and converts the oceans into a global water closet and avenue to other lockers, just like South Africa became for Grotius' Netherlands.

Where *mare liberum* originates a few years after the Dutch East India Company, the Dutch colonial seeds are soon thereafter spread to South Africa in 1652. One space on the ocean became the same as any other in its function and purpose. Thus, with a natural law of European privileged trade and accumulation via a World Ocean, all other purposes, histories, and geographies are erased or shrouded. See, for example, Hegel's view on Africa as a subject of such globalization that is only possible after social relations and human–ocean relations are commodified and open up the world to barbaric subjugation:

> Africa is not interesting from the point of view of its own history. ...
>
> Man [in Africa] is in a state of barbarism and savagery which is preventing him from being an integral part of civilization. ... [Africa] is the country of gold which closed in on itself, the country of infancy, beyond the daylight of conscious history, wrapped in the blackness of night.
>
> (Hegel, quoted in Abdi 1999: 151)

Of course the "blackness of night" appears to be a crude reference to skin color, and blackness equating the undeveloped, the empty, and the savage. Colonizing the "heart of darkness" then is rationalized by erasing geography through the sea, making European development the end of history, and replacing other purpose(s) with a singular global purpose of free access to the rest of the world's spaces and homes as naturalized right. Such erasure connects Grotius to Stephen Biko—where Biko led Black South Africans to see "blackness of their skin" as the cause of their collective oppression and articulate a Black Consciousness to reinstate not just political power in the face of Apartheid (apartness), but to reinstate pre-colonial South African purposes and ontologies (see Abdi 1999).

Colonial and neo-colonial periods expunge the meanings of the local connection of inlet to stars of the South Pacific, or the organic functions of a living water. Perhaps this is the most powerful reducer of modernity where all life and home is made to serve one master, making the habitation of multiple "overseas" spaces (see Luke, this volume) less palpable because there is no perceptible loss of purpose or function to the then colonial and now globalized "Northern" minds. Enterprise, use, and free access to habitat and home underlies the structure of contemporary political order, which means that this very order must maintain a hegemonic hold on ontological notions of not just the ocean or of social relations, but of all-inclusive ecology (human and non-human) itself.

Plumwood agrees that a main explanation for how

> the rationalist culture of the west has been able to expand and conquer other cultures as well as nature was that it has long lacked their respect-based constraints on the use of nature—a thought that puts the "success" of the west in a rather different and more dangerous light.
>
> (Plumwood 2002: 117)

The success is "more" dangerous because it leads in a boomerang effect back to the West where ecological collapse presses hard on the doors of the West threatening broad social collapse, and the West will not be immune regardless of how remote it tries to make itself. Nonetheless, without the Grotian or Seldenian ocean, the colonial nations could not have gone across the sea to siphon off resources, and *ultimately create the structure of a world capitalist system we now live in.* Imagine the power of the current core states, such as those in the G-8, without a colonial legacy to found their current power, and through this image we can imagine a counterfactual position for the modern power of the sea. Certainly, this power of the sea was not lost on Alfred Thayer Mahan, who knew that control of the ocean was a prerequisite for extending national and imperial power. Control the sea, control the world, was his modern contribution. In order to control the sea, it has to be something ontologically that can be controlled, such as the "heap of matter that Nature could not bring to perfection."

Thus, the modern power of the sea is first found in Ovid's "Art," what we might now call normalizing. Normalizing one ontology over another is a form of power that begets more power, material and non-material. Of course, in addition to setting up and providing the foundation for initial and continued colonial expansion, the Grotian ocean sets up an open access space filled with an infinite basket of fish where the fate and destruction of international fisheries was indisputably set. From this legacy we inherit our fisheries crisis, because nations inherited the Grotian mandate to dispose of the fish as they wished without any interference from other nations under the auspices of war, justified to Grotius in an immutable and universal Law of Nations. Again, it is not the open access that sets up crisis, but open access *for* enterprise.

In addition, the conceptual framing of the sea sets forth the ability to materially control people with the sea. The "forward positioning" of the US fleet around the world is one example of this use. The expansion of US power and that of other expansionary militaries are dependent on the Grotian legacy and modern disposal of the Sea Mother, and it is hard to imagine a power more forceful than the idea that banishes gods to a cabinet, lays the foundation for hundreds of years of political domination, and which all the while gives permission and capacity to empty the life from the place from which life itself emerged.

This is at least one way to tell the story of the power—and death—of the sea.

Notes

1 "Ancient" here does not indicate extinct, but a depth of history, time, and persistence.
2 It is unclear whether "the lot" means that the crew as well were sold, but they were "declared forfeited and confiscated" (Grotius (1916).
3 The emptiness here refers to agency—the ocean has no agents or agency, but is filled with resources, like fish.
4 It was not until later that a 3-mile territorial sea excluded these coastal areas.
5 Emphasis is in the original. The 1972 version of this text maintains this spelling, which is maintained in the quotes; though the same is not true of the version (from the same publishers) of Grotius.

References

(1494) 'Treaty between Spain and Portugal concluded at Tordesillas; 7 June 1494,' The Avalon Project at Yale Law School, 1996–2007, online at http://avalon.law.yale.edu

Abdi, A. A. (1999) "Identity Formations and Deformations in South Africa: A Historical and Contemporary Overview," *Journal of Black Studies*, 30: 147–63.

Acheson, J. M. and Wilson, J. A. (1996) "Order out of Chaos: The Case for Parametric Fisheries Management," *American Anthropologist*, 98: 579–59.

Alcock, F. (2002) "Bargaining, Uncertainty, and Property Rights in Fisheries," *World Politics*, 54: 437–61.

Ames, K. (1994) "The Northwest Coast: Complex Hunter-Gatherers, Ecology, and Social Evolution," *Annual Review of Anthropology*, 23: 209–29.

Bastien, J. W. (1985) "Qollahuaya-Andean Body Concepts: A Topographical-Hydraulic Model of Physiology," *American Anthropologist*, 87: 595–611.

Berkes, F., Kislalioglu, M., Folke, C., and Gadgil, M. (1998) "Exploring the Basic Ecological Unit: Ecosystem-Like Concepts in Traditional Societies," *Ecosystems*, 1: 409–15.

Committee on the Human Dimensions of Global Change, National Research Council (2002) *The Drama of the Commons*, eds. E. Ostrom, T. Dietz, N. Dolsak, P. C. Stern, S. Stovich and E.U. Weber, Division of Behavioral and Social Sciences and Education, Washington, DC: National Academy Press.

Connery, C. L. (2001) "Ideologies of Land and Sea: Alfred Thayer Mahan, Carl Schmitt, and the Shaping of Global Myth Elements," *Boundary*, 2: 28.

——(2006) "There was No More Sea: The Supersession of the Ocean, from the Bible to Cyberspace," *Journal of Historical Geography*, 32: 494–511.

Enloe, C. (1996) "Margins, Silences and Bottom Rungs: How to Overcome the Underestimation of Power in the Study of International Relations," in S. Smith,

K. Booth, and M. Zalewski (eds.) *International Theory: Positivism and Beyond*, Cambridge: Cambridge University Press.

Grotius, H. (1916) "The Freedom of the Seas or The Right Which Belongs to the Dutch to Take Part in the East Indian Trade," ed. J. B. Scott, New York: Carnegie Endowment for International Peace/Oxford University Press.

Isbell, B. J. (1985) *To Defend Ourselves: Ecology and Ritual in an Andean Village*, Prospect Heights, IL: Waveland Press.

Jackson, J. B., Kirby, M. X., Berger, W. H., Bjorndal, K. A., Botsford, L. W., Bourque, B. J., Bradbury, R. H., Cooke, R., Erlandson, J., Estes, J. A., Hughes, T. P., Kidwell, S., Lange, C. B., Lenihan, H. S., Pandolfi, J. M., Peterson, C. H., Steneck, R. S., Tegner, M. J., and Warner, R. R. (2001) "Historical Overfishing and the Recent Collapse of Coastal Ecosystems," *Science*, 293: 629–39.

Jackson, M. (1993) *Indigenous Law and the Sea*, Washington, DC: Island Press.

Jacques, P. (2006) *Globalization and the World Ocean*, Lanham, MD: AltaMira/Rowman and Littlefield.

Jacques, P., Ridgeway, S., and Witmer, A. R. (2003) "Federal Indian Law and Environmental Policy: A Social Continuity of Violence," *Journal of Environmental Law and Litigation*, 18, 223–50.

James, E. O. (1969) *Creation and Cosmology: A Historical and Comparative Inquiry*, Leiden, the Netherlands: E. J. Brill.

Johannes, R. (1978) "Traditional Marine Conservation Methods in Oceania and their Demise," *Annual Review of Ecology and Systematics*, 9: 349–64, at 352.

Luke, T. (2006) "Alterity or Antimodernism: A Response to Versluis," *Teleos*, 137: 131.

Maclachlan, C. M. (1991) *Spain's Empire in the New World: The Role of Ideas in Institutional and Social Change*, Berkeley: University of California Press.

Merchant, C. (1980) *The Death of Nature: Women, Ecology, and the Scientific Revolution*, San Francisco, CA: Harper & Row.

Oliver, J. (1997) "The Taino Cosmos," in S. Wilson (ed.) *The Indigenous People of the Caribbean*, Tallahassee: University Press of Florida.

Plumwood, V. (2002) *Environmental Culture: The Ecological Crisis of Reason*, New York: Routledge.

Prager, E. and Earle, W. S. (2000) *The Oceans*, New York: McGraw Hill.

Reinhard, J. (1985) "Sacred Mountains: An Ethno-Archaeological Study of High Andean Ruins," *Mountain Research and Development*, 5: 299–317.

Scott, C. and Mulrennan, M. (1999) "Land and Sea Tenure at Erub, Torres Strait: Property, Sovereignty, and the Adjudication of Cultural Continuity," *Oceania*, 70: 146–76.

Selden, J. (1972) "Of the Dominion, Or, Ownership of the Sea," in L. Silk (ed.) *The Evolution of Capitalism*, New York: Arno Press.

Sponsel, L. (2000) *Identities, Ecologies, Rights, and Futures: All Endangered*, Westport, CT: Greenwood Press.

Steinberg, P. E. (2001) *The Social Construction of the Ocean*, New York: Cambridge University Press.

Part II
From the local to the global

5 Multi-level governance and the politics of scale

The challenge of the Millennium Ecosystem Assessment

Christoph Görg and Felix Rauschmayer

Introduction

Over the last years, Multi-Level Governance (MLG) has become a buzzword, and not only for environmental policy. Informed by previous research on federalism, this new form of political steering (Hooghe and Marks 2001; Heinelt et al. 2002; Bache and Flinders 2004) became paradigmatic for the European integration process and decision making in that supranational entity. If EU environmental policy represents a "unique system of multilevel environmental governance" (Jordan 2005: 2), it is questionable whether the EU model is transferable to other regions. Moreover, in research about environmental governance, in the EU and beyond, the term "level" denotes existing institutional systems or procedural processes at specific spatial dimensions such as *international* or *supranational* institutions (Multilateral Environmental Agreements, European Commission, etc.), *national* authorities or democratic institutions (e.g. national parliaments), or *local* decision making processes. The different levels are simply taken as given! The *production* of these spatial levels, i.e. the production of social space on a specific spatial scale—e.g. the production of Europe in a historical process—and its meaning for the relationships between the different levels, is regularly excluded in MLG approaches. Analyses therefore underestimate or often simply neglect the processes of up-scaling and down-scaling of decision making through the strengthening or weakening of existing levels and/or the construction of new levels. MLG approaches therefore often miss the associated impacts on policy making. It is exactly this question—how the scalar dimensions of social and political processes are produced—that is emphasized by approaches from critical geography dealing with the *politics of scale* (e.g. Smith 1995; Swyngedouw 1997; 2004; Brenner 2001; 2004; Brenner et al. 2003; Heeg et al. 2007). The question of scale has also become prominent in a variety of issues regarding environmental problems. For environmental governance, in particular, the question of how to connect socio-economic, political and ecological scales is critical (Cash and Moser 2000; Meadowcroft 2002; Bulkeley 2005). The emergence of "beyond-the-border-problems," environmental problems, where the causes and consequences are split between different countries and political authorities, pose vexing challenges. In these cases, the gains and losses related to environmental threats, as much as the costs of political responses, are often distributed among different regions or spatial scales. To address these distributional effects, the power relations of the different actors involved at these different scales have to be taken into account. Transboundary environmental problems therefore raise questions of how to connect the scale, the interplay and the fit of environmental regimes and institutions (Young 2002). Furthermore, as analyzed in the politics of scale, power relations connected to the relationships between different levels of decision making are important. The central question of the "politics of scale" approaches used in critical geography—the production of spatial scale and the relevance of the production processes for environmental governance, however, is seldom mentioned in the literature on environmental governance (Brown and Purcell 2005; Bulkeley 2005).

Recent discussions about environmental governance will be analyzed below in order to demonstrate that the production of scale is often neglected and that this disregard has profound impacts on the way the notion of MLG is used. The concept of scale will be introduced to address this shortcoming and to deal with the complex transformations which give rise to notions of multi-level governance. Moreover, a better understanding of the scale issues in Multi-Level Environmental Governance can improve our understanding of the rescaling of politics in general. It will be argued that scale-related thinking has some advantages to explain the complex transformation connected with multi-level politics. In particular, the analysis of how distributional conflicts within and between different levels are resolved—or regulated without really being resolved—could benefit from the politics of scale approach. Above all, this approach uses the notion of power and domination to explain how the power relations connected with distributional conflicts are inscribed in political institutions.

The integration of the notions of power and domination into governance approaches, however, is a challenge. Governance approaches are marked by a problem-solving bias which tends to exclude questions of domination (Mayntz 2005), too easily assuming that actors or institutions are *actually interested in solving problems*. This problem-solving bias is an important gap in recent governance approaches. When we examine distributional conflicts within and between different levels we have to address the question whether actors are genuinely interested in solving problems—or whether they are more interested, considering possible losses, in merely handling the consequences of the problems (in material as much as in political terms) without actually trying to solve the problem effectively. To do this, we have to take into account the power relations between the actors' diverging interests, and how the interests are inscribed in institutional measures—that is: how much they were able to influence the measures adopted—and thus the structural selectivities inscribed in the institutional responses on different scales.

This argument will be supported by referring to a very important example of environmental assessments and environmental policy making: the Millennium

Ecosystem Assessment. The Millennium Ecosystem Assessment (MA), published its main results in 2005 (see MA 2003; 2005a; 2005b; 2005c) and provides an excellent overview of a broad range of empirical issues connected with the question of scale in environmental sciences and policy. Moreover, it offers important methodological tools to move forward towards an integration of social and ecological scales, using multi-scale assessments and focusing on cross-scale interactions.

A much closer look at the results of the assessment as well as at the approaches applied, however, makes it obvious that some questions remain unresolved and that several new challenges have emerged. This article has made use of a valuable study at the Helmholtz Centre for Environmental Research-UFZ which analyzes the relevance of the MA for Germany (see Beck et al. 2006). In this study, we became aware of the methodological gains connected with the MA approach as well as of the impulses this approach gives to multi-level environmental governance.

Nevertheless, in their present form, the policy options discussed within the MA do not acknowledge that the societal externalization or "misplacement" of environmental effects is a specific "beyond-the-border" or "trans-local" environmental problem of particular importance to industrialized countries. The term "misplacement" addresses the impacts on ecosystem services in other parts of the world while providing human well-being for a particular society in a specific region or nation-state. Thus, the term emphasizes the relevance of cross-scale interactions and the power relations involved for governance strategies at the regional and/or local level. To fully grasp these cross-scale interactions, it is necessary to analyze how socio-spatial dimensions are produced by social processes, rather than dealing with them simply as givens. In the conclusion, we will discuss the degree to which the misplacement of environmental threats is due to power relations within and between different social scales and its impact on the local level.

Scale and levels in environmental governance

The terms *scales* and *levels* are used very differently in environmental governance. Not only can we observe differences between different disciplines and sub-disciplines and for different approaches (see for a rough overview: Gibson et al. 2000; Giampietro 2003; Evans et al. 2003; Cash et al. 2006), but often both terms are used without a clear distinction. The remaining vagueness of both terms constitutes a major concern for any systematic analysis of the natural and social processes going on simultaneously and with interdependencies on several scales and at several levels on these scales (Rotmans 2003). Regarding the basic understanding of scale, Gibson et al. (2000: 218) offered a definition of *scales* "as the spatial, temporal, quantitative, or analytical dimensions used by scientists to measure and study objects and processes." *Level*, in contrast, normally is used as a concept that denotes specific units of analysis, e.g. a system of institutions, located on a specific scale. If local, regional, national and global are dimensions used to measure social or biophysical processes (i.e. scales), then the local, the national and the global levels consist of social, economic or political institutions which give a particular level a certain durability. Starting from these definitions, however, it becomes clear from the outset, that a concrete *place* or *location* is never solely affected by a single scale or a single level of decision making, though even the relevance of this fact is seldom acknowledged. On the contrary, in a specific town or community, global markets, national laws and regional measures operate as much as locally oriented actors. Thus, we should not confuse the meaning of scale as an "analytical dimension used by scientists" (Gibson et al. 2000: 218) with a concrete spatial unit which can only be understood as constituted from a variety of processes occurring simultaneously at different scales, with careful attention paid to their interplay (see below).

Recently, the environmental governance discourse took up the scale issue in different ways and for many purposes, informed by a variety of disciplines and approaches, from political international relations theory (Young 2002), political economy (Adger et al. 2005) through institutional economics (Berkes 2002), resource management and integrated assessment (Rothman and Rotmans 2003). Two purposes are particularly relevant: (1) scale as a device to analyze the structure of environmental problems and to design policy responses; and (2) scale as an attribute of socio-economic and political processes crucial for decision making in a globalizing world. The MA deals carefully with the first one, but only mentions the latter without tackling it sufficiently. Moreover, it is only in the first notion that scale can be understood as a given, whereas the second implies that the production process of and the changing configuration between scales must be taken into account.

Regarding the structure of environmental problems and related responses, Cash and Moser (2000) distinguished the main challenges as (a) institutional fit problems, (b) scale-discordance problems, and (c) cross-scale dynamic problems. The first challenge (a) is perhaps the most intensively studied, giving rise to concepts of international regime formation (Young 2002) as much as to analyses of the fit of social and ecological scales (e.g. Young et al. 2005). At the core of the challenge lies the notion of tension between biophysical and institutional scales; biophysical scales could mean ecological, chemical or other natural conditions (e.g. watersheds), whereas institutional scales could include political, socio-economic or cultural institutions crucial for policy responses. The EU Water Framework Directive, for example, requires that water management be restructured on the scale of entire river basins, which causes institutional change in many EU member states (WFD Art. 35; see Moss 2004). In spite of the advantages in theory and practice, understanding the mismatch between institutional scales and the dynamics of biophysical systems remains a major challenge (Holling 1995; Folke et al. 1998).

The second, the scale-discordance challenge (b) refers to distributional questions: gains and costs differ depending on the scale chosen. What is seen as a global threat like climate change—where some policy responses would create global benefits—may have opposing distributional effects at national or local scales (Cash and Moser 2000: 112). This may be even more important for biodiversity-related issues: the conservation of biodiversity establishes a global good which sometimes comes at the expense of local communities whose use of biological resources for food or shelter are then restricted. The production of global goods, thus, can produce vulnerability and poverty at the local level. This problem gives rise to two further questions: how to deal with the issues of poverty, global inequalities and the power relations involved in the scale issue, and how to deal with the interplay of multiple spatial scales in natural and societal terms and the up-scaling and down-scaling of environmental problems (Adger et al. 2005).

The third challenge, the question of cross-scale interactions (c), addresses in particular this last question, requiring an analysis of the vertical interplay of spatial scales and institutional responses (Berkes 2002; Young 2002). Cross-scale interactions differ when focusing on natural or societal processes. To understand natural interlinkages better, one has to investigate causal feedback loops from the local to the global and back. The most important recent example is the interplay between global climate change and the regional climate, where the global–regional interplay causes highly different impacts at the regional level (see IPCC 2007). For cross-scale interactions in social processes, however, these interlinkages are much more complex and to some degree beyond causal determination. Furthermore, one must define what constitutes a local level of decision making, and whether this local level is a well demarked entity. A community or a specific nature conservation site could be, and frequently is, affected by processes operating at all scales, from the local to the global. Conflicts about logging at the Clayoquot Sound at Vancouver Island in Canada have not only local, but also national (e.g. forest laws) and global dimensions (e.g. global timber markets, boycott campaigns, etc.; see Magnusson and Shaw 2003). And there is not only an external restriction of regional or local processes, but an active involvement of processes at other societal scales at the lower scales. Local land use decisions, for example, are not only restricted by national law and global markets. Furthermore, a broad variety of actors can be observed at the local level itself, some of whom are acting at a local scale while others are more nationally or globally oriented—from local tourism managers and local fishermen or indigenous peoples up to national timber industry representatives or international NGOs organizing global campaigns. While the local level of decision making is influenced by these actors, some act at a local scale while others act on other scales. These actors are struggling with the question concerning how the conflict should be framed and constituted as a political space: as a local conflict, a case for regional measures or national laws, or as part of global environmental change (Magnusson and Shaw 2003; see, concerning conflicts about genetic resources, Brand et al. 2008). Regarding social scales (at least), we therefore *cannot* assume that spatial scales are *fixed* and *given* entities, *nor* can we assume that they are even *clearly separated*. On the contrary, we have to analyze the processes of how the actions of different and conflicting interest groups constitute social scales and how they overlap or even conflict with each other. It is most important, therefore, to determine which kind of actors with which interests and which power relations are involved in an issue in order to better understand the spatial dimension of the conflict. Moreover, social and political scales are not strictly separated from each other, so that we must also analyze the ways in which they are intrinsically interconnected. Political scientists deal with both problems under terms like "glocalization" or "politics of scale."

Scale as an attribute of social and political processes becomes a crucial issue connected to the analyses of globalization processes and of the "hollowing out of the nation-state" (Jessop 2002). The institutions at the national scale have long been understood as the most important levels of decision making; however, over the last years, processes of up-scaling and down-scaling of statehood involving the transfer of authoritative power and political responsibility to lower levels (e.g. urban) or higher levels (e.g. supranational or international regimes; see Brenner et al. 2003) have become increasingly important. According to Brown and Purcell (2005), recent work in radical political geography is not so much engaged in environmental issues, although some exceptions exist in the work of Eric Swyngedouw (1997; 2004) and Roger Keil (Desfor and Keil 2004; Keil and Debbané 2005), for example. We nevertheless can draw on work on the "politics of scale" to respond to the two questions addressed above: How are local, national and global scales intrinsically interconnected? Moreover, how do social processes produce social scales?

The first issue is highlighted by the concept that local and global processes are not strictly separated processes but deeply intertwined or mutually constituted—what Swyngedouw (1997) calls "glocalization." They are deeply intertwined because what happens at one scale is not only connected to other scales (e.g. the influence of global markets on local land use change for agriculture), but is to some degree itself part of processes of other scales: national governments agree to global treaties and, thus produce global institutions; global or regional agreements enforce or weaken the rights of local actors; local and regional resource use decisions produce global climate change; national law stimulates or resolves local conflicts; and so on. Moreover, local and global scales can constitute each other mutually, because processes at one scale constitute the processes at the other: the globalization of finance, for example, is produced in cities, which are not exclusively local units but also global cities (Sassen 1994; Brenner and Keil 2006). Global environmental change as a whole is a result of a huge number of decisions taken at the local level (e.g. land use change), which are also influenced by global processes (e.g. global markets for soy, biofuels or meat are linked to the deforestation of the Amazon region). Two notions, therefore, are crucial to our approach: first, it is not scale itself, but *societal processes* (e.g. economic, political and cultural dimensions of environmental conflicts) that should be seen as a starting point for analyses (Brown and Purcell 2005); and, second, we must not look at only a single scale, but at the *relationships between scales* (Brenner 2001).

Both notions are important in order to understand the "politics of scale." Whereas in most integrated assessment and environmental policy literature, space is defined as a physical entity and spatial scale as a measurable spatial unit,[1] the "politics of scale" approach goes beyond this geophysical condition. It consequently understands that scales are produced by social processes, which means by actors engaged in conflicts or negotiations, creating agreements, or regulating social tensions and contestations. In particular, the "politics of scale" approach addresses not only the power relations determining the selection of one scale or another but also those resulting from this choice. For example, the scale of resource management to deal with commons has strong implications on power relations; and the shift from local to global levels is not politically neutral. Recent attempts to respond to environmental threats at the global level, focusing on international agreements and organizations like the World Bank, were criticized as constituting a new class of global resource managers (Goldman 1998; 2005). Thus, the challenge emerges of how actors operating at the local scale can enforce their interests. This challenge is particularly pressing for managing public goods or commons. Over the last years, local and regional natural resource management institutions have received the greatest attention as the ostensibly appropriate scales to avoid the so called "tragedy of the commons" (Ostrom et al. 1999). Moreover, alliances of local actors, also called translocal actor coalitions (Martello and Jasanoff 2004: 12), have become influential even at the international level. Networks of indigenous peoples' organizations, for example, were able to articulate their interests at the international level and became influential actors in the negotiations on the Convention on Biological Diversity (Brand et al. 2008). Thus, neither the international level nor the local level can be seen any longer as separate entities, but have to be viewed as constituted by conflicts operating *at* every bit as much as *between* the different levels of decision making. These conflicts and the cross-scale interactions associated with them give rise to still further challenges for environmental governance. In the following section, we will first explain these challenges by referring first to the example of the MA, before arguing how these challenges could be addressed as an expression of the politics of scale in natural resource use management.

Multi-scale assessments and scale interactions in the MA

The Millennium Assessment (MA) was carried out between 2001 and 2005 to assess the consequences of ecosystem change for human well-being. The linkages between ecosystems and human well-being were assessed by the ecosystem services, i.e. the benefits people obtain from ecosystems (MA

2005a). The MA is characterized by a reflexive and innovative approach to scale issues. Not only does it take questions of data sampling and integrated assessment seriously, but also looks at cross-scale interactions and questions related to the social implications of particular levels of decision making, including the different kinds of knowledge involved (see Reid et al. 2006). Moreover, even the power relations within and between scales are mentioned as important dimensions that shape the impact and outcome of environmental governance. Nevertheless, the mismatch between social and natural scales is not dealt with substantially, but only mentioned as one remaining research need (Carpenter et al. 2006).

In the following, we want to show that the MA integrates most approaches to the scale issue, but fails to take in the "politics of scale" (and to some degree even the notion of "glocalization"). Moreover, reducing the understanding of spatial scale to physical terms is a crucial shortcoming in the MA, as it ignores the social and political construction of scales. This has important implications, as we will show in the succeeding section, concerning the consequences of MA results for a nation-state like Germany.

The MA conducts integrated assessments not only at a global scale, but also at multiple scales. Moreover, it highlights the significance of the sub-global dimensions of ecosystem change and biodiversity loss (MA 2005c: 31). The understanding and the impacts of, as well as the policy responses to, global environmental problems such as climate change or biodiversity loss, differ significantly at regional or local scales. This is even more the case, though, when focusing on ecosystem services for human well-being. Regional, national or even local assessments, therefore, are not case studies but assessments in their own right. The MA understands relationships between the scales as nested hierarchies (see Figure 5.1), where the lower level is part of higher levels (MA 2005c: 31).

A multi-scale approach, however, is not only necessary for technical reasons regarding data sampling and evaluation. The MA mentions three other reasons. First, the needs of decision makers at different levels are different, e.g. a "global assessment cannot meet the needs of local farmers" (MA 2003: 43). Second, the selection of a specific scale is crucial to analyzing distributional effects: winners and losers are different at different scales and "[t]he choice of scale is not politically neutral, because the selection may intentionally or unintentionally privilege some groups" (MA 2003: 122). Finally, a multi-scale approach enables the evaluation of cross-scale interactions, because conclusions at one scale could be more easily reflected at other scales (MA 2003: 43), and similar results on different scales seem to confirm the robustness of the results (MA 2005c: 10). The use of Ecosystem Services (ESS) varies on different scales, and a multi-scale analysis gives information about the distribution of gains due to increased and decreased use of ESS and the induced change in human well-being. Defining gains and losses demands consideration of the perceptions at different levels: Enhanced carbon sequestration is considered a gain on the global scale, but can be perceived a

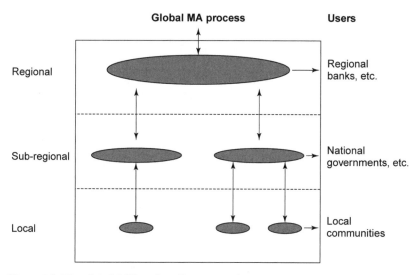

Figure 5.1 The global Millennium Ecosystem Assessment process

loss on a local scale (MA 2005a: 86). Such multi-scale information is important for the elaboration and implementation of political responses to the endangerment of ecosystems.

Besides these advantages, the MA has an important shortcoming which arises from the problem solving bias of environmental governance as much as from the basic understanding of scale. In the MA, scale is used as a "physical dimension," measurable in meters, whereas the term level "is used to describe the discrete levels of social organization, such as individuals, households, communities, or nations" (MA 2003: 108, referring to Gibson et al. 2000). Furthermore, the MA distinguishes the scale of observation from the scale of the phenomenon and states that both are independent of each other (MA 2003: 108, referring to Gibson et al. 2000).

Both arguments are far from trivial. Regarding the latter, each phenomenon, and in particular large entities like ecosystems or landscapes, do not simply exist as separate units of scientific observation. Where observation constitutes functional processes as separate and limited phenomena, ecosystems do not exist as such, but are scientifically constructed (Jax 2005). The first argument is more important: Whereas the physical dimensions of space are key for ecological and social processes, spatial scales for societal processes are not restricted to physical dimensions measurable in meters. Global decision making often occurs in small offices or at telephone- or internet-based conferences. Moreover, geographical units—like regions or communities—do not consist of a single social scale. In every urban or rural region, a dynamic mix of locally, nationally, and globally oriented actors and processes can be found: implantation of transnational companies, national or state police offices negotiating with locally oriented farmers or workers, and so on (see above for the case of Clayoquot Sound). What the MA refers to as "discrete levels of social organization," are not discrete but mutually overlapping. These levels, such as "households, communities, or nations," seen in their spatial, or their scalar existence, are not given entities. Social, political and cultural patterns determine whether these levels are perceived as separated entities. For example, what is seen as a household varies over history and between different cultures. Moreover, historical conflicts and decision making determine the borders of "households, communities, or nations." This means that their identity is constituted discursively or symbolically and their borders politically (or via military violence, like most national borders).

For the same reasons, it is problematic to assume that multi-scale assessment should deal with nested units in a hierarchy of geographical levels (as shown above). We cannot assume that all processes operating in a community are part of regional or even national markets (as they may be exported and sold in other regions of the world; see below); nor that measures taken at the national level always support the local level, as they may often contradict the interests of local resource users. Even when analyzing environmental issues, we cannot suppose that smaller spatial units, like landscapes or watersheds, are part of one single spatial unit at a higher scale (like a nation-state). Particularly if socio-economic or political processes are addressed, it is not helpful to assume that they are part of the same scale or that they operate in nested hierarchies.

For these reasons, questions of social scales cannot be reduced to the physical dimension of space, nor can scalar issues at social levels be tackled only in such a hierarchical way, as was done in the MA. The stated difficulties of applying the MA framework at the local scale (MA 2005c: 73) may have emerged from these difficulties. First, cross-scale interactions at social scales are often as important as those at ecological scales. Therefore, one cannot deal with the local scale (in the language of the MA, the scale on which household or community levels act) separately from other processes. The question whether, at the community level, gains from ESS are appropriated by local or global actors has to be answered empirically. For example, the gains from biodiversity protection might be accumulated by a global tourist company, whereas the local community might lose its provisioning services, such as food, water, timber, and fiber, and not even receive any jobs from the company. To state that direct interactions between social and natural processes mostly occur at the local scale (see Figure 5.2; MA 2003: 121) ignores the fact that social levels at smaller scales do not exist separated from other scales, as discussed above. Moreover, when we look at global ecological scales, we must analyze the impact of different social processes, located at different social scales, on global or continental environmental conditions. Direct interactions with the natural world or ecosystems are mostly expressed through actions by institutions at the local scale (e.g. land use change), but caused by social processes at every social scale (e.g. global markets, national laws or regional policies, etc.). Reducing these interactions to the local scale is a very prominent example of the "local trap": the assumption that the local scale has something inherently specific, which is criticized by Brown and Purcell (2005).

The "misplacement" of environmental degradation—the relevance of the MA for Germany

Looking at the relevance of the MA for Germany, we found the methodological approach very useful and that it could confirm some MA results. In particular, the need for a multi-scale assessment was covered by the fact that the availability of ESS in Germany faces different threats than at the global scale. In Germany, water availability is not a major problem, and even climate change is not supposed to change this, contrary to the status and trends in many parts of the world (Beck et al. 2006: 53). Moreover, the need for reflexive analyses of cross-scale interactions and for decision making at different levels seemed very helpful to us. In particular, decisions on different political levels from the community level up to global market processes affect land use changes, the most important direct driver of ESS in densely inhabited countries like Germany. More recently, global climate change has become another important direct driver.

On the other hand, we found that the MA did not mention one kind of cross-scale interaction, which is very important for Germany (as for all industrialized countries): the impact of imported products, which add to human well-being in Germany, on ecosystem services in the parts of the world supplying the imported products. These cross-scale interactions are far from trivial because they raise important methodological challenges, in particular concerning the connections between ecological and social scales. Regarding the former, an assessment of the relevance of the MA for Germany would deal with the status of ecosystems only within its political borders. For the social and political scale, such an assessment must involve scale-interactions with ecosystems beyond these borders, taking into account the Germany-induced impacts on ecosystems in other parts of the world (Beck et al. 2006). These impacts, however, are often very damaging and possible threats to ESS in other parts are mostly ignored in environmental impact analyses (see also Sachs et al. 2005). We call this kind of societal externalization "the *misplacement* of environmental degradation." Misplacements are forms of externalizations via the natural and social environment across social scales, when impacts of political or social decisions on ESS and human well-being in other parts of the world are ignored (see Figure 5.2). The impact of producing shrimp for future export to Germany is an example of such a misplacement, where the increase of human well-being in Germany through shrimp consumption is directly connected to the degradation of mangrove forests and increasing environmental vulnerabilities in Africa, Latin America or Southeast Asia (MA 2005c: 521; Beck et al. 2006: 44, 88). Such misplacement is referred to in approaches like the "ecological footprint" or the "ecological rucksack" (Wackernagel and Rees 1996). However, these approaches also take into account only one dimension of scale interactions through data collection and fail to tackle the cross-scale interactions (glocalization) and the implications of the politics of scale (see Figure 5.2; Beck et al. 2006: 88).

Another example of the misplacement of environmental degradation, the impact of the purchase of fishing rights by the European Union on regional fisheries on the West African coast, is mentioned briefly in the MA (MA 2005b: 13; 2005c: 490–92; Beck et al. 2006: 79; Kaczynski and Fluharty 2002). But even in this case, the cross-scale interactions concerning socio-economic and ecological processes are much more complex than mentioned in the MA. Obviously, the cash payments connected with EU fishing rights contribute to the national budgets of the related African countries. At the same time, these fishing agreements lead to competition between locals fishing with small-scale traditional vessels and big trawlers from abroad. This example shows that the over-exploitation of fish stocks at local levels is connected with decision making at a supranational, national and global scale. The example also shows that while the degradation of ESS in a specific region can undermine the livelihood conditions at the local scale, it can simultaneously generate livelihood gains not only at the national scale, but also at a *foreign* local scale, i.e. in Germany. The example also highlights potential issues at the global scale: because the government of Morocco receives payments for the territory of Western Sahara, an occupied West African country, such payments could yet violate international laws and UN Security Council decisions (see www.fishelsewhere.org). The West African fisheries example explains the importance of the interaction of national and global scale processes for local processes and determines, to some degree, the options available for local decision making.

In looking at a less tangible example, the benefits arising from the valorization of genetic resources, it appears highly doubtful as to whether locally based actors can, in fact, prevail in decision making at the local level. The valorization of genetic resources, i.e. heritable properties of an organism valuable for medicinal purposes or in agriculture, is negotiated in the Convention on Biological Diversity as the regulation of access and benefit sharing. In this case, locally based actors like small farmers or forest dwellers, who may have particular knowledge about their local environmental conditions, are in conflict with large international companies operating at the global scale, and with national or regional authorities, interested in generating additional income. In many parts of the world, strategies aimed at exports and at getting the highest cash value for resources will dominate at the local or regional scale (as for example in the case in the state of Chiapas in southern Mexico; see Brand et al. 2008: ch. 5). The interaction of ecological and social processes, thus, cannot be dealt with at a specific, separated local scale but must take into account the interconnection between all scales. In these interconnections, the power relations between different regions and

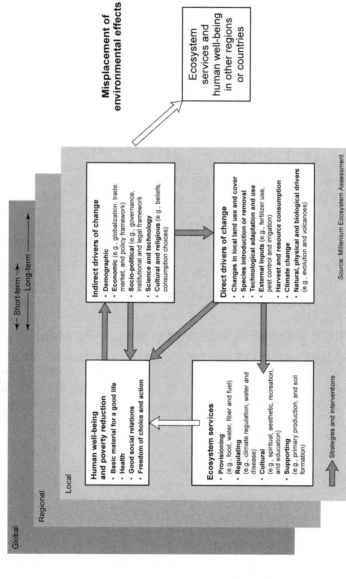

Figure 5.2 Conceptual framework of the Millennium Ecosystem Assessment.

Source: Millennium Ecosystem Assessment.

nation-states as much as between supranational regions and local communities are of central importance.

To fully grasp the complex decision making processes we also cannot reduce our perspective to a narrow problem-solving approach. We have to take into account the economic interests and the power relations involved when we seek to understand how specific decisions respect or reflect the interests of different actors. In the negotiations between the EU and West African countries, obviously the economic and political power of the EU prevailed over the interests of the locally based fishermen. We are confronted, thus, with a constellation in which environmental challenges are strongly related to power relations across scales. In distributional conflicts linked to scale interactions we cannot assume that the problems can be regulated by an environmental management in favor of all interests concerned. On the contrary, in dealing with the question of who appropriates which ESS, we have to deal with specific gains and losses, herewith impacting on global inequality (Görg 2007b). Using ESS, for example, by way of importing shrimp to Germany or other countries, contributes to attenuating or deepening poverty, ethnic marginalization and gender imbalance. All this has profound spatial or scalar implications. The misfit of institutions and ecosystems is at the base of the problem, but with power and income disparities frequently linked to it, and the impacts in Germany and in the region exporting the ESS (e.g. shrimp or fish) show cross-scale interactions in themselves. The production and interaction of local, national, regional and global scales, thus, has to be taken into account.

Outlook: the politics of scale in environmental governance

It has been argued recently, though for different reasons, that the "politics of scale" approach could inform environmental governance (Meadowcroft 2002; Bulkeley 2005; Brown and Purcell 2005; Görg 2007a). Two arguments are particularly important: first, the "politics of scale" approach provides a more comprehensive understanding of scale-interactions by focusing on the "mutual imbrications of all scales" (Brenner 2004: 7); and, second, the approach highlights the social processes producing social scales (and their relationships with each other), particularly emphasizing the power relations within and between scales. Moreover, what is missing in most governance approaches is a specific reference to constellations in which opposing actors are not really interested in problem solving, thus producing what Bob Jessop (2002) called *governance failures*. For our purpose, one governance failure is particularly important: the misplacement of ecological degradations connected with asymmetric power relations. It is a general weakness of governance approaches that they inherited a narrow perspective from earlier approaches to political steering. As Renate Mayntz (2005) has argued, this narrow steering perspective ignores the broader societal context in which governance takes place. In particular, the power relations involved in decision making and the forms of societal domination tend to be ignored. This is especially problematic where distributional conflicts are involved. Thus, the question, "In favor of which interests are environmental problems regulated?" has to be taken into account.

Distributional conflicts, thus, are important for cross-scale interactions, as mentioned above. This notion leads back to the questions raised at the beginning: how can the emergence of MLG be explained? This question can be answered by focusing on the transformation of the nation-state strongly connected with neoliberal globalization (Hirsch 2001; Jessop 2002; Brenner et al. 2003; Brand et al. 2008). Political-administrative regulation and control functions are increasingly shifting from the nation-state to subnational, regional, and also inter- and supranational levels. A system is coming into being of less strongly institutionalized bodies of regulation, which differ but also intersect and overlap in their ranges of activity, as compared, for example, to those of the federal system in a nation-state. Beside this vertical interplay between these new regulatory entities, we have to consider that these bodies and activities are related to very different sectors of society and to problem areas (like climate change and ESS) which are different from, although not independent of, one another. Moreover, each problem area has its own specific constellation of actors, interest structures and power relations. Thus, the horizontal interplay between these institutions and of measures taken or proposed at different levels is also important. Referring to societal processes (e.g. economic, political, and cultural dimensions of environmental conflicts) as a starting point for analysis (as postulated by Brown and Purcell 2005, see above), means dealing with the specific constellations of actors at different levels and in different sectors, problem areas, the actors' respective interests and their power relations.

The relationships between these actor constellations are critically important. Specific actor constellations at the national level enable certain countries like the USA or Germany to handle climate change in a specific way, for example to promote "biofuels" as a strategy to reduce the dependency on fossil fuels. Such strategies have strong impacts on other socio-economic (e.g. food prices in Mexico) and environmental processes (in particular biodiversity change; see GRAIN 2007; TWN 2007). Moreover, because of their relative strength, such actor constellations (also called "relationships of social forces," see Brand et al. 2008) could also weaken the influence of other actors (like nature conservation groups). This is also the case when specific governance strategies which are institutionalized in one country or region (like the EU's Common Agricultural Policy or its fishery policy as mentioned above) have a strong impact on ESS and related social actors in other regions.

It follows that socio-political struggles are always, among other things, about the dominance of a certain scale within the geographical-institutional asymmetric setting or about the reconfiguration of that constellation ("re-scaling"). The continuing struggles for dominance and the re-scaling process are a reason for the growing awareness of multi-level decision making as much as for research toward overlapping areas of regulation and their interplay. Driven by "social strategies and struggles for control and empowerment" (Swyngedouw 1997: 141), these processes can either result in new relations of dominance or deepen existing ones, e.g. between the EU and African countries and communities. Thus, cross-scale interactions and their impact at the local or regional scale represent a particularly important example of what has been called a "politicized environment" (Bryant and Bailey 1997)—the way power relations are inscribed in the use of the natural resources and ESS by different countries or communities.

The power relations between spatial units are inscribed into the structure of multi-level environmental decision making. This is the environment-related consequence of the production of "new state spaces" (Brenner 2004) by re-scaling elements of state power and thereby creating new and more complex relationships between different scales of state politics. Such a global multi-level system includes power relations at and between different scales. It is important to note that these scales are not independent of one another, but exert a mutual influence. They are also not directly derivable from each other; neither the global (as sometimes assumed by globalization theories) nor the local naturally prevails (see Bernt and Görg 2007). Sometimes it is easier at the local scale to bring the interests of the actors based there to bear on an issue. But, even in this case, the local level does not exist independently from the other scales. For this reason, we should resist the "lure of the local" (Mitchell 2001) and avoid the "local trap" (Brown and Purcell 2005). Although the international scale plays an increasingly important role, the relations of the scales to one another are not complementary per se, and we should not assume that the local scale is privileged per se. On the contrary, the local sale is increasingly produced by global processes, and this dynamic needs critical investigation.

Note

1 This notion of space is the dominant one; even scale sometimes is defined as an "analytical dimension used by scientists," see above. See (MA 2003: 108; Reid et al. 2006: 7; for an overview: Evans et al. 2003: 5).

References

Adger, W. N., Brown, K., and Thompson, E. L. (2005) "The Political Economy of Cross-Scale Networks in Resource Co-management," *Ecology and Society*, 10(2): online.

Bache, I. and Flinders, M. (eds.) (2004) *Multi-Level Governance*, Oxford and New York: Oxford University Press.

Beck, S., Born, W., Dzioch, S., Görg, C., Hansjürgens, B., Henle, K., Jax, K., Köck, W., Neßhöver, C., Rauschmayer, F., Ring, I., Schmidt-Loske, K., Unnerstall, H., and Wittmer, H. (2006) *Die Relevanz des Millennium Ecosystem Assessments für Deutschland*, UFZ-Report, Leipzig: UFZ (Helmholtz Centre for Environmental Research, UFZ).

Berkes, F. (2002) "Cross-Scale Institutional Linkages for Commons Management: Perspectives from the Bottom Up," in E. Ostrom, T. Dietz, N. Dolsak, P. C. Stern,

S. Stonich, and E. U. Weber (eds.) *The Drama of the Commons*, Washington, D.C.: National Academy Press.

Bernt, M. and Görg, C. (2007) "Searching for the Scale—Skalenprobleme als Herausforderung der Stadt-und Umweltforschung," in S. Heeg, B. Röttger, and M. Wissen (eds.) *Politics of Scale. Räume der Globalisierung und Perspektiven emanzipatorischer Politik*, Münster, Germany: Westfälisches Dampfboot.

Brand, U., Görg, C., Hirsch, J., and Wissen, M. (2008) *Conflicts in Environmental Regulation and the Internationalization of the State. Contested Terrains*, London and New York: Routledge.

Brenner, N. (2001) "The Limits to Scale? Methodological Reflections on Scalar Structuration," *Progress in Human Geography*, 25(4): 591–614.

———(2004) *New State Spaces. Urban Governance and the Rescaling of Statehood*, Oxford and New York: Oxford University Press.

Brenner, N., Jessop, B., Jones, M., and Macleod, G. (2003) *State/Space: A Reader*, Oxford, Berlin and Malden, MA: Blackwell.

Brenner, N. and Keil, R. (eds.) (2006) *The Global Cities Reader*, London and New York: Routledge.

Brown, C. and Purcell, M. (2005) "There's Nothing Inherent about Scale: Political Ecology, the Local Trap, and the Politics of Development in the Brazilian Amazon," *Geoforum*, 36: 607–24.

Bryant, R. L. and Bailey, S. (1997) *Third World Political Ecology*, London and New York: Routledge.

Bulkeley, H. (2005) "Reconfiguring Environmental Governance: Towards a Politics of Scales and Networks," *Political Geography*, 24: 875–902.

Carpenter, S. R., DeFries, R., Dietz, T., Mooney, H. A., Polasky, S., Reid, W., and Scholes, R. J. (2006) "Millennium Ecosystem Assessment: Research Needs," *Science*, 314: 257–58.

Cash, D. W., Adger, W. N., Berkes, F., Garden, P., Lebel, L., Olsson, P., Prichard, L. and Young, O. (2006) "Scale and Cross-Scale Dynamics: Governance and Information in a Multilevel World," *Ecology and Society*, 11(2): online.

Cash, D. W. and Moser, S. C. (2000) "Linking Global and Local Scales: Designing Dynamic Assessment and Management Processes," *Global Environmental Change*, 10: 109–20.

Desfor, G. L. and Keil, R. (2004) *Nature and the City*, Tucson: University of Arizona Press.

Evans, T., Ostrom, E., and Gibson, C. (2003) "Scaling Issues in the Social Sciences," in D. S. Rothman and J. Rotmans (eds.) *Scaling in Integrated Assessment*, Lisse, The Netherlands: Swets Zeitlinger.

Folke, C., Pritchard Jr., L., Berkes, F., Colding, J., and Svedin, U. (1998) *The Problem of Fit Between Ecosystems and Institutions*, IHDP Working Paper no. 2, Bonn, Germany: IHDP (International Human Dimensions Programme on Global Environmental Change).

Giampietro, M. (2003) "Complexity and Scales: The Challenges for Integrated Assessment," in D. S. Rothman and J. Rotmans (eds.) *Scaling in Integrated Assessment*, Lisse, The Netherlands: Swets Zeitlinger.

Gibson, C. C., Ostrom, E., and Ahn, T. K. (2000) "The Concept of Scale and the Human Dimensions of Global Change: A Survey," *Ecological Economics*, 32: 217–39.

Goldman, M. (ed.) (1998) *Privatizing Nature: Political Struggles for the Global Commons*, London: Pluto Press.

———(2005) *Imperial Nature: The World Bank and Struggles for Social Justice in the Age of Globalization*, New Haven CT and London: Yale University Press.

Görg, C. (2007a) "Landscape Governance. The 'Politics of Scale' and the 'Natural' Conditions of Places," *Geoforum*, 38(5): 954–66.

———(2007b) "Räume der Ungleichheit. Die Rolle gesellschaftlicher Naturverhältnisse in der Produktion globaler Ungleichheiten am Beispiel des Millennium Ecosystem Assessments," in C. Klinger, G.-A. Knapp, and B. Sauer (eds.) *Achsen der Ungleichheit. Zum Verhältnis von Klasse, Geschlecht und Ethnizität*, Frankfurt and New York: Campus Verlag, 131–50.

GRAIN (2007) "Stop the Agrofuel Craze!," *Seedling* (agrofuels special issue), July: 2–9.

Heeg, S., Röttger, B., and Wissen, M. (eds.) (2007) *Politics of Scale. Räume der Globalisierung und Perspektiven emanzipatorischer Politik*, Münster, Germany: Westfälisches Dampfboot.

Heinelt, H., Getimis, P., Kafkalas, G., Smith, R., and Swyngedouw, E. (2002) *Participatory Governance in Multi-level Context*, Opladen, Germany: Leske Budrich.

Hirsch, J. (2001) "Die Internationalisierung des Staates. Anmerkungen zu einigen aktuellen Fragen der Staatstheorie," in J. Hirsch, B. Jessop, and N. Poulantzas (eds.) *Die Zukunft des Staates*, Hamburg, Germany: VSA-Verlag.

Holling, C. S. (1995) "Sustainability: The Cross-scale Dimension," in M. Munasinghe and M. Shearer (eds.) *Defining and Measuring Sustainability*, Washington, DC: UNEP/World Bank.

Hooghe, L. and Marks, G. (2001) *Multi-Level Governance and European Integration*, Lanham, MD: Rowman and Littlefield.

IPCC (Parry, M. L., Canziani, O. F., Palutikof, J. P., van der Linden, P. J., and Hanson, C. E., eds.) (2007) *Climate Change 2007: Impacts, Adaptation and Vulnerability. Contribution of Working Group II to the Fourth Assessment Report of the Intergovernmental Panel on Climate Change*, Cambridge: Cambridge University Press.

Jax, K. (2005) "Function and 'Functioning.' Ecology: What Does It Mean?", OIKOS, 111:3, pp. 641–48.

Jessop, B. (2002) *The Future of the Capitalist State*, Cambridge: Polity Press.

Jordan, A. (2005) "Introduction: European Union Environmental Policy—Actors, Institutions and Policy Processes," in A. Jordan (ed.) *Environmental Policy in the European Union*, London: Earthscan.

Kaczynski, V. M. and Fluharty, D. L. (2002) "European Policies in West Africa: Who Benefits from Fisheries Agreements?" *Marine Policy*, 26(2): 75–93.

Keil, R. and Debbané, A. M. (2005) "Scaling Discourse Analysis: Experiences From Hermanus, South Africa and Walvis Bay, Namibia," *Journal of Environmental Policy and Planning*, 7(3): 257–76.

MA (Milennium Ecosystem Assessment) (2003) *Ecosystems and Human Well-Being: A Framework for Assessment*, Washington, DC: Island Press.

———(2005a) *Ecosystems and Human Well-being: Synthesis report of the Millennium Ecosystem Assessment*, Washington, DC.: Island Press.

———(2005b) *Our Planet—Summary for Decision Makers*, Washington, DC: Island Press.

———(2005c) *Ecosystems and Human Well-being: Multiscale Assessments. Findings of the Sub-global Assessments Working Group of the Millennium Ecosystem Assessment*, Washington, DC: Island Press.

Magnusson, W. and Shaw, K. (2003) *A Political Space*, Minneapolis: University of Minnesota Press.

Martello, M. L. and Jasanoff, S. (2004) "Introduction: Globalization and Environmental Governance," in S. Jasanoff and M. L. Martello (eds.) *Earthly Politics: Local and Global in Environmental Governance*, Cambridge, MA: MIT Press.

Mayntz, R. (2005) "Governance Theory als fortentwickelte Steuerungstheorie?" in G. F. Schuppert (ed.) *Governance-Forschung*, Baden-Baden, Germany: Nomos Verlagsgesellschaft.

Meadowcroft, J. (2002) "Politics and Scale: Some Implications for Environmental Governance," *Landscape and Urban Planning*, 61: 169–79.

Mitchell, D. (2001) "The Lure of the Local: Landscape Studies at the End of a Troubled Century," *Progress in Human Geography*, 25(2): 269–81.

Moss, T. (2004) "The Governance of Land Use in River Basins: Prospects for Overcoming Problems of Institutional Interplay with the EU Water Framework Directive," *Land use policy*, 21: 85–94.

Ostrom, E., Burger, J., Field, C. B., Norgaard, R. B., and Policansky, D. (1999) "Sustainability—Revisiting the Commons: Local Lessons, Global Challenges," *Science*, 284(5412): 278–82.

Reid, W. V., Berkes, F., Wilbanks, T. J., and Capistrano, D. (eds.) (2006) *Bridging Scales and Knowledge Systems: Concepts and Applications in Ecosystem Assessment*, Washington, DC: Island Press.

Rothman, D. S. and Rotmans, J. (eds.) (2003) *Scaling in Integrated Assessment*, Lisse, The Netherlands: Swets Zeitlinger.

Rotmans, J. (2003) "Scaling in Integrated Assessment: Problem or Challenge?" in D. S. Rothman and J. Rotmans (eds.) *Scaling in Integrated Assessment*, Lisse, The Netherlands: Swets Zeitlinger.

Sachs, W. and Santarius, T., with Aßmann, D., Brouns, B., Linz, M., Moll, S., Ott, H. E., Pastowski, A., Petersen, R., Scherhorn, G., Sterk, W., and Supersberger, N. (2005) *Fair Future. Begrenzte Ressourcen und globale Gerechtigkeit*, Report, ed. Wüppertal Institut für Klima, Umwelt, Energie, Munich: C. H. Beck.

Sassen, S. (1994) *Cities in a World Economy*, Thousand Oaks, CA: Pine Forge Press.

Smith, N. (1995) "Remaking Scale: Competition and Cooperation in Prenational and Postnational Europe," in H. Eskelinen and F. Snickars (eds.) *Competitive European Peripheries*, Berlin, Heidelberg and New York: Springer.

Swyngedouw, E. (1997) "Neither Global Nor Local. 'Glocalization' and the Politics of Scale," in K. R. Cox (ed.) *Spaces of Globalization: Reasserting the Power of the Local*, New York and London: Guilford Press.

——(2004) "Scaled Geographies. Nature, Place, and the Politics of Scale," in E. Sheppard and R. B. McMaster (eds.) *Scale and Geographic Inquiry: Nature, Society, and Method*, Oxford: Blackwell.

TWN (Third World Network) (publisher) (2007) *Thirld World Resurgence*, 200 (issue topic: "Biofuels: An Illusion and a Threat").

Wackernagel, M. and Rees, W. E. (1996) *Our Ecological Footprint: Reducing Human Impact on the Earth*, Gabriola Island, British Columbia: New Society Publishers.

Young, O. R. (2002) *The Institutional Dimensions of Environmental Change: Fit, Interplay, Scale*, Cambridge, MA: MIT Press.

Young, J., Báldi, A., Benedetti-Cecchi, L., Bergamini, A., Hiscock, K., van den Hove, S., Koetz, T., van Ierland, E., Lányi, A., Pataki, G., Scheidegger, C., Török, K., and Watt, A. D. (eds.) (2005) *Landscape Scale Biodiversity Assessment: The Problem of Scaling. Report of an Electronic Conference*, Vacratot: Institute of Ecology and Botany of the Hungarian Academy of Sciences.

6 The internationalized state and its functions and modes in the global governance of biodiversity

A neo-Poulantzian interpretation[1]

Ulrich Brand

International environmental politics is usually analyzed from a perspective of more or less functioning cooperation. Problems should be dealt with cooperatively through political institutions, agreed targets and rules, capacity-building and effective implementation at the national level. Scientific knowledge is considered crucial in order to understand—and, in many cases like climate change, to make visible—complex problems. Moreover, discourses over nature and environmental problems play an important role in the formation of interests and policies. Conflicts and different interests are considered to be reconciled through *arguing*, *bargaining*, and *learning* in political processes.

On the other hand, socioeconomic developments and social forces, with their heterogeneous interests, values and world views, are rarely taken into account. Moreover, problems are seen as emerging objectively and the state is often seen as a neutral agency which intends to solve problems. This text seeks to illustrate the following: If the existence of structural conflicts and contradictions as well as the socioeconomic embeddedness of politics is integrated into the analysis, the picture of global environmental politics becomes more realistic and the obstacles of the development toward a more democratic and just sustainability more obvious. In addition, those dimensions can be considered more constructively when the state is not understood as a neutral and homogeneous entity.

In this text I would like to focus on one aspect of that ambitious claim and on one specific conflict field: The role of the state in the global governance of biodiversity. Biodiversity politics is, despite its special features, exemplary for global environmental politics. The first part of this paper will introduce Nicos Poulantzas' theory of the state and reformulate the theory for an understanding of central aspects of international politics. After this, the internationalization of the state is linked to the concepts of hegemony, power and knowledge. The conflict field of the appropriation of biodiversity is briefly introduced and, in the second part, the role of international politics is outlined. Finally, two modes of international politics are analyzed: the asymmetric relationship among two international political institutions and the strategic selectivity of one of them.

Theoretical considerations

It might be problematic to label an approach with the name of one theorist: Foucauldian, Gramscian or neo-Gramscian—and now a "neo-Poulantzian" approach to a critical theory of International Political Economy (IPE) or the internationalized state is proposed. I do not intend simply to "apply" Poulantzas—who wrote in the 1970s against the backdrop of late Fordism and focused on the nation-state—in order to understand the actual phase of globalized capitalism and its profound transformation of the state. Central insights are taken as one pillar of a complex theory of the internationalized and globalized state. However, in this contribution the focus lies on Poulantzas and the state apparatuses of the internationalized state.

The focus of the second part of the theoretical considerations is the relationship between power, knowledge, hegemony, and the internationalized state. Against the backdrop of the discussion of post-Fordism, the concept of a "knowledge-based economy" is introduced and linked to the internationalized state.

Aspects of a neo-Poulantzian research agenda

I would like to highlight several aspects of Poulantzas' theory, which was strongly developed in his latest book, *State, Power, Socialism* (1978/1980/ 2002). It was supposed to be the missing fourth volume, on the state, of Marx's *Capital*. The intention at this point is not to outline the whole theory but rather emphasize those dimensions of his theory which are thereafter used to support this article's argument. The innovation in Poulantzas' theory is the way in which he links the institutional materiality of the state with the other structures of capitalist societies and with social struggles and forces which today give us some tools to conceptualize the internationalization of the state.

First, the state is a social relation which is institutionally separated from the rest of society; disposes over specific and impersonal means of power; and fulfills certain functions and materializes in apparatuses and discourses (see below). This is not very specific but is the argument of many state theories. However, Poulantzas understands the state as a part of the social division of labor and not as something neutral and completely apart from capitalist society. The state is constitutive for other social relations, especially production and class relations, and vice versa. Therefore, the structure and actions of the state cannot be explained by themselves but rather by considering the (changing) social context.

Besides this "structural" perspective, Poulantzas argues—second—that social forces and their strategies, political and social struggles as well as the relations of social forces are constitutive for capitalist societies and therefore necessary to consider for an adequate understanding of the state. Struggles take place all over society among different forces, which are not pre-constituted but forces constituted through struggles, and are more or less visible, more or less intense, and more or less strategic. The economic process itself, under-stood as formal and informal production as well as social reproduction, is an ongoing struggle. Past and current struggles are inscribed in the state and, at the same time, the state marks out the multiple terrains of struggles in the relations of production, through the education process and the assignments of the roles of individuals, etc.

Since the state is part of society with its social forces and power relations and, at the same time, a specific institutional and discursive ensemble, Pou-lantzas argues, third, that the state is the "material condensation of societal relations among different forces" (Poulantzas 1978/1980/2002: 159), which is expressed within the state in a specific form. Struggles and compromises of the past are inscribed in the state while the state shapes the relationships between forces and is part of the struggles, of the social division of labor, and of capitalist, as well as non-capitalist, power, productive and reproduc-tive relations. The state as an institutional ensemble is central for the exercise of political power. Poulantzas calls the state the "relay station and bastion" of the economic, political and ideological power of dominant forces (i.e. for him classes; Poulantzas 1978/1980/2002: 73). But state power, its means and its legitimacy, are closely linked to societal power.

The state is not just the condensation of societal power relations but the *material* condensation of it. This means that it has its own materiality (i.e. apparatuses), and changes in the relations between forces need to fit into the materiality of the different apparatuses. The condensation of specific forces does not take place in "their" particular apparatuses but in a specific way in all of them. Those apparatuses develop their own modes of action, have certain resources, knowledge and competences, and they are selective.

Specific policies can be understood as unstable compromises among social forces which are formulated through specific state apparatuses. Even if the social power bases of specific forces are reflected in the state apparatus and state policies, state policies develop their own (ir-)rationality which is not a mere reflection of societal constellations. The state bureaucracy develops complex forms of action and has its own competences, clientele and a con-sciousness of its problems. Even if the state gets its resources from society (especially through taxes), it develops its own modes of power, action (state capacities), and forms to deal with its resources.

Fourth, the state is not a homogeneous organizational ensemble, because within the apparatuses societal contradictions are inscribed and struggles take place. Therefore, its different apparatuses are in relationships defined by tension (e.g. the ministry of the environment and of the economy). Domi-nant, or hegemonic, forces intend to convert those state apparatuses to dominant ones where their interests are concentrated and dominant appara-tuses tend to represent the interests of dominant forces (Poulantzas 1978/ 1980/2002: 169).

The unification of a state is an ongoing, unstable and contested process and it manifests itself in "global and massive policies towards hegemonic classes or fractions." Bob Jessop emphasized later that the state itself needs to create a certain coherence of its orientations and relations (which are never complete nor stable) in order to formulate not overly contradictory policies. He calls this "state projects" (1990: 9, 315).

> Its [the concept of state projects; U.B.] essential theoretical function is to sensitize us to the inherent improbability of the existence of a unified state and to indicate the need to examine the structural and strategic factors which contribute to the existence of state effects.
>
> (Jessop 1990: 9)

Poulantzas saw this aspect but he did not give the same attention to it as Jessop did later.

Against the backdrop of the outlined aspects it can be argued that the internationalized state, its apparatuses and discourses, are material condensations of societal relations of forces "of second order" (Brand and Görg 2008, Brand et al. 2008). These power relations are inscribed into the structure of the international state apparatuses. Most of all the forces are national-governmental actors—which are themselves material condensations at the level of the respective nation-states and condense those competing forces to "a national interest"—but also business associations, private corporations, NGOs, representatives of social movements.

The state "fulfills" different social functions, which is a fifth dimension: repressive, ideological, economic and political.[2] For Poulantzas, the "general political function of the state" is to ensure that social struggles take place in a well ordered way, and second, that social cohesion and consensus are created. The state is crucial in organizing the forms of struggle and actively promoting consensus. Here, the state does not act in a neutral way toward the different social forces but, according to tendency, it organizes the dominant forces—which are divided and in competition among each other and have problems formulating coherent strategies—and de-organizes those that are dominated.

Poulantzas was mostly interested in the analysis of economic state functions; (i.e. the reproduction of property and market relations) of the labor force and infrastructure; of the environment; and, with all of them, the conditions for capital accumulation (as well as gender and/or ethnic relations).

An overall function of the state is to be the political center-stage of the organization of social hegemony and the establishment of a dynamic mode of development (i.e. in terms of regulation theory: an accumulation regime which is embedded in the institutions of a mode of regulation). Dominant social forces intend to universalize their interests in society and to become hegemonic (i.e. to exercise domination via political, moral and intellectual leadership—especially promising and securing growth and progress by pursuing their accumulation strategies—and consensus and through accepted institutions). This is the reason why Poulantzas calls the state a "strategic field" for social forces since interests—and we can add norms and identities—are generalized through the state. Consensus does not mean that there is no conflict but rather that conflict takes place under broadly accepted rules and that the existing balances of forces and an accepted leadership of specific forces have accepted the initiative to maintain social dynamic and change within certain margins.

Bob Jessop (2003) highlights one aspect of the production of hegemony, which is the role of economic, political, and social *imaginaries*. They produce discursive images of the social and the possibilities to act socially, materially and temporal-spatially. For the production of hegemony, it is at the very least essential that the multitude of actors has no contradicting images of the world in order to interact with each other.

Finally, another productive concept is that of "strategic selectivity," which meets the need to examine how state power is exercised in and through practices and forces. The continuous interplay of strategies and structures must be analyzed, and therefore Jessop developed his strategic-relational approach (Jessop 1990: 4). Strategic selectivity means that state actions have consequences for social forces and their capacity for action. But it is not exclusively based on the state:

> Instead it depends on the relation between state structures and the strategies which various forces adopt towards it. The bias inscribed on the terrain of the state as a site of strategic action can only be understood as a bias relative to specific strategies pursued by specific forces to advance specific interests over a given time horizon in terms of a specific set of other forces each advancing their own interests through specific strategies.
>
> (Jessop 1990: 10)

Beyond Jessop it can also be argued that strategic selectivities, as part of condensed relationships of forces, are inscribed in international political institutions. In their political constitutions as well as their ongoing functioning, certain topics, decisions and policies are considered to be important and gain attention, resources and knowledge. The access to international political institutions differs among actors with their aims and strategies. Priorities and counter-priorities are set in the particular international political institutions or in relationship with others; some policies are undertaken more symbolically or are compensated (cf. a critical-feminist analysis of international political institutions, Prügl 2004).

The internationalized state, power and knowledge

Poulantzas did not pay attention to the emerging international political institutions, their modes and/or functions. However, some functions that were important during (central and peripheral) Fordism at the level of the nation-state are transferred to other spatial levels—international or local, to political institutions within these realms, and/or, at least partially, to private actors like private firms. The transformation of the state (system) involves changing socioeconomic and cultural conditions and changing constellations of forces. Neoliberal politics is decisively a strengthening of world-market oriented capital and a weakening of other capital groups and of the representatives of wage-earners (cf. Plehwe et al. 2006). The state today is analyzed as a "national competition state" (Hirsch 1997) or a "post-national Schumpeterian workfare regime" (Jessop 2002).

The post-Fordist mode of development can be identified as a "knowledge-based economy" (Jessop 2003). In the present phase of capitalism we do not live in a "post-industrial" society, but the forms of industrialization refer in a much more systematic way to different forms of knowledge. While during Fordism the Tayloristic mass production of consumer goods and the commodification of the material conditions of production wage-earners was decisive (Aglietta 1979); today the production and appropriation of knowledge is much more important (Drahos and Braithwaite 2003; Hirsch 2002). The so-called life-science industries based on the systematic production and appropriation of knowledge are linked to rationalization processes of social work (R & D, in the production process, services). Knowledge is inscribed in certain technologies and with that an instrument of power. Therefore, to give an example, in the field of biodiversity politics the conflicts about the introduction of GMO seeds are of utmost importance.

States become more important in the production and diffusion of knowledge through educational, technological and other policies, and they are crucial to secure knowledge through intellectual property rights. But this is ambiguous since on the one hand the commodification of knowledge is important; and on the other hand the development of knowledge is a common process and the enclosure of knowledge can be a threat to further innovations (Brand et al. 2008; Hirsch 2002). In addition, the state promotes the economic imaginary of a knowledge-based economy. This is also the case at the regional level; the most explicit case here is the Lisbon Strategy of the EU.

Knowledge also becomes more important in political processes themselves. Expert knowledge helps to legitimize political (non-)decisions. Peter Haas argued that experts are not only called when they are needed but that experts themselves can lay the foundations for a future policy field. *Epistemic communities* in that sense are defined as "a network of professionals with recognized expertise and competence in a particular domain and an authoritative claim to policy-relevant knowledge within that domain or issue-area" (Haas 1992: 3; cf. the critique by Forsyth in this volume). Environmental problems are not objectively given but constructed in policy processes and as parts of knowledge fields (Fischer 2000; Hajer 1995). Levy et al. (1993) argued that one major task of international politics is not to create large bureaucracies but rather *open-ended knowledge creation* and the worldwide circulation of information. Environmental politics is one of the most prominent fields where the role of expertise and scientific knowledge is examined, given the complexity and uncertainty of problems and adequate forms to deal with them (Conca and Dabelko 1998; Fischer 2003; Lander 2006; Lipschutz and Conca 1993). In recent years, the concrete linkages between scientific knowledge and political processes (i.e. the science–policy interfaces) have gained more attention (cf. for biodiversity politics van den Hove and Sharman 2004).

It is not by chance that the Intergovernmental Panel on Climate Change (IPCC) plays an important role for the Framework Convention on Climate Change or the Subsidiary Body for Scientific, Technical and Technological Advice (SBSTTA) for the CBD. An actual example is the Millennium Ecosystem Assessment, the goal of which is "to establish the scientific basis for actions needed to enhance the conservation and sustainable use of ecosystems and their contributions to meeting human needs" (BSR 2005: preface). Another example is that of the World Bank, which defines itself more and more as a "knowledge bank" (cf. the contribution of Michael Goldman).

One role of knowledge and experts is the framing of problems, thereby creating pathways to deal with them reasonably and legitimately. This is not an entirely open process, but rather there are pre-constituted ("larger") pathways designed to manage these problems. For example, the state and the international intergovernmental system are considered the appropriate forums to deal with specific grievances. We could call it a certain knowledge of the state and its competencies. In the last few decades this knowledge changed in the sense that for many problems private actors and interests— not the state—have become the more adequate and acceptable forms to deal with such problems. But there is still a "master frame" which consists of a perception that international politics come into play when national actors are not able to deal with dilemmas.

To summarize, the internationalized state with its heterogeneous apparatuses at different spatial levels is important in manifold senses: it gives a specific discursive structure, economic imaginaries and eco-governmentality—as part of societal power relations and knowledge—a certain continuity and "arms" them by law, money and force. The state is not the only instance, of course. But it is a crucial one. Through a power-shaped knowledge structure, specific state and hegemonic projects are more likely to be successfully pursued. The argument is that international state apparatuses become more important in the reproduction of social relations and inherent forms of knowledge.

Power and knowledge in the global governance of biodiversity

Genetic resources and post-Fordist societal relationships with nature

The conflict structure of the appropriation of biodiversity was developed along with modern capitalism (i.e. they are a crucial part of it). But the conflicts became manifest only in particular moments or cases because existing power structures and hegemonic interpretations of nature and its appropriation were not seen as problematic. Concerning biodiversity, the "gene flow" from the Global South to the Global North—for example, via scientific collection—was largely for free and was supposed to serve scientific progress (Crosby 1986). In fact, the hereditary characteristics were not only "stored" in zoological or botanical gardens and gene banks or used scientifically but also commercialized. This was the case in the agricultural and pharmaceutical sector—but it was generally not seen as a problem (Kloppenburg 1988).

A manifest conflict has developed since the 1970s when the erosion of genetic and species diversity was politicized by environmental movements, NGOs and experts. Around the UN Food and Agricultural Organization (FAO), discussions and policies began to halt the erosion of plant genetic resources.[3] With the Convention for International Trade in Endangered Species of Wild Fauna and Flora (CITES), initial measures were taken for species protection.

A second dynamic has developed since the 1980s. With the development of new biotechnologies, especially genetic engineering, the interest in genetic resources grew. Research centers' and private companies' interest in "genetic material"—existing *ex situ* particularly in gene banks or *in situ* (i.e. in the field)—grew enormously. Via bioprospecting and the screening of DNA, the "green gold of the genes" of plants, animals and micro-organisms (i.e. its potential economic value) was explored and exploited by a self-proclaimed *life-science industry*. This is a costly process. R & D costs under conditions of hard competition might be reduced through the reference to "traditional" uses and knowledge of biodiversity.

The "oil of the 21st century" (World Resources Institute) is sometimes considered as the centerpiece of a new growth model. The dynamic forces behind these economic-technological and political-legal processes come especially from the United States and some from Europe. Corporations like Monsanto, and public research institutes in the USA, are at the top of biotechnological developments. Since the 1980s, the Supreme Court (with an important decision allowing the patenting of life—the so-called Chakrabarty case, when the first patent on a micro-organism was legally accepted) and the US Patent Office make R & D in the field of genetic engineering and its patenting possible. These processes have consequences not only for production and consumption globally, but also for the lives of local farmers and indigenous peoples.

As a result of complex institutional and discursive struggles, economic practices, and national state policies, a "valorization paradigm" emerged in the field of the appropriation of biodiversity which functions as the hegemonic economic imaginary (cf. in detail Brand et al. 2008). Biodiversity and its hereditary characteristics are an important "raw material" for socioeconomic dynamics and part of a search process for a post-Fordist mode of development. The dominant forces establish an unstable compromise and the relationships of forces among different actors are absorbed by the international state apparatuses.

We can identify emerging "post-Fordist societal relationships with nature" in the sense that they are dominant in orientation and represent institutional practices and ways of justifying the appropriation of nature and dealing with the ecological crisis (Brand and Görg 2001; 2008). The centerpiece of post-Fordist societal relationships with nature, which have continuities as well as discontinuities with previous phases, is the further commodification of nature. Aspects of nature conservation are not completely left out but, as an overall tendency, protection is articulated with valorization strategies.

In the field of biodiversity politics, knowledge becomes important in a complex manner. First of all, the screening, use and development of the hereditary characteristics of plants, animals and micro-organisms is an increasingly high-tech process in which both modern scientific knowledge and technology play a crucial role. Second, the knowledge of how local communities and indigenous peoples use parts of nature is important because it helps the modern actors in the screening process; but local knowledge is also considered important for the conservation of biodiversity (cf. for the role of local knowledge, Luke and Forsyth [Chapters 2 and 9] in this volume).

In sum, the conflicts over genetic goods are considered to be of such importance because genetic resources may be a centerpiece of a new growth model and therefore a basis for hegemony. But this commodification process is not a purely technological-economic one but rather embedded politically and culturally. Moreover, we can observe here specific "politics of scaling" (i.e. different actors try to strengthen the spatial level of action and institutionalization where they think they can best pursue their interests). The following focuses on political aspects at the international level.

Global governance of biodiversity: the example of the CBD

In international biodiversity politics, the nodal points of the internationalized state are the following ones: the CBD; FAO and its International Treaty on Plant Genetic Resources for Food and Agriculture (IT-PGRFA), which came into force in 2004 after long deliberations; the agreement on Trade Related Aspects of Intellectual Property Rights (TRIPS) of the WTO; and the World Intellectual Property Organization (WIPO). Moreover, bilateral and regional agreements continue to be developed in order to create a legal framework, especially to secure access to genetic resources and intellectual property rights, the latter in case of the potential production of commodities.[4] I focus on the CBD and link it to the WTO's TRIPS agreement.

The core of biodiversity politics is the protection and use of ecosystems, species and the inner-species diversity (i.e. the hereditary characteristics of plants, animals and micro-organisms). Therefore, the CBD has three main goals (article 1 of CBD; www.biodiv.org): the protection of biological diversity, its sustainable use, and a fair and equitable sharing of the benefits deriving from the use. These main goals are linked to the accessibility of genetic resources and technology as well as intellectual property rights. Compared to other international agreements, the role of indigenous and local communities (the concept of indigenous peoples is avoided in official documents) plays an important role.

The dynamics of international politics is less about the protection of or an end to the erosion of biodiversity, but rather lie in the complex interests of its commercialization. As we saw above, the described socioeconomic and technological developments need to be secured politico-legally: the appropriation of biodiversity needs a certain legal security.

The CBD as a framework convention needs to be transferred into national law and should guide concrete policies of protection, access agreements for bioprospecting, benefit-sharing, etc. It is a terrain in which different actors can create consensus about (a) what the problems and their causes are, (b) how they should be dealt with, and (c) where and what experiences with the implementation are made. Of course, the dimensions (a) and (b) are highly controversial but the consensus-building function cannot be disregarded. The self-description of the CBD's "toolkit" is the ecosystem approach, programs of work and guidelines for action (Secretariat of the Convention on Biological Diversity 2006: 45ff.).

Finally, one fact should not be forgotten: in many cases, the appropriation of biodiversity, and especially its hereditary characteristics, takes place without regulation. Therefore noteworthy NGOs and local people still denounce cases of *biopiracy* (cf. the recent overview in GRAIN 2005).[5]

Two modes of politics: strategic selectivity and asymmetry among political institutions

I would like to highlight two modes of politics in order to show that international biodiversity politics is part of a comprehensive hegemonic and state project. The first is the strategic selectivity of the CBD as a political terrain, an actor and a discourse, and the second is the asymmetric structure of international politics. The fact that IPI are "material condensations of relation of forces of second order" is made clear in both modes. Among other things, I want to show that the mode of strategic selectivity is only understandable when the embeddedness of politics is considered within a larger framework.

Strategic selectivity has to do with structured terrains and with the strategies different actors adopt toward the state and its particular apparatuses. Concerning the mode of strategic selectivity, I refer to three crucial aspects of the appropriation of genetic goods that are dealt with in very different ways: (a) the "hot topics" of access, benefit-sharing and intellectual property rights; (b) the downplayed and re-articulated issue of the rights of indigenous peoples and local farmers; and (c) the important fact that there were always coercive forms of biodiversity appropriation, which is presently of great importance.[6]

The hot topics: access to genetic resources, benefit-sharing and intellectual property rights

Questions of access to biological diversity and especially to genetic resources, benefit-sharing (ABS), and intellectual property rights are the outstanding conflicts in the CBD process. Despite all differences, it can be stated that Northern research institutes and corporations are interested in genetic goods that are located in Southern countries and they want established rules concerning IPR in case these genetic goods produce marketable products.[7] These Northern countries are largely supported by their governments, some of which promote conservation issues as well. The local population in countries with notable biodiversity is willing to share goods and knowledge but people are skeptical with respect to the possible negative consequences for their lives and the environment. Southern governments want to participate economically in the development of drugs, cosmetics and seeds and want to establish technological capacities. However, the claims of local actors might be present in some way in state politics. Additionally, it is important to note that in many cases other land use interests (e.g. logging or monoculture farming) are given priority (cf. Secretariat of the Convention on Biological Diversity 2006: 23ff.).

In recent years, through international negotiations, a line of compromise was established between Northern and Southern governments, i.e. to promote the commercialization of biodiversity, especially with respect to genetic resources. An important requirement is the principle of "national sovereignty" over genetic resources. Not by chance, one decisive innovation of the CBD is the invention of "national sovereignty" over national and genetic resources (article 15.1. of the CBD); before the dominant principle was that of a "common heritage of humankind" which, in fact, was in many cases overshadowed by the private appropriation of genetic goods (Görg and Brand 2000). Against this backdrop, the aim to grant access to *in situ* existing genetic goods is not controversial among governments. However, conflicts arise when it comes to the concrete conditions of access and benefit-sharing mechanisms which should be "fair and equitable" (article 1; then made more precise in articles 8(j) and 15.7. of the CBD).

With the so-called Bonn Guidelines on Access and Benefit-sharing of 2001, a further compromise among the governments was established.[8] However, the implementation process proved insufficient because the guidelines were non-binding and the focus was on access and IPR—and not on benefit-sharing. Therefore a Group of Like-Minded Megadiversity Countries, formed in 2002, proposed a binding protocol to the CBD.[9] But this proposal was denied, and at the COP7 in 2004 in Kuala Lumpur a less-binding ABS regime was promoted by the relevant governments (Decision VII/19), which was further negotiated in March 2006 at COP8 in Curitiba.

Closely linked to ABS questions are those of IPR. The CBD has several provisions with respect to these questions. They are negotiated in the WTO as well and for some years the WIPO proposed a Patent Agenda to harmonize international IPR regulations (Correa and Musungu 2002; WIPO 2002; Wissen 2008). The processes will be key for an ABS regime, and, given the actual legitimation problems of the WTO, it is possible that the Patent Agenda of the WIPO might become a kind of a "counteroffensive" of the powerful countries.

The functionalization of indigenous peoples and local communities

In comparison with other international political forums, the CBD recognizes the role of indigenous or traditional knowledge and communities in its famous article 8(j) (the concept of how indigenous peoples use their traditional knowledge is avoided in official documents): knowledge and its uses are seen as important and should be protected, and indigenous peoples should participate in political processes and in mechanisms of benefit-sharing. The so-called farmers' rights in the International Treaty on Genetic Resources for Food and Agriculture (ITPGRFA) of the FAO hold a similar status. This has to do with the fact that the struggles of indigenous peoples for recognition intensified in the 1980s on many levels: 1992 was a peak year of consciousness-raising and organizing as it marked five centuries since the beginning of the *conquista* in Latin America. The start of the Zapatista rebellion in Mexico in 1994 was a continent-wide signal. The recognition of indigenous peoples was evidenced by democratization processes in many countries. Second, it became clear that indigenous peoples and local communities were important for the conservation of biological diversity. Third, it became more and more obvious since the 1970s that traditional forms of agriculture created an enormous genetic diversity of seeds, a process which is undermined by "modern" agriculture and which is often characterized by monoculture and a reduction of agro-diversity. But in order to produce even more modern (i.e. new high-yielding seeds), genetic diversity is crucial as an "input."

However, the political and legal recognition of indigenous peoples and local communities is superposed by the fact that a realization of these principles is left to national legislation processes (and respective power relations). Additionally, the CBD principle of national sovereignty concedes national governments—and not local peoples—the rights over genetic goods. The recognized "participation" of indigenous peoples and local communities is not backed by legally recoverable rights in international or national legal processes or the negotiation of access agreements. Alternative approaches like "traditional resource rights" or "community rights" are discussed but not realized.

The experiences of recent years show that indigenous peoples and local communities are, according to tendency, functionalized: Their role is to conserve biodiversity and the knowledge concerning how to use it—this is explicitly stated in article 8(j). In many cases indigenous peoples and local communities serve as helpful "indicators" in bioprospecting processes. Even the World Bank declared traditional knowledge as the "most underutilized resource in the development process."[10] While this is recognized, the means to protect and develop the conditions of their own existence are undermined—not only through the CBD and the described developments but through broader social processes like the industrialization of agriculture, oil exploitation or massive logging operations.

Indigenous peoples and local communities have no rights because the national governments claim to represent them. The danger of a functionalization of the local becomes clear, among other things, with the many initiatives of capacity-building (i.e. to educate groups with respect to the relevance of biodiversity and of political processes). Capacity-building does not only improve the ability to deal with complex issues, but also to improve the conditions of the valorization of genetic goods.

Another form of functionalization is that the claims of indigenous peoples and local communities somehow become a negotiation token for Southern governments in international processes or in the negotiation of access agreements.

Absent from political deliberations: the militarization of biodiversity appropriation

The ignorance of important social and political developments becomes clear when considering the growing militarization of the appropriation of biodiversity. This takes place especially in regions where specific forms of nature appropriation meet the resistance of local people and where an appropriation under legal-political conditions is difficult. It is obvious in the case of oil but it also takes place in the field of biodiversity or genetic resources (Ceceña 2006). At stake is the securing of "strategic resources" for economically and politically dominant actors. Part of this includes overall strategies of the U.S. government, especially in Latin America, to control regions like Mexico and Middle America, the Amazon basin and the Cono Sur. Plan Colombia is the most visible case that the region is controlled by military and para-military; in recent years Paraguay became a second center (see Ceceña and Motto 2005).[11] Besides the control of important resources, counter-insurgency strategies play a role. The justification is the establishment of "continental security," the "war against terrorism" and the necessary interventions against "failed states" (cf. Barnett 2003). Under the heading of "environmental security" people and regions are controlled militarily and in part via satellite (Acselrad 2002).

All those aspects do not play a minor role in the CDB or WTO deliberations.

The ambivalence of coherence: CBD and WTO

Apart from the outlined examples of a strategic selectivity, another dimension is crucial in international politics: the asymmetric relationship among different state apparatuses. Politically, the tensions between different forums are seen as problematic under the heading of a "lack of coherence." From a neo-Poulantzian perspective, the lack of coherence has to do with the contradictions and tensions among different policy fields (environmental, agricultural or trade politics; cf. Petit et al. 2000) and also with the specific material condensations of balances of forces in the specific IPI and with the asymmetry among the IPI.

This is especially the case between the WTO-TRIPS agreement and the CBD. Tensions and asymmetries can be observed in at least four areas. One major expression of the asymmetry occurred during years the CBD did not get an official status at the WTO and TRIPS council—although it was several times requested. Behind those inequalities stand different balances of forces. The Northern countries accord the WTO an enormous importance. Their interests are especially condensed in this apparatus, and they are able to resist provisions which are not in their interest (e.g. the EU and the liberalization of trade in agriculture). Southern countries or governments as condensations of relations of forces in respective countries do (and must) accept the uneven rules of the game (like China, Brazil, and India) and try to promote certain interests like exports of agricultural goods in the case of Brazil.

(1) The TRIPS agreement, which was negotiated parallel to the CBD, has much stronger provisions with respect to intellectual property rights (Drahos and Braithwaite 2003 on the TRIPS negotiation). Within specific time limits, all member countries must adopt minimum standards to protect intellectual property. Article 27 says that everything can be patented with some exceptions mentioned in article 27.3(b) which allows states to develop a *sui generis* system for the protection of innovations out of plants and animals (except the important micro-organisms). *Sui generis* means "own system," which must not contradict TRIPS (Dutfield 2001). This topic became highly politicized in recent years but the WTO still pushes for its implementation (recently, at the Hong Kong ministerial conference of the WTO, the deadline to implement TRIPS for thirty-two so-called least developed countries was extended to 2013).[12]

(2) The WTO promotes an agro-export model which is oriented toward the world market, industrialized, and based on chemical inputs. Economies of scale, open markets, and economic profit dominate environmental considerations by far. Locally situated and often sustainable agriculture is in many cases overtaken by transnational agrobusiness, and the WTO promotes that. The dominant orientation is even intensified by the so-called Singapore Issues in the WTO on investment, competition, public obtaining, and administrative trade issues. This makes concrete effects of the CBD less probable.

(3) Another problem of WTO dominance is in the field of biosafety. The Biosafety Protocol was negotiated for a long time in the CBD and came into force in 2003. But the WTO provisions on free trade can be used against biosafety, especially against the important principle of the precautionary approach in articles 1 and 24 of the Biosafety Protocol, which is not recognized by the WTO.

(4) A fourth tension is still a potential one, but might gain major relevance in the next years. This is the influence of the GATS agreement (General Agreement on Trade in Services) on biodiversity politics. The recently published Millennium Ecosystem Assessment put the concept of *ecosystem*

services at the center of environmental discussions (BSR 2005; MASR 2005). Within this framework, GATS, which as a specific state apparatus favors a clear commercialization and privatization strategy, could claim its relevance to biodiversity. This means that, with the concept of ecosystem services, the privatization of nature could be promoted further political-institutionally.[13]

In sum, the negotiation dynamics of the WTO are characterized by a will to claim for all issue areas. It is the strongest international apparatus of the internationalized state and condenses asymmetrical relations of forces in an outstanding way. For example, forests and genetic goods can become part of the non-agricultural market access agenda (NAMA) as *environmental goods*. And, in the World Bank and the IMF, the WTO has strong allies (cf. Oxfam 2005).

In contrast to a perceived lack of coherence as a problem for effective politics from a neo-Poulantzian perspective, it becomes clear that incoherence among apparatuses is a characteristic of international politics itself.

Functions of the internationalized state in biodiversity politics

After this brief outline, I would like to systematize in the following several functions of international political institutions (IPI) like the CBD as part of the internationalized state. The (contested and never complete) fulfillment of these functions is a precondition for a hegemonic and dynamic constellation.

(1) The most important economic function is the following: The intergovernmental institutions intend to develop a legal framework and are therefore part of a "global constitutionalism" (Gill 2003), i.e. the internationalization of the Western-bourgeois property and legal regime.[14] This process is full of tensions but the overall tendency is in the interest of "modern" actors and their accumulation strategies (i.e. pharmaceutical and agricultural companies and research institutes and "their"—mainly Northern—governments). The state is part of a complex search process aimed at creating economic growth. This function is full of tensions as well because the individual states—which act in and intend to cooperate through agreements like the CBD—are at the same time in a competitive relationship.

Another economic function which Poulantzas mentioned and which is obvious in biodiversity politics is the link between different modes of production. The most advanced process of capitalist valorization and production (i.e. techno-economic processes of genetic engineering) is linked to forms of "traditional" use of nature and "traditional" knowledge.

(2) A second function of international politics that seems quite obvious but should at least be mentioned is that of securing national sovereignty, because international politics takes place through the acknowledgement of states as legal and legitimate entities. This is important because it enables the respective states to act on their own territory. The CBD is a good example, in that in the early 1990s, when the problems of biodiversity erosion and the economic

importance of genetic resources were acknowledged, this international agreement invented national sovereignty over genetic (and biological) resources.

(3) The internationalized state creates specific institutional terrains in order to deal with different conflicts. When, in the 1970s and 1980s, erosion, environmental discourses, and the development of new technologies took place, the importance of a comprehensive political terrain became obvious. In this sense, the CBD is—like the WTO—a "post-Fordist" (and "post-Cold War") IPI because it takes into account perceived and politicized problems, new actors, interest constellations and new modes of politics. The CBD is an unstable compromise and not a neutral terrain, but rather asymmetrically structured. I want to show briefly—and incompletely—some dimensions of the inscribed strategic selectivity: specific actors have uneven access and the different topics are dealt with in uneven ways. The actions of the international state apparatuses (CBD and WTO in our case) have different effects for actors and their capacities to act.

(4) According to Poulantzas it can be argued that the internationalized state gives certain balances of forces a form (i.e. it gives the relationship among states, private corporations, and local actors like indigenous peoples continuity through the structured political terrain). Of course, there are constant struggles to change the "rules of the game" and the power relations linked to them. But once the terrains are set up, the state apparatus itself becomes part of the struggles.

(5) Finally, it is worth considering that IPI fulfill an intellectual function in the sense that they create knowledge and organize orientation and consensus. It is not just an outcome of constellations of forces or an instrument of dominant forces but is itself part of the game which creates knowledge, gives orientation and sometimes has unintended consequences.

One aspect for the nation-state that was emphasized by Poulantzas is not so important at the international level: the creation of social cohesion. Even if there is a lot of talk about a world-society, an important feature at the international level are the conflicts, competition and identity-formation vis-à-vis other societies. Therefore, the creation of social cohesion is a function which is already fulfilled at the national level, even if there are slow processes working toward a regional alliance like that of the EU.

Global governance of biodiversity as a hegemonic project

The CBD and the WTO-TRIPS agreement were not developed after an established agreement but they are an integral part of such agreements (as the FAO is in the field of agriculture). In fact, there have previously existed other political regulations for international action concerning conservation (CITES, the establishment of gene banks and their coordination through the CGIAR system) or the exchange of seeds (FAO—International Undertaking) which provided some international guidance for managing the erosion and appropriation of biodiversity.

As I said before, the question of social cohesion or internal unity of the state does not seem crucial at the international level. The spatial and therefore political, economic and cultural fragmentation of the world-society is a quite obvious phenomenon. However, there are competing state projects inscribed in different apparatuses because of specific material condensations of social relations of forces. The state project of the WTO concerning IPR or the general maintenance of biodiversity is quite different from that of the CBD. As we saw, one major discussion in the (weak) state apparatus has been the failure to implement the CBD. This has to do with the competing interests concerning the various (local) uses of nature—timber, monocultures—as part of the export-oriented macroeconomic model as well as with the predominance of the WTO.

Incoherence in international politics is, according to the outlined perspective, less the inability of nation-states or international political institutions to control political processes but rather of contradictions, tension and the inability to create consensus among the dominated. Until now, the heterogeneous state apparatuses have been a form of international politics and a dimension of uncertainty themselves. According to this line of thought, the potential for a coherent Global Governance is rather weak. This creates possibilities for significant actors in international biodiversity politics (cf. Brand et al. 2008: ch. 6).

This fact articulates with another result of empirical studies: what we can observe in recent years, especially in the field of IPR, is an attempt to "forum-shift" dominant actors toward bilateral agreements and WIPO.[15] The latter UN organization gained importance precisely after the failure of the third ministerial conference of the WTO in late 1999 in Seattle, where the non-implementation of the TRIPS agreement by many Southern governments—expected in many countries by January 2000—was one of the reasons for the crisis. WIPO announced in 2001 a *Patent Agenda* which is now being developed as a state apparatus which might concentrate the interests of dominant actors (cf. the detailed study of Wissen 2008).

Interestingly, at the level of international politics, the relationship between forces and their strategies on the one hand and state apparatuses on the other are much more obvious. For example, a WTO ministerial conference makes the conflicts and differences visible, whereas at the national level many processes are rather non-transparent.

Even if there is no coherent state project, the global governance of biodiversity in the sense of a political-institutional framework is *part* of a hegemonic project. This is developed step by step and as a technological, economic, cultural, environmental and political search process. The dominant strategies to commodify nature in a new way are clearly formulated by the biotechnology industry and "their" governments, the significance of which is contested. It is clear that strict "modern" IPR are crucial since the value of drugs, seeds and cosmetics is not so much the product itself which could be reproduced from others but the monopoly to commercialize it. One capital fraction is not interested in strong regulations of access and benefit-sharing but maintains the traditional forms to act without political regulation. Today this is labeled as biopiracy but it takes place all over the world. Other companies pursue the strategy to develop international regulations for the appropriation and use of biodiversity and its genetic goods.

Of course, this project is not isolated but part of the neoliberal and neoimperial restructuring of the world. The export-oriented model of many economies is at the core of this project. But the effects of this model are different in vulnerable and indebted countries of the periphery, on the one hand, or in core countries or strong countries of the periphery, like China, on the other. Therefore, considerations of sustainability are in all countries at the edge of political developments. The hegemonic societal project is the valorization of nature at almost any cost and this becomes part of nation-state projects as well as of the project of international politics.

It is hegemonic in the sense that the relevant actors—especially most governments in the North and South—accept the political terrains to develop rules for the appropriation of biodiversity, to pursue with them their interests and to accept these terrains as sites to deal with their conflicts. The valorization of nature is the base line of the compromise. It can be called hegemonic because there is a certain consensus that, under the labels of Sustainable Development and Global Governance, environmental problems can be dealt with in a certain way: with modern knowledge and technology, with the existing institutional and ideational framework, and relations between forces (of countries, classes, and other groups).

Moreover, the weakness of the CBD, compared to the WTO and the power of the export-oriented growth model, is widely accepted. The same national governments who act in the WTO through their ministry of economy or trade and in the TRIPS agreement through ministries of economy or justice, act in the CBD through their environmental ministries. Usually, at the national level there is a hierarchy among these state apparatuses which internationally is reproduced asymmetrically (not as a clear hierarchy).

What is the aim of biodiversity conservation? Has this topic been completely left out? No, on the contrary it is present through specific policies. There are conservation policies being implemented, especially the finance mechanism of the World Bank-based Global Environmental Facility. In addition, the CBD produces information, raises awareness and shapes national legislation processes. However, in many cases conservation policies themselves are re-interpreted through and articulated with the valorization paradigm.

In recent years, the political actors themselves understood the asymmetric development of the CBD toward ABS and IPR and the ongoing erosion of biodiversity. Therefore, at the COP6 in 2002 in The Hague and at the "Rio +10" conference in 2002 in Johannesburg, the "2010 Biodiversity Target" was agreed upon, which means that the erosion of biodiversity should be "significantly" reduced by that year (cf. Potsdam Recommendations 2006; Secretariat of the Convention on Biological Diversity 2006).

The hegemonic and state project is contested. Especially in the field of intellectual property rights, long-lasting struggles of social movements, as well as critical NGOs and experts, were able to formulate a strong critique of the provisions of the famous article 27.3(b) of the TRIPS agreement. We will see in the future whether the de-legitimization of WTO is strengthened or whether it is able to reconstruct itself as the crucial international state apparatus (after the ministerial conference in Hong Kong in December 2005 the latter is possible). International politics is not only a question of more or less effective institutions and processes but also—although less as at the national level—of legitimacy.

Open questions

This outline of a neo-Poulantzian approach to a critical IPE needs, of course, sophistication and development. I shall just name some of the many questions I have.

One is the assumption that the apparatus of the internationalized state exists at the international level of intergovernmental organizations and agreements. Nation-states are considered as actors in international politics. Does this make sense? Would it be more fruitful to also consider nation-state apparatuses as parts of the international state apparatus, especially those of powerful states like the USA, the EU or Germany? What is the shape and role of the "transnational environmental states" (Goldman 2001) in the Global South?

In discussing this rather general outline, there is a need to consider whether the differences among these particular policy fields are greater than assumed here and, if so, the possibility that my insights would be limited to a generalization. One could argue that the role of the state differs from policy field to policy field (in Germany this position is prominently represented by Mayntz and Scharpf 1995). Even historical-materialist approaches should take this fact more into account as well as the differing micro-policies and the strategies of actors. The counter-argument here is that, from a historical-materialist perspective, hegemonic projects and processes of coordination and generalization are necessary because the accumulation process requires a certain coherence, i.e. a historic bloc or overall mode of development. The state remains part of these developments and an analysis of the state needs to consider the broader context. Power and its material and immaterial resources lie not in the state apparatus itself but come from the nation-states, which themselves get their resources from their respective societies.

Another question is how a "relative autonomy" of the internationalized state apparatuses in the sense of their capacities might develop with respect to the constitutive forces (i.e. the representatives of nation-states and given the fact that the resources come from the nation-states and they acquire them from their respective societies). Then the question of the role of international state officials emerges, as well as the question of the concrete forms of strategic selectivity of the international state apparatus.

This paper has focused on international political institutions. However, this needs to be integrated in the framework of a critical IPE. A lot of work is being done here, especially from the so-called neo-Gramscian approach to IPE: hegemony and the role of dominant social forces in the making of world order, production relations and states are the central topics. Moreover, regulation theory offers some useful analytical tools to consider the relationship between macroeconomic developments and social as well as political institutions. A further elaboration should consider Marxist form analysis in order to understand how the existence of capitalist forms (capital and wage labor, commodities, money, the state) shape—not determine!—social and political processes. The abstract concept of the political and value form helps us to understand the direction of capitalist development and the problems in developing alternatives. However, a more detailed analysis of societal and political transformations is needed. At the international level and with respect to the transformation of the state and politics, a neo-Poulantzian approach might lead to a more detailed and sophisticated understanding of the actual dynamics.

Notes

1 I would like to thank the participants of the workshop, especially Gabriela Kütting, for their comments; and Wendy Godek for her careful editing of the text.
2 This is not a functionalistic argument because those functions are fulfilled through struggles and might fail. In this case, social dynamics and stability are in danger and a crisis may take place.
3 The concept of "genetic resources" itself is problematic because parts of nature are constructed instrumentally as something which can be valorized economically (cf. Heins and Flitner 1998).
4 Cf. in detail Brand et al. 2008; LePrestre 2002. There is also a systematic overview given of the actors and their interests and strategies.
5 However, the concept of biopiracy became contested itself because it has—at least—three meanings. The first is that the appropriation of biodiversity, its components and the knowledge required to use it is illegitimate when local communities, farmers and indigenous peoples are neither involved nor informed and cannot decide what is going to happen. The second is that biopiracy exists as long as the provisions of the CBD are not fulfilled. This understanding is frequently criticized by local actors, since very often approval by state actors is considered as sufficient to fulfill the requirements of the CBD. The third meaning is that of the pharmaceutical and agricultural industries, which intend to denounce the use of their products and innovations secured by IPR without paying for it (cf. Campaign against Biopiracy of BUKO 2005).
6 Another "hot topic"—that of GMOs and genetic use restriction technologies (GURTS)—has been left out.
7 A lot of genetic goods are already in Northern countries, i.e. in gene banks, botanical or zoological gardens. The collections which were transferred prior to 1993 are not subject to the CBD.
8 The Draft Guidelines for Access and Benefit-Sharing were developed and presented by the Swiss government after a survey among the relevant actors; then in a consensus-building process it became an official regulation of the CBD as the Bonn Guidelines on ABS (2001, adopted in 2002).

9 The Group of Like-Minded Megadiversity Countries is an informal coordinating mechanism of countries like Brazil, Mexico, Columbia, India or the Philippines where a lot of biodiversity is situated *in situ*. At the beginning there was the idea to form a cartel in the negotiation processes.

10 See www.worldbank.org/afr.ik quoted after: 'System and national experiences for protecting traditional knowledge and practises, Background Note by the UNCTAD-secretariat. TD/B/COM.1/EM.13/L'.

11 Another prominent, although exceptional, example is Iraq, where not only the oil sector but the entire seeds sector is restructured toward the interests of US corporations.

12 Another example of an asymmetry within the CBD is that between the important Working Group on Access and Benefit Sharing and the less important group on Traditional Knowledge and Indigenous Peoples. The latter requested consideration when topics related to their agenda were dealt with in the ABS Working Group. This was denied.

13 Friends of the Earth International (2002) mentioned this risk a few years ago in a policy paper, and indeed some years ago the EU Commission and the Swiss government proposed to integrate the "protection of biodiversity and landscape" as an environmental service into the GATS negotiations.

14 "This can be understood as a term intended to describe the varied and complex efforts, especially by forces of the political right and those of neo-classical economists and financial capital, to develop a politico-legal framework for the reconstitution of capital on a world scale, and thus for the intensification of market forms of discipline. ... The new constitutionalism seeks to reinforce a process whereby government policies are increasingly accountable to (international) capital, and thus to market forces (especially those exercised in and from financial markets." (Gill 1995: 78–79).

15 The concept of a "forum-shift" means that dominant actors try to shift from one political forum to another when they can pursue similar interests in a better way (cf. Braithwaite and Drahos 2000; for international biodiversity politics, cf. Brand et al. 2008).

References

Acselrad, H. (2002) "Die ökologische Herausforderung. Zwischen Markt, Sicherheit und Gerechtigkeit," in Christoph Görg and Ulrich Brand (eds.) *Mythen globalen Umweltmanagements. "Rio + 10" und die Sackgassen nachhaltiger Entwicklung.* Münster, Germany: Westfälisches Dampfboot, 48–73.

Aglietta, M. (1979) *A Theory of Capitalist Regulation: The US Experience*, London and New York: New Left Books.

Barnett, T. (2003) *The Pentagon's New Map*, www.nwc.navy.mil/newrulesets

Braithwaite, J. and Drahos, P. (2000) *Global Business Regulation*, Cambridge: Cambridge University Press.

Brand, U. and Görg, C. (2001) "The Regulation of the Market and the Transformation of the Societal Relationships with Nature," *Capitalism, Nature, Socialism*, 12 (4): 67–94.

——— (2003) "The State and the Regulation of Biodiversity International Biopolitics and the Case of Mexico," *Geoforum*, 34: 221–33.

———(2008a) "Post-Fordist Governance of Nature. The Internationalisation of the State and the Case of Genetic Resources: A Neo-Poulantzian Perspective," *Review of International Political Economy*, 15(4): 566–88.

————(2008b) "Sustainability and Globalisation: A Theoretical Perspective," in J. Park, C. Conca, and M. Finger (eds.) *The Crisis of Global Environmental Governance: Towards a New Political Economy of Sustainability*, London and New York: Routledge, 13–33.

Brand, U., Görg, C., Hirsch, J., and Wissen, M. (2008) *Contested Terrains: Conflicts about Genetic Resources and the Internationalisation of the State*, London and New York: Routledge, forthcoming.

Brenner, N. (2004) *New State Spaces: Urban Governance and the Rescaling of Statehood*, Oxford: Oxford University Press.

BSR (Business for Social Responsibility) (2005) *Millennium Ecosystem Assessment: Ecosystems and Human Well-being: Biodiversity Synthesis Report*, Washington, DC: World Resources Institute.

Campaign against Biopiracy of BUKO (2005) *Grüne Beute, Biopiraterie und Wider-stand—Argumente, Hintergründe*, Aktionen, Grafenau and Frankfurt am Main: Trotzdem-Verlag.

Ceceña, A. E. (ed.) (2006) "Los desafíos de las emancipaciones en un contexto militarizado," Buenos Aires: CLACSO.

Ceceña, A. E. and Motto, C. E. (2005) "Paraguay: eje de la dominación del Cono Sur," Buenos Aires: Observatorio Latinoamericano de Geopolítica, CLACSO.

Conca, K. and Dabelko, G. D. (eds.) (1998) *Green Planet Blues: Environmental Politics from Stockholm to Kyoto*, Boulder, CO: Westview.

Correa, C. and Musungu, S. F. (2002) "The WIPO Patent Agenda: The Risks for Developing Countries," South Centre. www.southcentre.org/publications/wipopatent/toc.htm

Crosby, A. W. (1986) *Ecological Imperialism*, Cambridge: Cambridge University Press.

Drahos, P. and Braithwaite, J. (2003) *Information Feudalisms: Who Owns the Knowledge Economy?* New York: The New Press.

Dutfield, G. (2001) "Biotechnology and Patents: What Can Developing Countries Do About Article 27.3(b)?" *Bridges Monthly Review*, 5(9): 17–1.

Fischer, F. (2000) *Citizens, Experts, and the Environment: The Politics of Local Knowledge*, Durham, NC and London: Duke University Press.

Friends of the Earth International (2002) "Implications of WTO Negotiations for Biodiversity," Briefing, April, Amsterdam.

Gill, S. (1995) "Theorizing the Interregnum: The Double Movement and Global Politics in the 1990s," in B. Hettne (ed.) *International Political Economy: Understanding Global Disorder*, London and New Jersey: Zed Books, 65–99.

————(2003) *Power and Resistance in the New World Order*, New York: Palgrave.

Goldman, M. (ed.) (1998) *Privatizing Nature: Political Struggles for the Global Commons*, London: Routledge.

Goldman, M. (2001) "Constructing an Environmental State: Eco-governmentality and other Transnational Practices of a 'Green' World Bank," *Social Problems*, 48 (4): 499–523.

Görg, C. and Brand, U. (2000) "Global Environmental Politics and Competition Between Nation-States: On the Regulation of Biological Diversity," *Review of International Political Economy*, 7(3): 371–98.

————(2003) "Post-Fordist Societal Relationships with Nature: The Role of NGOs and the State in Biodiversity Politics," *Rethinking Marxism*, 15(2): 264–88.

————(2006) "Global Regulation of Genetic Resources and the Internationalization of the State," *Global Environmental Politics*, 6(4): 101–23.

GRAIN (Genetic Resources Action International) (2005) *Whither Biosafety? In these days of Monsanto Laws, Hope for Biosafety Lies at the Grassroots*, www.grain.org/articles/index.cfm?id = 9

Haas, Peter M. (1992) "Introduction: Epistemic Communities and International Policy Coordination", *International Organization*, 46(1): 1–35.

Hajer, M. A. (1995) *The Politics of Environmental Discourse: Ecological Modernization and the Policy Process*, Oxford: Clarendon Press.

Harvey, D. (2003) *The New Imperialism*, Oxford: Oxford University Press.

Heins, Volker and Flitner, Michael (1998) "Biologische Ressourcen und Life Politics," in M. Flitner, C. Görg, and V. Heins (eds.) *Konfliktfeld Natur. Biologische Ressourcen und globale Politik*, Opladen, Germany: Leske Budrich, 13–38.

Hirsch, J. (1997) "Globalization of Capital, Nation-states and Democracy," *Studies in Political Economy*, 54: 39–58.

———(2002) "Wissen und Nichtwissen. Anmerkungen zur 'Wissensgesellschaft,'" in O. Brüchert and C. Resch (eds.) *Zwischen Herrschaft und Befreiung*, Münster, Germany: Westfälisches Dampfboot, 43–54.

Jessop, B. (1990) *State Theory: Putting the Capitalist State in its Place*, Cambridge: Polity Press.

———(2002) *The Future of the Capitalist State*, Cambridge: Polity Press.

———(2003) "Postfordismus und wissensbasierte Ökonomie, Eine Reinterpretation des Regulationsansatzes," in U. Brand and W. Raza (eds.) *Fit für den Postfordismus?* Münster, Germany: Westfälisches Dampfboot.

Kloppenburg, J. R. (1988) *First the Seed: The Political Economy of Plant Technology, 1492–2000*, Cambridge: Cambridge University Press.

Kütting, G. (2000) *Environment, Society and International Relations: Towards More Effective International Environmental Agreements*, London and New York: Routledge.

Le Prestre, P. (ed.) (2002) *Governing Global Biodiversity: The Evolution and Implementation of the Convention on Biological Diversity*, Aldershot, UK: Ashgate.

Lander, E. (2006) "La Ciencia Neoliberal," in A. E. Ceceña (ed.) *Los desafíos de las emancipaciones en un contexto militarizado*, Buenos Aires: CLACSO, 45–94.

Levy, M. A., Keohane, R. O., and Haas, P. M. (1993) "Improving the Effectiveness of International Environmental Institutions," In: P. Haas, R. O. Keohane, and M. A. Levy (eds.) *Institutions for the Earth*, Cambridge, MA: MIT Press, 397–426.

Lipschutz, R. (2004) *Global Environmental Politics: Power, Perspectives, and Practice*, Washington, DC: CQ Press.

Lipschutz, R. D. and Conca, K. (eds.) (1993) *The State and Social Power in Global Environmental Politics*, New York: Columbia University Press.

MA (Millennium Ecosystems Assessment) (2005) *Millennium Ecosystem Assessment Synthesis Report*, Washington, DC: Island Press.

Mayntz, R. and Scharpf, F. W. (eds.) (1995): *Gesellschaftliche Selbstregelung und politische Steuerung*. Frankfurt and New York: Campus.

McCarthy, J. and Prudham, S. (2004) "Neoliberal Nature and the Nature of Neoliberalism," *Geoforum*, 35: 275–83.

Oxfam (2005) "Kicking Down the Door: How Upcoming WTO Talks Threaten Farmers in Poor Countries," Oxfam Briefing Paper no. 72, Oxford: Oxfam.

Paterson, M. (2000) *Understanding Global Environmental Politics*, New York: Palgrave.

Petit, M., Fowler, C., Collins, W., Correa, C., and Thornström, C-G. (2000): "Why Governments Can't Make Policy: The Case of Plant Genetic Resources in the International Arena," draft MS.

Plehwe, D., Walpen, B., and Neunhöffer, G. (eds.) (2006) *Neoliberal Hegemony: A Global Critique*, London and New York: Routledge.

Potsdam Recommendations (2006) "Potsdam Recommendations on the Convention on Biological Diversity, Submitted by the Eminent Experts," Workshop on Implementation of the Convention on Biological Diversity, Potsdam, Germany, December 13–15.

Poulantzas, N. (1975) *Politische Macht und gesellschaftliche Klassen*, Frankfurt am Main, Germany: Europäische Verlagsanstalt.

———(1978/1980/2002) *State, Power, Socialism*, London: Verso, 1980; quoted from the recent German edition (2002) *Staatstheorie: politischer Überbau, Ideologie, sozialistische Demokratie*, Hamburg, Germany. First published 1978.

Prügl, E. (2004) "International Institutions and Feminist Politics," *Brown Journal of World Affairs*, 10(2): 69–84.

Secretariat of the Convention on Biological Diversity (2006) *Global Biodiversity Outlook 2*, Montreal. Online. Available at www.biodiv.org/GBO2

Strange, S. (1988) *States and Markets*, London: Pinter Publishers.

Swyngedouw, E. (2004) "Globalisation or 'glocalisation': Networks, Territories and Rescaling," *Cambridge Review of International Affairs*, 17: 25–48.

van den Hove, S. and Sharman, M. (2004) *Interfaces Between Science and Policy for Environmental Governance: Lessons and Open Questions from the European Platform for Biodiversity Research Strategy*, MS.

WIPO (2002) 'WIPO Patent Agenda. Options for the Development of the International Patent System,' Memorandum of the Director General. A/37/6. www.wipo.int/eng/document/govbody/wo_gb_ab/doc/a37_6.doc

Wissen, M. (2008) "Politicizing Intellectual Property Rights. The Conflicts around the TRIPs agreement and the World Intellectual Property Organisation," in U. Brand, C. Görg, J. Hirsch and M. Wissen (eds.) *Contested Terrains: Conflicts About Genetic Resources and the Internationalisation of the State*, London and New York: Routledge, ch. 4, forthcoming.

Young, O. R. (1999) *Governance in World Affairs*, Ithaca, NY and London: Cornell University Press.

7 Reinventing the future

The global ecovillage movement as a holistic knowledge community

Karen Litfin

Within the field of global environmental politics, a distinction is commonly made between top-down and bottom-up approaches. Top-down approaches typically focus on international environmental treaties and institutions, with the primary policy agents being technical experts and norm entrepreneurs working in states and international organizations. Bottom-up approaches generally focus on social movements and global civil society, with the primary agents being nongovernmental organizations directing their actions toward states, international organizations or, increasingly, firms. In both cases, the empirical focus tends to gravitate toward institutions and states, thereby privileging a state-centric understanding of politics. Consistent with the other chapters in this volume, this chapter seeks to simultaneously elucidate and complexify our understanding of global/local linkages. Yet it also offers a potentially more hopeful reading of the knowledge/power nexus by shifting the focus to small-scale place-based, yet tightly networked, collective efforts toward self-empowerment in response to the life-alienating forces of technocracy, the administrative state and global capitalism.

While this top-down/bottom-up distinction is a useful one, it overlooks an important group of actors who do not fit easily into the field's understanding of politics: those who are pioneering ecologically sustainable ways of living. From the perspective of global environmental politics, there are three good reasons to sidestep the lifestyle politics of ecovillages. First, their numbers are relatively small, and their actions barely register on the radar screens of media coverage and political officialdom. Second, for the most part, these individuals tend not to be organized beyond their local communities, and so therefore have little national or transnational influence. Third, as the few scholars who are attentive to such phenomena as the voluntary simplicity movement and the local currency movement are quick to note, these groups do not actively counter the broader institutional and structural dynamics that foster unsustainable ways of living (Princen et al. 2002). Yet there is a powerful counterbalance to these good reasons: if current human systems are unsustainable, it is prudent to look to those who are pioneering sustainable living practices. To ignore communities that are actually reducing their ecological footprints dramatically, that are creating models of sustainability literally from the ground up, would be intellectually negligent and pragmatically unwise.

In response to the gradual disintegration of supportive social and cultural structures and the creeping global ecological crisis, small groups of people the world over are coming together to create modes of living in harmony with each other, with other living beings, and with the Earth. If these communities were isolated experiments, disconnected from one another and from larger social and political processes, they might not be of interest to the study of global environmental politics. Since 1995, however, with the formation of the Global Ecovillage Network (GEN), thousands of these communities have come together for the purpose of sharing and disseminating information about sustainable living practices. Network members include large networks like Sarvodaya (11,000 villages applying ecological design principles in Sri Lanka) and the Colufifa network of 350 villages in Senegal; the Ladakh project on the Tibetan plateau; ecotowns like Auroville in South India and the Federation of Damanhur in Italy; small rural ecovillages like Gaia Asociación in Argentina and Huehuecoyotl, Mexico; urban rejuvenation projects like Los Angeles Ecovillage and Christiania in Copenhagen; permaculture design sites such as Crystal Waters, Australia, Cochabamba, Bolivia and Barus, Brazil; and educational centers such as Findhorn in Scotland and the Centre for Alternative Technology in Wales. These communities trace their roots to diverse lineages (Dawson 2004):

1 The ideals of self-sufficiency and spiritual inquiry that have historically characterized monasteries and ashrams, and which are also prominent principles in the Gandhian movement;
2 The "back-to-the-land" movement and, later, the co-housing movement;
3 The environmental, peace and feminist movements;
4 The appropriate technology movement;
5 The alternative education movement.

In this chapter, I characterize ecovillages, emerging in an astonishing diversity of culture and ecosystems, as a planetary knowledge community grounded in a holistic ontology and seeking to construct viable living systems as an alternative to the unsustainable legacy of modernity. As a global knowledge community, the ecovillage movement is remarkable both for its unity and its diversity. Ecovillages have taken root in tropical, temperate and desert regions, their religious orientations include all the major world religions, plus paganism and atheism. Their specific practices vary according to cultural and ecological context. What unites the network as a knowledge community is its members' commitment to a supportive social environment and a low-impact way of life. To achieve this, they integrate various aspects of ecological design and building, green production, renewable energy, community-building and spiritual practices. Beneath this commitment to social and ecological sustainability, one may discern a worldview premised upon holism and radical interdependence. This basic ontological commitment is what unites the global ecovillage movement, forging a shared epistemic bond across widely disparate communities. This holistic worldview, drawing upon strands of systems theory, Gaian science, permaculture and perennial philosophy, may be understood as a form of constructive postmodernism. As such, the global ecovillage movement represents a pragmatic knowledge community in terms of its commitment to both a set of practical living skills and a common worldview.

The ecovillage movement may be understood as a conscious and pragmatic response to the material and ideational crisis of modernity, a response that is grounded in a holistic ontology. Modernity may be characterized as a historically specific story about the triumph of human reason over superstition and the vagaries of nature; about history as a progressive march toward the material liberation of humanity; about the possibility of a reductionist approach to knowledge; and about the possessive individual, replicated in the sovereign state, as the locus of political authority (Litfin 2003: 36). From a holistic perspective, the social and environmental consequences of this story make it an increasingly unviable one, thereby necessitating new ways of living premised upon a sense of deep connection to the human and biotic community. Whereas the scientific metaphors that inform the story of modernity are rooted in atomism and the machine, the metaphors that inform the worldview of the global ecovillage movement are the organism and living systems.

Increasingly, the dark side of modernity is inescapable: in the ever-deepening disparity between the conspicuous consumption of the North and the grueling poverty of the South; in the myriad forms of pollution that threaten air, land and sea; in the mass extinction of species; and in the feverish pursuit of security that seems to generate only greater insecurity. Whereas from a conventional social science perspective these problems are taken as distinct fields of study, from a systems perspective they are interrelated symptoms of "the global problematique," or

> the problem of all problems, not merely the sum of the problems of pollution, war, famine, alienation, resource depletion, urban crowding, and exploitation of the Third World by the First. It is a systemic construct that assumes causal connections among these problems, connections that amplify the disturbance of the meta-system.
>
> (Haas 1983: 39)

From a systems perspective, the seemingly separate problems that constitute the global problematique cannot be effectively addressed in isolation (Luhmann 1990).

Taking a systemic approach to the global problematique, the ecovillage movement addresses the interrelated problems of social alienation and ecological degradation by building sustainable communities locally from the ground up while simultaneously constituting a global network for education and social change. Combining a supportive social environment with a low-impact lifestyle, ecovillages are consciously seeking to birth new ways of living that transcend the modern dichotomies of urban vs. rural settlements, private vs. public spheres, culture vs. nature, local vs. global, expert vs. lay-person, affluence vs. poverty, and mind vs. body. In this sense, they represent a postmodern perspective, but one that seeks to construct a viable alternative rather than merely a deconstruction of modernity. Ecovillage participants aim to create diverse models of living, compatible with their local social and physical contexts, that will be "successfully continuable into the indefinite future" (GEN 2004). They build upon varying combinations of three interrelated dimensions—ecology, community, and spirituality.

While the movement is relatively small, comprising several hundred relatively new ecovillages in industrialized countries and networks of perhaps 15,000 traditional villages in the developing world that are introducing ecovillage design principles, it is a rapidly growing movement. If the dominant human systems on the planet are not sustainable, as increasingly seems to be the case, then the rise of the global ecovillage movement is of urgent practical consequence. As a living expression of a worldview fundamentally different from that of secular modernity, the ecovillage movement is also of theoretical interest for the history (and implementation) of ideas.

In this chapter, I first explore the role of systems theory in the global ecovillage movement, focusing on Gaia theory and permaculture. The former adopts a holistic understanding of the Earth system, or Gaia, with living systems (including human systems) inextricably intertwined with one another and with geological and chemical systems. Gaia theory, as a widely accepted scientific model, at once revives the ancient image of a living Earth, and endows it with scientific legitimacy. In contrast to the mechanistic worldview of modernity, Gaia is conceived (either literally or metaphorically, depending upon the source) as an organism. The global ecovillage movement has been powerfully inspired by Gaian thinking and imagery. Permaculture, a variant of systems theory informed by elements of perennial agriculture and deep ecology, offers a holistic and practical approach to human and natural systems as mutually enhancing.

I then investigate how both the individual and the global are constituted within the holistic ontology that informs the movement. While holism represents a real challenge to the atomistic ontology of modernity, the eco-village movement does not do away with individualism; rather, it puts a primary emphasis on individual responsibility while conceiving of the individual as inextricably embedded in larger living systems. I will also suggest that whereas, from a perspective of conventional political logic, a focus on individual responsibility might be considered an ineffective organizing strategy in the face of unsustainable global structures and processes, this focus is far more compelling when considered in light of a holistic ontology. Likewise, from a systems perspective, the global ecovillage movement's affirmative strategy of building alternative systems rather than simply opposing existing ones turns out to have a persuasive internal logic. Moreover, if ecovillages were merely isolated phenomena, perhaps we might take a passing curiosity in them as efforts to address the global problematique on the scale of local communities. Yet they are also linked together as a global movement through the Global Ecovillage Network (GEN), whose primary purpose is information exchange among thousands of ecovillages and related projects, as well as education for social change in the larger world.

Unlike many of the chapters in the volume, my analysis does not envision environmental knowledge as solely an instrument of hegemonic domination over local communities. While the sprouting of alternative knowledge/power practices at the margins may not portend the unraveling of hegemony, the ecovillage movement's self-empowering pragmatic approach offers a small opening in the knowledge/power window through which we might envision new possibilities. The ecovillage movement seeks to offer a coherent response to the material and ideational crises of modernity, addressing the global problematique at the interconnected levels of individual responsibility, local communities and global action. The conceptual underpinnings of the movement lie in its ontological commitment to holism and radical interdependence, a commitment that unites the movement across cultural, religious, geographic and socieoeconomic lines. In Tim Luke's terms, the ecovillage movement represents a "resurgence of the lived, the local and the living."

The following section outlines the holistic worldview of the ecovillage movement, especially as it is expressed in two strands of systems theory: permaculture and Gaia theory. I then turn to an analysis of the place of the individual in the ecovillage movement's pragmatic holism, followed by a discussion of the degree to which the movement is politically engaged on a transnational level. Finally, I conclude with a brief inquiry into the question of whether ecovillages are an effective response to the global problematique.

Holism in the ecovillage movement

As GEN president and Findhorn ecovillage resident Jonathan Dawson observes, "two broad—and, to some degree, overlapping—approaches can be discerned in the ways that various ecovillages have sought to create low-impact settlements" (2006: 39). The "low-tech" approach reduces needs and costs by emphasizing manual labor and using locally available and recycled materials. The "high-tech" approach involves state-of-the-art environmental technologies that are often more expensive and travel farther than conventional alternatives. A striking feature of both is their "holistic and integrated character, enabling them to increase internal resource flows and reduce the need for external inputs" (Dawson 2006: 43). Gray water and kitchen waste are recycled into community gardens; human manure is composted into landscape soil; rainwater is harvested for garden and home use; woody waste from community forests warms the homes of the residents. To the extent that ecovillages are able to generate a local economy based upon community resources, money circulates internally and automobile use decreases. Central to each of these elements of ecovillage life is the creation of virtuous cycles, as opposed to vicious cycles, which regenerate the land, enliven the community, and sustain its members in a cohesive whole comprised of integrated human and natural systems.

One expression of this holism, which mostly predates the ecovillage movement and powerfully informs it, is permaculture. As initially developed by its Australian founders, Bill Mollison and David Holmgren in the 1970s, permaculture focused on small-scale sustainable agriculture and integrated systems at the household level (Holmgren and Mollison 1978). Over the next two decades, the concept was adapted to diverse social and ecological contexts, becoming a small but global movement spanning North and South. Permaculture takes a systems approach to what it sees as the interrelated dimensions of human systems: land stewardship, buildings, agriculture, economics, tools and technology, culture and education, health and spiritual wellbeing. Most important, permaculture promotes bottom-up social change rooted in design principles observable in nature, starting with the individual and the household as the drivers for change at the market, community, and cultural levels. The original permaculture vision of "permanent" agriculture has evolved into one of sustainable culture premised upon low-energy human support systems designed in harmony with ecosystems, and has been expanded by the ecovillage movement from the household to the community level.

The systems perspective of permaculture is fundamentally related to its understanding of the primacy of energy flows. Responding in part to the growth of the new science of ecology and in part to a dawning awareness of industrial society's fossil fuel dependency, permaculture has from the beginning emphasized the importance of energy flows and cyclical processes. From this perspective, all elements of human and other living systems can be understood in energetic terms: food, trees, soil, buildings, modes of transportation, water—*all* are embodiments and conductors of energy. The key to permaculture is in the wise husbandry of energy resources. Permaculture farming places an enormous emphasis on enhancing soil fertility through composting, thereby minimizing the loss of energy. Likewise, the perennial edible landscapes associated with permaculture, including food trees, berries and herbs, decrease the energy input required for food production. Similarly, there is a strong emphasis on promoting the growth of forests because trees, more than any land species, accumulate biomass rapidly and thus represent a tremendous storehouse of energy.

A related permaculture concept is minimizing waste through closing cycles of production and consumption. If human systems were designed according to nature's design principles, there would be no waste. Indeed, the notion of waste is a human construct, and is deeply implicated in the growth of modern industrial societies. Permaculture seeks to minimize waste in all aspects of human settlements through such low-energy technologies as composting toilets, the composting of food and agricultural waste, the use of renewable energy resources, the recycling of gray water into food production, and the use of local organic building materials such as cob, straw bales, and compressed earth blocks. Ecovillages, which grew in part from the permaculture movement, have become demonstration sites for these and other low-energy earth-friendly technologies.

From an ontological perspective, permaculture is deeply skeptical of modernity's notion of progress in the linear march of time, seeking instead to reorient human culture to the cyclical notion of time rooted in natural processes. Seen through the eyes of modernity, the permaculture movement has an essentially pessimistic view of the trajectory of human culture. Permaculturalists believe that some degree of technological and economic collapse is likely within the coming decades, and is a current reality for many people around the world. The permaculture vision of sustainable agriculture is premised upon the decline and eventual elimination of the "fossil fuel subsidy." The "end of oil scenarios" now coming into mainstream parlance have been commonplace among permaculturalists since the 1970s. According to this view, the profligate expenditure of energy that has spurred industrial societies, largely in the form of fossil fuels, will soon come to a peak, resulting in a climax of "postmodern cultural chaos" and a subsequent "descent culture" (or permaculture) toward an eventual low energy sustainable future in the coming centuries (Holmgren 2002: xxix). This descent, however, will not be a return to preindustrial societal forms, primarily because modernity has created an information-rich culture premised upon learning and change. Modern society, from a permaculture perspective, is a "fast-breeder system that generates new information, knowledge, innovation and culture" (Holmgren 2002: 22). Thus permaculture systems, pioneered by individuals who are the beneficiaries of this "fast-breeder system," are information and design-intensive. This macro-level perspective informs the entire pragmatic permaculture agenda and has had a strong influence on the ecovillage movement. Their use of low-energy building materials, their commitment to wind, solar and biomass energy systems, and their preference for using human (as opposed to machine) energy—all of these practical applications come as a natural corollary to this macro-vision.

Many key permaculture concepts, which follow from their systems perspective on energy, have found a welcome home in the ecovillage movement. Some of these include (Holmgren 2002: viii):

1 Design from nature; design from pattern to details;
2 Catch and store energy;
3 Make the smallest intervention necessary;
4 Use small and slow solutions;
5 Apply self-regulation and accept feedback;
6 Produce no waste;
7 Use and value diversity;
8 Integrate rather than segregate.

Permaculture is essentially a practical approach to the design of integrated human and natural systems, which the ecovillage movement has adopted and tailored to local contexts and community life. Not surprisingly, most of GEN's Living and Learning Centers include permaculture courses in their curricula.

The ecovillage movement is also influenced by certain intellectual strands of systems thinking. One powerful scientific expression of a systems approach is Gaia theory, a now widely accepted view of the Earth as a holistic, self-regulating biogeochemical system.[1] Gaia theory at once revives an ancient symbol, endows it with scientific legitimacy, and inspires the political imagination (Litfin 2005). As a symbol of wholeness, interdependence and dynamic complexity, Gaia offers an alternative to the atomistic, reductionist scientific metaphors that inform modern social thought.

Both as conceptual underpinning and imaginal metaphor, Gaia circulates widely in the ecovillage movement. For instance, there are ecovillages with "Gaia" on several continents, and "whole earth" images are popular in ecovillages everywhere. In the 1990s, Ross and Hildur Jackson, two founders of GEN working in Denmark, started three "Gaian" entities: Gaia Trust, which funnels financial assets from investments into seed grants for ecovillages; Gaia Technologies, which develops sustainable technologies, and Gaia Villages, to conduct research on the global ecovillage network. More recently, the leadership of GEN has formed a collective, Gaia Education, which has developed a four-week comprehensive course on Ecovillage Design Education. This curriculum is now available as a distance-learning course through the Open University of Catalonia in Spain. A related venture is Gaia University, which began offering undergraduate and graduate degree programs in Integrated Eco-Social Design in 2006. If any icon can be said to elicit universal appeal in the global ecovillage movement, it is Gaia. Whether that allure is primarily rational, aesthetic or emotive is beyond the scope of this essay; for now, it is sufficient to note its ubiquity and to comment more generally on some plausible reasons for this appeal.

Paradoxically, Gaia theory is simultaneously at the cutting edge of Western science even as it represents a return to the ancient organismic worldview. Gaia theory brings the premodern idea of a living Earth into the realm of falsifiable science, conferring upon the "anima mundi" the mantle of scientific legitimacy. Yet Gaia theory departs from conventional science in some important ways. Whereas past science, divided into separate disciplines of biology, chemistry, and physics, provided an inventory of the Earth's parts, Gaia theory offers us a view of the Earth as an integrated whole—a complete, dynamic and self-sustaining living system. Gaia is, at a minimum, a symbol of wholeness, interdependence, and dynamic complexity. For many, Gaia also evokes a sense of awe and reverence, restoring a sense of connection to the cosmos that Western culture abandoned when it adopted a mechanistic worldview. By evoking a sense of the sacred, Gaia challenges modernity's utilitarian and reductionistic orientation, while grounding its holism in an integrative approach to Earth's geological, hydrological, atmospheric and biological systems.

Gaia theory offers scientific grounding for a radical ontology of inter-dependence and a more intimate perspective on globalization. Like ecovillage designers, Vaclav Havel takes inspiration from Gaian science for a globalized approach to human thinking and living. He observes that we experience a sense of helplessness before the global problematique because "our civilization has essentially globalized only the surface of our lives" (Havel 1997: 167). Our external lives—our communication, transportation, financial exchanges, agri-culture and medicine—have become globalized, but our inner lives orbit inside the myopic constraints of egoism and parochial identities. Gaia theory, Havel suggests, calls us back from our isolation, connecting us to the wondrous whole of creation and calling us to a greater sense of responsibility. Embracing our embeddedness in the whole of creation and "trusting [our] own subjectivity as the principle link with the subjectivity of the world" (Havel 1997: 93), we claim our *responsibility* as *an ability to respond* to planetary challenges. This emphasis on individual responsibility within a symbiotically connected whole is an essential tenet of the global ecovillage movement, and seems to be a common thread across ecovillages in the diversity of their approaches to spirituality

Situating the individual in a whole-systems approach

Ecovillage designers address what they perceive to be the intertwined ecolo-gical, socioeconomic, and cultural-spiritual dimensions of the global pro-blematique through an integrated systemic understanding of the world. In this view, we are not atomistic individuals; rather, people are radically embedded in larger systems. The whole-systems approach of the ecovillage movement is not only pragmatic in its design from nature, but also serves as a source of meaning for the individual. Thus, ecovillagers view themselves as pioneering an alternative socioeconomic system to the unsustainable legacy of modernity. They seek to mend the modern split between people and the rest of nature by placing human existence within a holistic cosmology while simultaneously granting humans a special place as conscious designers of harmonious systems. And they seek to mend

> the divorce between head and heart that the current global economy enforces (whereby people often make consumer choices that they know to be socially or ecologically exploitative because they feel they have little choice). This ecovillage model enables people to bring back into alignment their desire for justice and sustainability with their aspiration to live well and happily.
>
> (Dawson 2006: 50)

In their whole-systems approach to sustainable development, ecovillage designers understand ecological, social and spiritual issues as fitting together into a holistic unity. In the words of one of the founders of the movement, ecovillagers see themselves as trying to "heal the fragmented aspect of the prevailing culture by living a holistic worldview" (Jackson and Svensson 2002: 106).

Rather than becoming lost in the whole, which from the atomistic perspective of modernity would be the inevitable fear, each individual inhabits the center of a series of concentric circles beginning with home and extending to community, ecosystem, nation and planet. One of the most compelling aspects of this holism is the deliquescence of the dichotomy between internal values and external action, revealed in a deep acceptance of personal responsibility for creating viable social and ecological structures (Mollison 1988: 1). First and foremost, an ontology of radical interdependence challenges the possessive individualism of modernity by integrating person and planet within the context of community. Recognizing their own complicity in replicating the social structures that threaten to unravel Earth's life-support systems, ecovillage participants accept responsibility for their own lives and seek to invent alternative social structures. As Jonathan Dawson puts it, a defining feature of ecovillagers is that "they are in the business of *wresting back control over their own resources* and, ultimately, their own destinies" (Dawson 2006: 35, emphasis in original).

Yet some observers are critical of ecovillagers' "life-style strategies" as a means of building sustainable democracies (Fotopoulos 2000). They see ecovillages as a self-indulgent, escapist and ineffective response to the powerful global structures that perpetuate socioeconomic injustice and environmental degradation. Without addressing the question of the effectiveness of the ecovillage strategy, which I take up in the next section, we should note that the ecovillage movement's perspective on political change is different from more mainstream understandings because it is rooted in a holistic worldview. From a mechanistic perspective, neither the lone individual nor tiny communities have the power to effectively counter enormous institutions; they are simply too small. Yet from a holistic perspective, the networks of interdependence within a system are so intricate and tightly interwoven that one can never say for certain that an individual's actions will be insignificant. Thus, for instance, ecovillage proponent J. T. Ross Jackson applies the systems thinking of chaos theorist Ilya Prigogine to the global ecovillage movement. Ross Jackson suggests that

> we are like individual molecules being perturbed on a global scale by a technology that is too powerful for us to handle in the dream state. We will have to wake up soon. ... And what would be the mechanism to bring this about? Prigogine's work suggests an answer—self-organizing systems! ... a grassroots local initiative, a decentralized explosion of energy with a global vision.
>
> (Ross Jackson 2000: 37–38)

A common metaphor in chaos theory is that of a butterfly's wings influencing planetary weather systems. From this perspective, it is quite possible that effective responses to the global problematique could come from the actions of individuals and small communities—especially if these local entities can organize themselves into a global network such as GEN.

From the holistic perspective of the ecovillage movement, the cosmos is holographic, with universal patterns replicated at every level of organization. Ecovillages, then, can be understood as "holons," integrating the social, ecological dimensions of human life in a single place. Thus, many ecovillages see themselves as microcosms of the world, with the individual playing a key role in hastening cultural change. Gaia Education, an educational initiative of GEN, articulates this systems theoretic perspective on the centrality of the individual for cultural transformation:

> In preparation for the emergence of a new worldview, "seed" people will begin to appear, inoculating the collective consciousness with new ideas and concepts—evolved interpretations about the nature of reality. Initially, these seed people will be perceived as a cultural "fringe," an idiosyncratic minority whose new interpretations can be easily discounted and disregarded because of their incongruity with established, officially sanctioned, interpretations of reality. Eventually, however, as the precepts of the old paradigm are revealed to be increasingly inept at managing and providing a meaningful context for the evolving, emerging situation, the seed people will gain credibility. ... Ecovillages are the "seed" communities of the not-too-distant future.
>
> (Gaia Education: Epilogue)

Seed people and seed communities sowing global transformation: again, the metaphors are organic, not mechanical, and the stimulus to change is individual action rippling across concentric circles and interconnected networks. This is a far cry from the conventional top-down view of meaningful change as coming from legislative and policy reform, or even the grassroots social movement model of social change through pressure and lobbying.

The global ecovillage movement is politically unconventional for another reason: it is an affirmative movement, not a protest movement. Rather than resisting what they oppose, ecovillages are building an alternative from the ground up. Like their emphasis on the individual, this positive approach also stems from their holistic worldview. If the world is radically interdependent, then establishing the alternative social structures on the ground may very well be a more effective strategy than simply saying "no" to unsustainable systems. This is particularly true if their perception of imminent crisis turns out to be valid. The permaculture understanding of systems also comes in here: smaller is safer. There is a pervasive wariness among ecovillagers of the scale and complexity of global social and technological systems, and a sense that empowerment and responsible action are most viable at the scale of the individual and community.

Global engagement

Despite this emphasis on lifestyle politics, an important consequence of the ecovillage movement's commitment to pragmatic holism is its engagement with the larger world. From a systems perspective, global engagement is a necessary corollary to a systemic understanding of the world because the individual and the community are always embedded in larger ecological and human systems. Ecovillages, unlike earlier intentional communities and back-to-the-land experiments, are not isolated enclaves; rather, they are, in general, deeply engaged in national and transnational politics. From my initial research, including visits to ecovillages on three continents, my sense is that ecovillagers tend to see themselves as engaged participants in planetary socio-ecological systems rather than utopian fugitives. This global engagement manifests itself in four primary ways. First, on a principled level, the movement has consciously constituted itself as a pragmatic response to the interrelated global dynamics of North/South inequity, global commodity chains, structural violence, and fossil fuel consumption. Second, at the level of action, ecovillage activists have been prominent players in the peace movement and the movement against neoliberal globalization. Even here, however, their emphasis is on establishing a positive example on the ground rather than simply opposing what they do not want. Third, many ecovillages in the North are deeply engaged in conflict resolution, sustainable development and human rights projects in the South. Fourth, in a more institutional vein, the movement has established itself since 1995 as a global network. GEN has established fourteen Living and Learning Centers on six continents in order to offer holistic education in sustainable living skills to people from around the world. GEN has also positioned itself as a significant presence for sustainability education among United Nations agencies.

Though ecovillages might look like isolated experiments or misguided attempts to withdraw from mainstream society, their deeper impetus comes from their analysis of the global problematique. In the words of two GEN founders, Hildur and Ross Jackson,

> The twentieth century was polarized by extreme wealth and poverty, disintegrating families, increasing violence and drugs, degraded environments, species depletion, no political leadership on a global scale, and democracy undermined by the power of corporations. The reasons for this situation include the spiritual (the loss of contact with the divine) and macro-economic (hitting the physical limits of a finite planet). It is all going to come to a crisis point, and change can only come from the bottom up.
>
> (Ross Jackson 2000: 60)

From a systems perspective, any effective response to the global problematique must simultaneously address its ecological, social, economic and spiritual causes, which is precisely the intention of ecovillages. The movement seeks to produce long-term fundamental change by creating viable alternatives on the ground. Again, in the words of Ross Jackson,

> The logic is simple. If the examples are good enough, they will be replicated. From then on, it is only a question of time until the strategy succeeds and ecovillages become the basis for a new culture based on a holistic paradigm ... Ecovillages are ideal vehicles for this task because they are by definition holistic, representing all the different aspects of sustainability in one place where it can be seen in an integrated solution.
>
> (Ross Jackson 2000: 64).

In this context, the fact that ecovillages are a conscious response to socio-ecological realities in the global North and South becomes centrally important. Within affluent countries, ecovillages seek to reinvigorate social life and decrease material consumption. In developing countries, ecovillages aim to preserve village life and enhance material living standards in a sustainable manner, thereby providing an alternative to poverty, urbanization and corporate-led globalization. Because a large number of people in developing countries still live in village settings, the foremost concern of Third World ecovillage movements is to incorporate appropriate technologies and community-building skills into existing villages. In industrialized countries, where small-scale communities have been overtaken by the forces of urbanization and suburbanization, ecovillagers find themselves starting more from scratch, establishing islands of relative sustainability in a sea of affluence, alienation and wastefulness. Yet, like their counterparts in the South, they seek to meld the best of new appropriate technologies, (e.g. solar, wind and biofuel energy sources) with traditional practices (e.g. mud building and organic farming). In both contexts, there is a shared motivation to create communities that can serve as a compelling response to the global problematique, succumbing to neither the affluence of the over-consuming North nor the grueling poverty of much of the South. Thus, the ecovillage movement represents an effort to forge a third way, applying and integrating the best practices of North and South with sensitivity to local context.

At the level of political action, opposition to economic globalization serves as a rallying point for ecovillagers around the world. Yet even in their opposition, they move beyond the politics of protest. For instance, during the 2005 G8 summit in Scotland, thousands of activists supported by a core group of Findhorn residents created a temporary ecovillage as a counterpoint to the unsustainable policies being promoted at the summit. The demonstration ecovillage included nine composting toilets, over twenty graywater systems, electricity generated by solar panels and wind turbines, and thirteen kitchens serving, as much as possible, fair trade, local and organic food. BBC News Online carried a front-page story under the headline, "Eco-Village Is 'Model for Us All'" (Mitchell 2005). Dawson suggests that the G8 action "illustrates the primary gift of ecovillages to the wider sustainability family; namely, the impulse to move beyond protest and to create models of more sane, just and sustainable ways of living" (Dawson 2006: 38).

Dawson also outlines how peace activism and international solidarity pervade the ecovillage ethic. Just to offer a few examples: Sarvodaya, GEN's largest member, has been an active peace broker in Sri Lanka's long-term civil war. Both Sarvodaya and Auroville assisted in tsunami relief work. Plenty International, an NGO created by The Farm in Tennessee, specializes in bringing soybean agricultural training to the Third World. Tamera ecovillage in Portugal, which considers itself a "research center for lived peace," is involved in conflict resolution work in Colombia and the Middle East. Ecovillagers in Denmark have partnered with ecovillagers in Senegal to send thousands of bicycles there (Dawson 2006: 15–18). Far from being exclusive enclaves of escapists, ecovillages are very often dynamic nodes of global engagement.

With the formation of GEN, an institutional context emerged to support this vision of global engagement and give the disparate movement a greater sense of cohesiveness. In 1995, Findhorn hosted a conference, "Ecovillages and Sustainable Communities," that drew over 400 people from over forty countries, with 300 more turned away for lack of space. Here, GEN was formally founded by a consortium of ecovillages from Europe, Asia, North America and Oceania (Bang 2005: 22). In the past decade, GEN has continued to expand, with community members in seventy countries; it has also divided into continental regions: GEN–Europe and Africa; GENOA–Oceania and Asia; and Ecovillage Network of the Americas.

Coincidentally, GEN got started just as the Internet was gaining widespread use. Given the global nature of the movement and the commitment of ecovillagers to minimize their use of fossil fuels, the Internet has been an indispensable organizing tool for the movement. The Internet has been key to disseminating information, sharing best practices, and organizing regional and global conferences. GEN has also developed a web-based Community Sustainability Assessment to measure how well ecovillages meet the criteria for a holistic vision of social and ecological sustainability.

This sense of wider responsibility is taken to another level through global outreach and the development of GEN's Living and Learning Centers. These ecovillage training centers, including three new ones at communities in Brazil, Senegal and Sri Lanka, offer full-immersion hands-on training in developing green technologies and living systems in a community and local cultural context. They teach a compendium of sustainable living skills, including organic gardening, living systems for water cycling, renewable energy sources, earth-friendly building from local materials, alternative economics, and community building and conflict resolution skills. GEN's initial partners in this venture are Sarvodaya in Sri Lanka, IPEC in Brazil and EcoYoff in Senegal, which are linked together in a South-South exchange network, and, in turn, with Living and Learning partners in the North. The intention is to create a learning web of shared resources in an evolving, collaborative system of experience, education and research to develop sustainable systems on the ground around the world. The orientation of the Living and Learning Centers is both global and local. Closely connected with an existing ecovillage, each Center models a comprehensive set of sustainable systems designed for its specific social and environmental conditions. This creates a practical base for whole-systems educational programs. Rich in experiential opportunities, the Living and Learning Centers' interactive learning community embody a "learn by doing," partnership pedagogy. The traditional skills and knowledge of each society are woven together with permaculture methodology and related appropriate technologies, forging workable solutions to the problems faced in each culture (Snyder 2006).

While these Living and Learning Centers are situated in strikingly diverse social and ecological contexts, even more striking is their common adherence to a systems theoretic perspective on the global problematique. The Centers exemplify the movement's holistic approach to the interrelated problems of North/South inequity, unsustainable resource depletion, war, hunger, social alienation and urbanization. Almost universally, their curricula emphasize permaculture design concepts and the interconnectedness of the social, ecological and spiritual dimensions of ecovillage living. Their commitment to a participatory pedagogy is rooted in an underlying belief that systemic change occurs from the bottom up, and can only be fostered though a pragmatic educational process that empowers individuals to take responsibility for their own lives.

GEN is increasingly visible as an organized presence at the transnational level. After gaining consultative status at the United Nations, GEN was the largest NGO presence at UN Habitat II Conference in 1996 (Ross Jackson 2000: 78) and is currently a significant player in the UN Decade for Education on Sustainable Development (2005–14). GEN's educational work at its Living and Learning Centers has received institutional endorsement from the United Nations Institute of Training and Research (UNITAR). GEN was also an active participant at the World Summit on Sustainable Development at Johannesburg in 2002, hosting several side events on ecovillage development. GEN's activities within the United Nations Economic and Social Council and its subsidiary bodies are detailed in its 2004 quadrennial report (GEN 2004).

The holistic vision of the ecovillage movement, while initially focused on sustainable living practices at the individual and community level, is increasingly expressing itself globally. Individual ecovillages are engaged in international solidarity networks for peace, human rights and sustainable development, and the movement itself has gained a transnational presence and cohesiveness through GEN. At all levels, from the individual to the global, the focus is on establishing ecologically and socially viable alternatives on the ground.

Lifestyle politics and the question of effectiveness

Even if ecovillages are internationally engaged and demonstrating the practical viability of a holistic worldview, their numbers and influence are so small that one must wonder if they should be taken seriously. They might offer a few lucky individuals a socially and ecologically harmonious way of living, but can the movement ever hope to be effective as a transformative force in the face of global capitalism and the culture of consumption? To consider the question of effectiveness, we must first know what the problem is that they seek to address and then be able to discern when it is being adequately met. As I suggested above, the ecovillage movement seeks to address not just one problem, but the global problematique as a systemically linked nexus that includes environmental degradation, hunger, war, social alienation and North–South inequity. If anything, these problems have only worsened since the inception of the ecovillage movement, and to the extent that there has been significant improvement, ecovillages cannot be credited. Yet, on a smaller spatial scale and a longer temporal scale, there are good reasons to be impressed by the actual and potential effectiveness of the ecovillage movement. First, ecovillages are demonstrating that it is possible to substantially reduce material throughput while enhancing the quality of life. This has two very important effects at the level of knowledge and discourse: (1) it undercuts the prevailing assumption that high levels of consumption are correlated with wellbeing; and (2) it demonstrates the practical viability of a holistic worldview. Second, in terms of long-term effectiveness, the ecovillage approach to systemic change bears a strong resonance with the anarchist strategy of *prefiguring*, or the creation of parallel structures for self-governance in the midst of the prevailing social order. Given the depth and breadth of the global problematique and the range of currently available options for addressing it, the strategy of prefiguring may well turn out to be an effective one in the long term.

At a minimum, ecovillages show that it is possible to live well while dramatically reducing consumption and waste. In a context where reductions in greenhouse gas emissions at the order of 60–80 percent are required to stabilize Earth's climate and the USA, the largest per capita emitter, refuses to be party to a treaty that would require it to reduce its emissions by only 5 percent, such a demonstration project is important. For instance, on my visit to Crystal Waters Permaculture Village in Australia, I found that the 230 residents there have been able to reduce their per capita solid waste by 80 percent. Jonathan Dawson cites two more detailed studies. A 2003 study by the University of Kassel found that the carbon footprints of Sieben Linden and Kommune Niederkaugungen were, respectively, 58 percent and 72 percent below the German average. Bear in mind here that the per capita footprint of Germany is already less than half of that of the USA. Studies at Cornell University and MIT found that the per capita ecological footprint of the suburban ecovillage at Ithaca, NY, was more than 40 percent lower than the national average. Jonathan Dawson cites three major reasons for these numbers. First is communality, or high levels of sharing and holding possessions in common. Second is the fact that ecovillages grow much of their own food and eat with the seasons, thereby reducing their food miles. Third, to the extent that ecovillages generate internal employment, they reduce their transport footprint (Dawson 2006/7: 1–2). Thus, at the local and individual level, ecovillages are highly effective in terms of reducing material through-put. Moreover, if ecovillage living offers a sense of meaning, satisfaction and personal integrity, then the movement is also effective on a subjective level. At the larger level of social discourse and received wisdom, their positive example helps to disentangle the good life from resource intensity while simultaneously demonstrating the practical viability of a holistic worldview.

While ecovillages may show that another world is possible on a very small scale, the question remains: can global systemic change come about through a network of communities committed to social and ecological sustainability? The short answer is that we don't know. There are good reasons to doubt that it can, yet also countervailing considerations to all of these good reasons. In the absence of more far-reaching forms of political engagement directed toward structural change, the ecovillage strategy of lifestyle politics is a doubtful one. Yet, as we have seen, much of the ecovillage movement is also working at that level. If ecovillages were isolated enclaves, we might also be dubious about their strategy. Yet, they have been globally linked since the formation of GEN and have also shown a tremendous commitment to education and outreach. So we must admit at least the possibility that the ecovillage movement could play an important role in the transition to a just and sustainable society.

In the present context, there are three other considerations that should make us pay attention to ecovillages. First is the dearth of compelling alternatives. There is at present no large-scale mass movement capable of adequately addressing the global problematique. And while elements of such a movement may be present, the ecovillage movement is already intersecting strongly with those elements. A strategy of prefiguring need not preclude engagement with electoral or protest politics. Second, the old leftist strategies of seizing state power have no place in the holistic worldview of the ecovillage movement. As Ted Trainer explains,

> We cannot expect to develop the sorts of communities that are required (for the transition to a just and sustainable world), with their great dependence on autonomous, skilled, conscientious, responsible and active citizens, via means that involve top-down control or authoritarian relations of any kind.
>
> (Trainer 2000: 277)

Third, and perhaps most important, if existing ways of living are not sustainable, then at some point they must change. Whether the impetus for change comes gradually as a consequence of the creeping ecological mega-crisis, or precipitously in the face of collapse of the petroleum economy, sweeping changes are inevitable. At that point, the viable alternatives already established on the ground will become enormously salient. This is precisely the rationale for prefiguring which, as political theorist Stephen Condit observes, represents "a causal engagement with the future which does not accept its determination by the prevailing social structures of the present" (Condit 2007: 24). A priori, there can be no way of knowing whether this strategy of prefiguring, of seeding a new society within the husk of the old, will be effective in the long run. Given the range of possibilities, it is at least worthy of genuine consideration.

Of course, the internal and external challenges facing the movement are colossal. If one takes seriously the systemic character of the global problematique, one can hardly avoid feeling overwhelmed by the immensity of the human predicament. And the ecovillage movement faces critical internal limitations. Because it is loosely organized and highly disparate in its membership and its approaches, it may not live up to its full potential as a global knowledge community. Many ecovillagers are, no doubt, simply "trying to build better circumstances for themselves, often ... in quite self-indulgent ways" (Trainer 2000: 277). In place of prefiguring, ecovillages "may settle for marginalization and reduce self-governance to mere self-gratification" (Condit 2007: 24). These are real dangers, and they should not be minimized. Nonetheless, because the ecovillage movement represents a global knowledge community giving practical expression to a holistic worldview, it offers a powerful counterpoint to modernity in ideational and material terms.

The ecovillage movement's commitment to *living* a holistic worldview makes it a unique kind of knowledge community, one that is grounded in individual empowerment, cooperative relationships, virtuous cycles and global engagement. No doubt, there are other examples of knowledge communities rooted in pragmatic holism; if the underlying significance of the global problematique in terms of consciousnesss is its challenge to modernity's atomistic worldview, then surely there must be. The participatory development movement comes to mind as one possibility, and perhaps ecovillages can be understood one strand of that multifarious movement. A key contribution of the ecovillage movement is its power of example. It has become commonplace to observe that current human systems, particularly those in the affluent North, are unsustainable. Yet, that recognition is rarely given its full weight: if they are not sustainable, then they will cease. The only questions are when and how. In that light, even if its seeds are sparsely sown, the pragmatic holism of the ecovillage movement takes on a different hue.

Note

1 For a basic explication of Gaia theory, see Lovelock 1979 and Margulis 1998.

References

Bang, J. (2005) *Ecovillages: A Practical Guide to Sustainable Communities*, Boston, MA: New Society Publishers.

Condit, S. (2007) "Practical Millenarianism: Norms of Anarchism in the 21st Century," Online. Available at www.joensuu.fi/kvl/pdf/philosophical_anarchism.pdf (p. 24).

Dawson, J. (2004) "Wholesome Living," *Resurgence*, 225 (July/August).

——(2006) *Ecovillages: New Frontiers for Sustainability*, Totnes, UK: Green Books.

——(2006/7) "Ecovillages Achieve Lowest-ever Ecological Footprint Results," *Global Ecovillage Network-Europe News* (Winter): 1–2.

Fotopoulos, T. (2000) "Limitations of Life-Style Strategies: The Ecovillage Movement Is Not the Way Toward a New Democratic Society," *Democracy and Nature*, 6(2): 287–308.

Gaia Education, "Ecovillage Design Education." Online. Available at www.gaiaeducation.org

GEN (Global Ecovillage Network). Available at www.gen.ecovillage.org

——(2004) "Quadrennial Report of the Global Ecovillage Network, 2004." Online. Available at http://ecovillage.org/gen/activities/un_ecosoc/ecosoc_index.html

Haas, E. (1983) "Words Can Hurt You: Or, Who Said What to Whom About Regimes?" in Stephen Krasner (ed.) *International Regimes*, Ithaca, NY: Cornell University Press.

Havel, V. (1997) *The Art of the Impossible: Politics as Morality in Practice*, translated by Paul Wilson, New York: Alfred A. Knopf.

Holmgren, D. (2002) *Permaculture: Principles and Pathways Beyond Sustainability*, Victoria, Australia: Holmgren Design Services.

Holmgren, D. and Mollison, B. (1978) *Permaculture One*, North Sydney, NSW: Transworld.

Jackson, H. and Svensson, K. (2002) *Ecovillage Living: Restoring the Earth and Her People*, Totnes, UK: Green Books.

Litfin, K. (2005) "Gaia Theory: Intimations for Global Politics," in Peter Dauvergne (ed.) *Handbook of Global Environmental Politics*, Cheltenham, UK: Edward Elgar, 502–17.

——(2003) "Towards an Integral Perspective on World Politics: Secularism, Sovereignty and the Challenge of Global Ecology," *Millennium: Journal of International Studies*, 32(1): 29–56.

Lovelock, J. (1979) *Gaia: A New Look at Life on Earth*, Oxford: Oxford University Press.

Luhmann, N. (1990) "The Autopoiesis of Social Systems," in *Essays on Self-Reference*, New York: Columbia University Press.

Margulis, L. (1998) *The Symbiotic Planet*, London: Weidenfeld and Nicolson.

Mitchell, L. (2005) "Eco-Village Is 'Model for Us All'," BBC News Online, July 5. http://news.bbc.co.uk/1/low/uk/4654077.stm

Mollison, B. (1988) *Permaculture: A Designers' Manual*, Tyalgum, NSW: Tagari Publications.

Princen, T., Maniates, M., and Conca, K. (eds.) (2002) *Confronting Consumption*, Cambridge, MA: MIT Press.

Ross Jackson, J. T. (2000) *We ARE Doing It: Building and Ecovillage Future*, San Francisco, CA: Robert D. Reed Publishers.

Snyder, P. (2006) "Living and Learning Centers." Online. Available at http://gen.ecovillage.org/activities/living-learning/snydernew.php

Trainer, T. (2000) "Where Are We, Where Do We Want To Be, How Do We Get Here?" *Democracy and Nature*, 6(2): 267–86.

Part III
From the global to the local

8 Water for all!

The phenomenal rise of transnational knowledge and policy networks[1]

Michael Goldman

How are the ideas and expertise that motivate global policy campaigns created? How are they debated and disseminated, and how do they contribute to policy change? This chapter follows the case of one global campaign, "Water for All," a major component of the UN Millennium Development Goals of providing safe water and sanitation to those who go without—estimated to be approximately 40 percent of the world's population. This campaign is remarkable in that its incarnation was only in the mid-1990s, and yet within a few years, a "global consensus" was formed as to what the best policy would be, and it has resulted in an abrupt sea-change in the way public supplies of water are delivered in major cities in the global South. The main actors of this, and many other recently contrived global policies, are working within transnational policy networks that, although quite new, are becoming quite effective and powerful. This chapter focuses on these networks in order to understand from where they derive their authority and power. The case of "Water for All" sheds light onto the larger trend of the production of, and reliance on, a new breed of "global experts" and their transnational networks, to define, interpret, and solve what are being unproblematically referred to as our "global problems."

On the drive from the Johannesburg airport to the wealthy white suburb of Sandton—host to the 2002 World Summit on Sustainable Development (WSSD)—colorful billboards suspended above the airport freeway depicted Black township boys splashing joyfully under a waterfall of clear blue water.[2] These ads cajoled summit delegates to taste and enjoy the city's tap water, boasting that it was as pure and clean as bottled water. But as the World Summit progressed, it became clear to me that these ads were not selling the idea of safe potable water to European delegates anxious about drinking water in the Third World, as much as they were selling South Africa's water systems to interested European bidders in town.

At the time of the 2002 World Summit, South Africa was reeling from a deadly cholera outbreak that erupted after government-enforced water and electricity cut-offs. At the outset of the epidemic, which infected more than 140,000 people, the government cut off the previously free water supply to 1,000 people in the rural KwaZulu Natal, for lack of a $7 reconnection fee. South

Africa has an ongoing water supply problem, as is evidenced by the 43,000 children who die annually from diarrhea, a disease epidemic in areas with limited water and sanitation services. The Wits University Municipal Services Project[3] conducted a national study in 2001 that identified more than 10 million out of South Africa's 44 million residents who had experienced water and electricity cut-offs. (These figures were disputed by South Africa's water ministry.) Epidemiologists interviewed by the study's authors say that these cut-offs were the catalysts of the national cholera crisis (Bond 2003; 2004).

These changes epitomized the politics of the World Summit agenda. As a follow-up to the momentous Rio Earth Summit in 1992, the mission of the Johannesburg World Summit was to assess the accomplishments and failures of the past 10 years and to agree upon a program for the future. The agenda emphasized five basic issues: water, energy, health, agriculture, and biodiversity. Even though a series of preparatory committee meetings was held in sites around the world (e.g. Jakarta, New York) in an effort to get public feedback and participation from a wide array of diverse actors, the final WSSD document read much like a World Bank policy paper, and a wish-list for the world's largest service sector firms: *Water privatization is the best policy to tackle the global South's poverty and water-delivery problems.* That such a seemingly diverse set of actors should carve out a document that is so "consensual" and full of "common sense" to many sectors and professional classes around the world—from the International Chamber of Commerce to environmental NGOs to South Africa's ANC—should give us pause.

This trend of solving the problem of water scarcity with water privatization reflects a major shift in the global development industry. From the 1950s through the 1970s—the period of national development—economic objectives in the global South emphasized repatriation and nationalization of natural-resource-based sectors. But since the debt crisis of the 1980s, and the full-throttle imposition of structural adjustment by the World Bank and IMF, Southern states have been forced to sell off their public enterprises, including those that had successfully produced national wealth, widespread employment, and social stability. By the 1990s, under the neoliberal logic of privatization, even the most essential public-sector services, such as education, electricity, transport, public health, water and sanitation, were being put on the auction block (World Bank 2003c; Hall and de la Motte 2005). The shift is fairly recent and yet widespread; it has received the cooperation and consent of a broad base of professional class networks ranging from chambers of commerce to development and environment NGOs. In the case of water, at the 1992 Earth Summit in Rio, privatization was hardly discussed; yet, just 10 years later at the 2002 World Summit on Sustainable Development in Johannesburg, it was the main event. Why and how did it become *the* solution to the problem of water scarcity for the poor, and how did it become so pervasive so fast? Is there a global consensus on its merit?

Giving birth to the global network

This story of the rapid transformation of epistemic models and policies on water crisis worldwide can best be understood within the context of the growth of the World Bank and the expansive global institutional terrain in which it currently works. For starters, it is important to appreciate that the World Bank of the 1950s and 1960s did not focus on what we currently understand as development or poverty alleviation: in those days, without much fanfare or press, the Bank loaned relatively small amounts of capital to Southern governments to pay for Northern contractors to build up basic capital-intensive infrastructure such as railroads and power plants—sectors that remained undercapitalized by the original European investors (for European firms' resource extraction and capital accumulation) due to the Second World War and subsequent colonial retreats by European governments and businesses. At that time, most people had never heard of the World Bank, nor had they run into its projects or economic and political ideas. In its first 25 years of existence (1944–69), the World Bank was largely run out of Washington, DC by Wall Street bankers, staffed by former colonial officers, and viewed as prudent, conservative, and risk-averse by Wall Street (Goldman 2005). That all changed in the late 1960s. Turmoil in the global political economy, with the US economy floundering from the high costs of its protracted war in Indochina, collided with the concerns of large institutional investors of OPEC petrodollars, Eurodollars, and Japanese yens looking for value and hesitant to invest in the United States or in their own "over-valued" home markets (Block 1977; Helleiner 1994; Kapstein 1994).

Contributing to this historical rupture were post-independence Southern countries suffering from both a precipitous drop in economic investment from the North and an increase in mass movements demanding the basic rights and access to public goods that liberation promised. In 1968, a humiliated President Johnson removed his troubled secretary of defense Robert McNamara from office and selected him as the World Bank president, a highly contentious move, but one that eventually bore fruit for select corporate sectors in the North and the development industry worldwide. McNamara transformed the World Bank from a small, reticent, and prudent investor into a completely different animal. In the first 5 years of McNamara's tenure, the Bank financed more projects (760 versus 708) and loaned more money ($13.4 billion versus $10.7 billion) than it had during the previous 22 years *combined* (Shapley 1993; George and Sabelli 1994). Together with his new treasurer Eugene Rotberg, McNamara invented a secure and profitable arena for huge institutional investors through a unique brand of bonds—very large, multi-denominational "global" World Bank bonds (Institutional Investor 1988).

Not only did this move spur a market for global bonds, and flush sources for raising capital, but it also offered to large Northern investors a new vision of the global South (commonly known as the Third World): untapped and unvalorized natural resources that could potentially fuel a tremendous growth spurt of Northern industrial output and profit. At the time, the World Bank did not have a global reputation or presence; its mission was not to fight poverty, and it was not considered a global storehouse of data and expertise on developing countries. These were all accomplishments of the McNamara era that we take for granted today. McNamara had to sell the idea to his board of directors that it made perfect sense to catapult past its slow-growth, multi-million dollar budget to a multi-*billion* dollar one. He proposed a massive lending portfolio with economic and political guarantees that would be quite attractive to Northern investors because these guarantees would minimize risk and maximize control over the procurements of capital goods and services necessary to build the Bank's projects. For example, he helped package the idea of the "green revolution" as the best offense against the rising tide of "red revolutions" sweeping across the postcolonial South (Kapur et al. 1997; McMichael 2000). For investors, the green revolution offered an enormous market for Northern capital goods such as dam turbines, irrigation equipment, tractors, and chemical- and petroleum-based seeds, fertilizers, and pesticides. McNamara's Bank was instrumental in transforming an agro-industrialization corporate agenda from US and European food production into a global food system (Bonanno et al 1994; McMichael 2000). While Wall Street began to smack its collective lips at this new high-risk/high-reward investment approach, Northern governments and a new "development community" of anti-poverty/anti-famine advocates were intrigued by the idea of a multi-billion dollar investment campaign to fight the global "war on poverty." After all, the bloody war in Indochina raged on, the US economy shrunk and real and imagined revolutionary fervor in the South fueled Northern Cold-War angst. The *idea* of investing in development became compelling.

Ironically, it was the demand side of World Bank expansionism that required even greater ingenuity and infrastructure. Since none of the Bank's capital is loaned without substantial obligations or strings attached, the potential borrowers of the global South—already economically vulnerable and politically dubious of these neocolonial ventures—had to be carefully courted and cultivated. True to his reputation as one of the US's "best and the brightest" (Halberstam 1972)—brilliantly transforming the moribund Ford Motor Company and then the US government's military complex (the Pentagon)—McNamara introduced the ideology of "global expertise" by creating new production sites for data analysis on borrowing countries and training in the nascent analytic approach of World Bank-style development. The idea of "growth with redistribution" became the mantra coming from his highly respectable senior economists (e.g. Hollis Chenery); programmatically, this call translated into the promotion of capital-intensive megaprojects as the surest vehicle for catalyzing high economic growth and poverty reduction. He matched the Bank's new increases in projects and capital loaned with new training institutes promoting the green revolution and the development project *writ large*, enlisting parliamentarians, engineers, professionals, and large-scale farmers. The Bank fell into the business of training Third World elites, setting up agricultural institutes, and creating quasipublic agencies like the Electrical Generating Authority of Thailand (EGAT) to directly oversee, for example, the capitalization and transnationalization of power production. The Bank "cultivated champions" at every node along the development production line, from Wall Street investors to the professional class actors who collect and analyze data, design and implement projects, and regulate them as government civil servants.

Under McNamara's leadership (1968–81), the Bank increased its commitment to train its own staff, members of borrowing state agencies, staff of NGOs, academics, and employees of engineering firms whom the Bank would then hire for its projects. Starting out by training just a few hundred of the world's elites in its first few decades, by the late 1980s, the Bank's training center was preparing thousands of professionals annually, with more than 3,000 in the field of economic development alone (Kapur et al. 1997). In those days, the center was called the Economic Development Institute because development economics was its core curriculum, and the primary knowledge good the Bank could market. But by the late 1990s, and with a change in name to the World Bank Institute (WBI), those numbers dramatically increased, as did the sites for and topics covered by its trainings. In 2002 alone, the Bank delivered 560 "learning activities" to "more than 48,000 participants in 150 countries through collaboration with more than 400 partner institutions," broadening "its reach to include parliamentarians, policymakers, technical specialists, journalists, teachers, students, and civil society leaders, as well as World Bank staff" (World Bank 2002). Under a broad rubric of technical titles, these training programs teach the types of expertise required to generate, tailor, and manage the lending efforts of the Bank, and contribute to the production of green neoliberalism around the world. On the topic of water privatization, the WBI's Water Policy Capacity Building Program alone has trained more than 9,000 professionals from ninety countries between 1994 and 2001. Almost half of the participants of the program surveyed (by the Bank) said that WBI-sponsored activities led to reform of water management policy in their own countries (Pitman 2002: 10).

But back in the early 1980s, the McNamara era's massive increase in capital loans hit a wall. As Western firms and investors profited from this new expansive development regime, borrowing governments could not possibly manage the large dollar-based loans with their local-currency-based economies (Babb 2005). The rise of a global debt crisis forced the World Bank to reinvent itself. Instead of collapsing under the weight of its borrowers' debts and inability to pay back their loans, however, the Bank successfully repositioned itself as the global arbiter of debt, and produced the next development regime, structural adjustment, which, in spite of the worldwide debt crisis it helped to engender, only broadened and deepened Bank power. Under this new Bank regime, the professional-class development component continued with a renewed vigor, but now with an expanded focus on macro-economic policy and government restructuring. "Growth with redistribution" was replaced with a neoliberal agenda of "economics first" led by newly hired senior economist Anne Krueger. Southern professionals were mobilized to help the Bank more directly intervene into the daily workings of government as well as transform macroeconomic policymaking, such as setting daily currency values. By the late 1980s, as this regime morphed into a neoliberal one, and so too did the apparatuses available for professional classes in borrowing countries, especially for those professionals made more vulnerable by their downsized states and a more inequitable and transnationalized economy. In its neoliberalization, the Bank extended its scope and influence beyond its traditional clients of contractors and government agencies to an expansive "civil society," which it actively helps to cultivate, albeit working within the highly circumscribed boundaries of development capitalism.

In contrast to the conclusions of many scholars on the dispersion of neoliberal ideas and policies (e.g. Jessop 2002; Peck and Tickell 2002), we can see that neoliberalism did not just start in Thatcher's Britain and Reagan's United States, and eventually spread to "the rest." Neoliberalism was (and is being) made through these highly contentious North/South political-economic and epistemic relations. The most pernicious (or perhaps pure) neoliberal policies have been experimented with first in the Bank's most vulnerable borrowing countries before ever hitting the shores of the USA or Britain. (One recent example is the elimination of agricultural subsidies forced upon Southern African nations as preconditions to access to World Bank and IMF capital and debt renegotiations, which precipitated the 2002–3 famine, even while the USA and Western Europe refused to give up their $300 billion annual agricultural subsidies.)[4] One of the major instigators of these neoliberal dynamics has been the World Bank. But, as the next sections show, the Bank and its borrowers are not the only actors neoliberalizing; rather they are joined by a swathe of elite transnational actors, including service-sector corporations, chambers of commerce, and development consultants and nongovernmental organizations. In the case of water, they are collectively promoting a "pro-poor" water agenda premised on the idea of inter-sectoral privatization (e.g. bundling services such as cable and telephone, water and electricity).

Networking for a new agenda on water

In 1990, fewer than 50 million people received their water from private water companies, and most water customers were in Europe and the United States. Just 10 years later, more than 460 million people were dependent upon a few global water firms for their water supplies, and the high growth areas were Africa, Asia, and Latin America. Industry analysts predicted that by 2015, nearly 1.25 billion people would be buying their water from Northern-based water firms (Shrybman 2002).[5] These days, a "highly indebted poor country" cannot borrow capital from the World Bank or IMF without a domestic water privatization policy as a precondition. The world's largest firms, French-based Suez and Vivendi (now Veolia Water), control about 70 percent of the global private water markets, and in the mid-2003 global economic downturn, competitors were being bought out and the market was becoming even more concentrated. Industry analysts predict that private water will soon be a capitalized market as precious, and as war-provoking, as oil (Global Water Report 1996; Barlow and Clarke 2002; Grusky 2002; International Consortium of Investigative Journalists 2002; Shrybman 2002; Public Citizen 2005). Dealing in water has become one of the most lucrative markets for transnational capital investors. According to one water analyst, "the global market for municipal and industrial water and sewerage goods and services is currently estimated to be in the region of US$200bn–$400bn per annum" (Owen 2001).

Spaces and flows of the new water discourse

Below is an excerpt from a (London) *Financial Times* article highlighting a report on water scarcity, released at a major global water conference by an eminent panel of experts.[6] "Poor Countries 'Must Raise Water Prices': World Commission Warning on Shortages of Vital Resources," reads the headline. The journalist reports:

> Prices paid by water consumers in developing countries must rise substantially to avoid life threatening shortages and environmental damage, according to an international report published yesterday.
>
> The report by the World Commission on Water, supported by the World Bank and the United Nations, calls for radical changes in the way in which water services are subsidized in some of the world's poorest and most disadvantaged regions.
>
> It says annual investment in water facilities need to more than double from $70bn–$80bn to $180bn to meet rising demand and reduce the numbers without clean water—1bn—and without sanitation—3bn—to just 330m by 2025.
>
> Governments unable to finance this huge investment must encourage the private sector—which provides less than five per cent of urban water to consumers in developing countries—to fill the gap. The single most effective stimulus for private sector investment would be to adopt "full cost pricing of water use and services" says the commission. ...
>
> [The report] warns: "Without full cost pricing the present vicious cycle of waste, inefficiency and lack of service for the poor will continue." Private parties also "will not invest unless they can be assured of a reasonable return on their investments. ...
>
> (*Financial Times* 2000)

The authors of the much-cited report to which this article refers, "A Water Secure World: Vision for Water, Life and the Environment,"[7] comprise an impressive list of the world's policy elites, collected together as an eminent panel of experts called the World Commission on Water for the 21st Century (WCW). Their message and "relational biographies" reveal an important story about these lofty goals of finding global solutions to a global water crisis (Dezalay and Garth 2002).

Formed in 1998, the World Commission on Water for the 21st Century has included former heads of state such as Mikhail Gorbachev of the USSR, Fidel Ramos of the Philippines, Ketumile Masire of Botswana, and Ingvar Carlsson of Sweden. It also includes former and current senior World Bank officials such as Robert McNamara (now co-chair of the Global Coalition for Africa), Mohamed El-Ashry, who is the CEO of the Bank's Global Environmental Facility, Enrique Iglesias (president of the Inter-American Development Bank), former World Bank vice president Wilfried Thalwitz, and Ismail Serageldin, who is both a senior World Bank environmental official and the WCW chair. Corporate leaders play an equally prominent role: also on the panel is Jerome Monod, chairman of the board of Suez, one of the world's largest water companies; and Maurice Strong, former CEO of Petro-Canada (the national oil company), Ontario Hydro, and other large natural resource and power firms, chair of the Earth Council, and a frequent commissioner and special envoy for the United Nations. From the foundation, NGO, and state sectors come dignitaries such as the president of the World Conservation Union (IUCN), Yolanda Kakabadse, president of the Rockefeller Foundation, Gordon Conway, former chair of the World Commission on Dams and former South African minister of water affairs, Kader Asmal, and the former president of Canada's foreign aid agency (CIDA) and current member of the Population Council, Margaret Catley-Carlson.

Well connected heads of major transnational research and policy institutes, most of which share the World Bank and the bilateral aid agencies of the North as an important source of funding, fill out the ranks.[8]

These recognizable names in both the business and development worlds have come together to form a new transnational policy network on water. This particular commission was started and is funded by another important actor in the network, namely the World Water Council (WWC).[9] The World Water Council, established in 1996, is a self-described "international water policy think tank" which aims to provide policymakers with up-to-date research and advice on global water issues. It is sponsored by UN and World Bank agencies, and is governed by board members hailing from the World Bank, CIDA, the United Nations Development Program, IUCN, Suez and other European water firms, and water-related professional associations. A 300-member group, the World Water Council played a pivotal role in organizing the second World Water Forum in The Hague, the third World Water Forum in Kyoto, and the fourth in Mexico City. It also produced the well circulated "World Water Vision" report quoted above with its unambiguous water privatization agenda for the future—one that mimics as well as extends the World Bank's policy position and economic analysis on water reform.[10]

Another important player in the transnational policy network on water is the World Business Council for Sustainable Development, or WBCSD.[11] Representing a coalition of 160 transnational corporations, the WBCSD is made up of some of the world's largest corporations involved in the business of water, energy, and waste management.[12] In August 2002, the WBCSD released an influential report entitled, "Water for the Poor," with a battle cry of "No Water, No Sustainable Development!" The report strongly endorses (as well as puts its own spin on) the Bonn Action Plan, a plan developed during the "multi-stakeholder" International Conference on Freshwater held in Bonn, Germany, in December 2001. In its "Water for the Poor" report, the World Business Council's main policy prescriptions reflect a political rationality that weaves together the needs of corporations and public institutions with those of the poor. From its perspective,

> Providing water services to the poor presents a business opportunity. New pipes, pumps, measurement and monitoring devices, and billing and record keeping systems will be required to modernize and expand water infrastructure. Industry not directly related to the provision of water services will be able to enter new markets because water for production, and to sustain a productive workforce, will be available. Thus this program has the possibility of creating huge employment and sales opportunities for large and small businesses alike.
> (World Business Council for Sustainable Development 2002: 9)

In short, everyone wins—the firms that join into partnerships with the global development community and governments to bring water to the poor, and those who are at the receiving end of the water pipeline. This is the same perspective the World Bank promotes in its professional training seminars and policy work.

Representatives of states, international financial institutions, development agencies, think tanks, and firms are not the only actors in the new and expanding transnational water policy network. The oldest and most prominent water NGO to get involved is WaterAid of Great Britain. WaterAid joins the World Bank and UN agencies in calling for "new millennium development goals" of halving the proportion of people without access to water and sanitation in the world by 2015.[13] WaterAid also endorses the increased participation of NGOs, civil society groups, and transnational water companies in water reform:

> One solution to this crisis is to call in the private sector. The idea is that more actors (not just governments) would enter the sector and deliver the services. In an environment of relatively free markets, the private sector can deliver not only investments, but also the reforms and efficiencies that are urgently needed in water and sanitation service delivery.[14]

In other words, the world's most influential water NGO has embraced the World Bank's and IMF's clarion call for water privatization as the most sensible way to avoid catastrophe.[15] Moreover, WaterAid also endorses the Bank's and IMF's controversial policy of using water privatization as a pre-condition for access to desperately needed capital and debt relief. That is, the latest structural adjustment policy for highly indebted countries—Poverty Reduction Support Credits (PRSC, which complements the Bank's larger program of poverty reduction strategies, or PRSP)—has water privatization commitments as one prevalent feature of its conditionalities for access to loans for "poverty reduction" and debt relief. On this topic, WaterAid writes:

> WaterAid has joined with other civil society groups in engaging with the PRSP program in some of the countries we work in to ensure that access to water and sanitation remains a priority in the PRSP. ... The PRSPs *present the clearest and most important opportunity* for translating these policies into plans that will be prioritized, resourced, implemented and monitored.[16]

The British public has its intimate connection with WaterAid, in the form of monthly pleas for charitable contributions for "pro-poor" water projects in the South, coming into everyone's home via the monthly water bill. WaterAid also has routine and high-profile promotional fundraisers that the British read in their major newspapers. Formed in 1981, it is one of the earliest and largest advocates for "water for all." WaterAid raises money from corporate and individual donations and works in fifteen countries in Africa and Asia helping to deliver water to the poor. In contrast to many other high-profile development NGOs, however, WaterAid was started by large water corporations, and is still supported heavily by them, along with individual donations and government support (from the UK and the European Union).[17] Almost every one of its trustees works or has worked for a major water firm: Vic Cocker is the retired CEO of Severn Trent, Hugh Speed is the vice president of Suez, David Luffrum and John Sexton have been directors at Thames Water, Stuart Derwent is from Southern Water, and Colin Skellet is the chair of Wessex Water. WaterAid is among the best networked of the water-related NGOs, and ran a number of panels at the World Water Forum in Kyoto, including one that tellingly asked, "How will the poor become *customers*?", which is precisely the question (and answer) the World Bank and the largest water firms have been pushing the past few years. WaterAid responds to the question with its own "successful" case studies on private sector participation and "the role of civil society in promoting a pro-poor agenda."[18]

Tracing the discursive genealogies and relational biographies of dominant global policy forums on water reveals the enormous role the World Bank has played in constituting and supporting these networks and their agendas.[19] Three of the highest-profile transnational water policy network actors were born from World Bank support: the Global Water Partnership, the World

Water Council, and the World Commission on Water for the 21st Century. All are key production nodes for transnational water conferences, training seminars, policy papers, and ultimately, a highly mobile set of global experts on water that comprise the leadership and establish the guiding principles of the new water reform movement. The Bank has also helped start and sustain the tri-annual World Water Forums,[20] and funded the International Symposium on Water,[21] the Global Panel on Financing Water Infrastructure,[22] the Water Media Network,[23] Water Utility Partnership-Africa,[24] and a variety of other high-level networks which bring together state, private sector, NGO, and corporate officials by region, theme, and agenda. As noted earlier, on water reform alone, the Bank has trained more than 9,000 professionals from ninety countries between 1994 and 2001 (Pitman 2002).

The World Bank and these key nodes in the global water policy network are educating journalists, development consultants, state officials, and the world at large on the necessity for water policy reform.[25] In 1998–99, Water-Aid, Vivendi, the World Bank, and the International Chamber of Commerce's Business Partners for Development organized a series of influential meetings on water and sanitation[26] in which they invoked the reports and arguments produced by these networks to make the case that these TPNs reflect widespread agreement on how to solve the crisis of water scarcity. At high-level meetings, forums, and policy-generating conferences throughout Europe, Asia, Latin America, and Africa, the topic of water reform moves forward, creating the appearance of worldwide consensus. Consequently, these uniquely situated and well funded transnational water policy networks have effectively filled the spaces and saturated the marketplace of ideas on water policy in global civil society. Who else can afford to attend global forums, speak up with reliable global data, and sit at these roundtables on water, but their own members? Indeed, a well known insider, the journalist John Roberts of one of the top industry newsletters, *Platts Global Water Report*, publicly scolded these network actors for considering themselves the leaders of a "global water community" (Roberts 2002). At the 4th International Symposium on Water, Roberts criticized symposium attendees for being too narrowly doctrinaire, and for appearing to the media as ideological advocates of water privatization, rather than as neutral sponsors of open dialogues on global water policy reform. Even to an insider, the self-referential work seemed a bit too gratuitous.

Creating a global consensus

Although the statements quoted above come from a seemingly diverse variety of interests and institutional standpoints—NGOs, transnational corporations, eminent experts, policy analysts from different regions of the world—their positions on global water policy reform, the strength of their voice, and their relational biographies in transnational policy networks (TPNs) have converged to create what they describe as a "global consensus" on water. The

TPN argument begins with the compelling "facts" that the global water commons is being threatened and the world's poor are suffering the most, due to their lack of access to water and their inability to become productive contributors to society in its absence. The second step has been to construct a narrow historical time frame and simple political landscape that governments inhabit. According to their analysis, the main actors causing the degradation of water service systems and depletion of the global water commons are inefficient and politicized (i.e. monopolistic and corrupt) governments, whose fatal flaw is to treat water *as if* it were a free natural resource. Governments' failure to price water properly so as to reflect its *true* cost has inculcated a culture of wastefulness amongst the world's populations, and as a result, water has become scarce. (As Peter Spillet, senior executive for Thames Water, phrased it, without a hint of irony, "clearly people do not understand the value of water and they expect it to fall from the sky and not cost anything") (Carty 2002). Yet because it is scarce, it has now become an arena that has begun to interest "value-seeking" corporations. According to this same Thames executive, "There is a huge growth potential [in privatizing water] ... We think there will be wars fought over water in the future. It is a limited precious resource ... So it's a very viable place to put your money" (Carty 2002).

To sum up, the majority of the world's water consumers supposedly lack access because of this history of government indifference and failure to charge people adequately for its use.[27] Indeed, the poor are in part impoverished *because of* this irresponsible government behavior. According to the political rationality of the transnational water policy network, this causal argument is applicable throughout the ailing South. To solve these problems, governments need—*at the very least*—to adopt international accounting methods for water services, submit to grading by international credit agencies, and, most important of all, put a market price on water. These standards should steer governments to invite experienced Northern private water companies, since the private sector is assumed to be more efficient, more capable of increasing water supplies, and more likely to improve conservation. This argument is one that has evolved since 1996, and has been contrived through the hard work of the vast transnational policy network of actors that present themselves, in this self-referential and inter-textual narrative, as neutral global-problem solvers trying to reverse water scarcity trends.

The major global water policy event of 2002, the World Summit on Sustainable Development in Johannesburg, reflected the realization of this global consensus, the product of 6 years' worth of transnational networking.[28] Although a number of sustainable development issues were on the agenda at the WSSD—including the famine in southern Africa, the HIV/AIDs crisis, and sustainable forestry and mining issues—the main working agenda was water privatization. Indeed, the Summit's main media event was the christening of the glamorous corporate- and UN-sponsored WaterDome. This gala spectacle was hosted by Nelson Mandela and the Prince of Orange, surrounded by the paparazzi and the global "water lords" identified above, and celebrated in ostentatious splendor the *public-private partnership* (PPP) agenda of the water lobby.[29] The water agenda aired at the WaterDome and the WSSD was identical to the one developed by the transnational water policy network, from the global diagnosis of a "world water crisis for the poor," to the solutions offered of greater efficiency in water service provision, better cost recovery, and a shift from public sector to private sector providers through "partnerships." The strength of this consensus can also be seen in the seemingly unrelated launching of the African Union as well as its bold report on the New Economic Program for African Development (Nepad), both of which embrace and echo the TPNs' precise analysis and plan of action for water. Throughout the continent, Africans are feeling the repercussions of these "global" mandates.

Imposing reforms

The most direct way the network's idioms, technologies, and "water action plans" get translated into action in borrowing countries is, of course, through the imposition of conditionalities on World Bank and IMF loans. In fact, almost all of the recent public utility privatization deals (outside of Western Europe and the United States) have occurred because of active Bank/IMF participation.[30] That participation comes in the form of a threat, since every government official knows that the Bank/IMF capital spigots can always be shut off for those governments refusing to conform to their loan conditions.[31] As overwhelming debt burdens have put tremendous pressure on borrowing-country governments and created dire social conditions in their countries (reflected in the 2002–3 famine in southern Africa), and as populist movements have demanded that their governments stop servicing these odious and unjust debts, the Bank and IMF are using the carrot of debt relief to foist water policy reform on borrowing-country governments.[32] In 2001, for example, all eleven of the World Bank's water and sanitation loans carried conditionalities that required borrowing governments to either privatize these services or dramatically increase cost recovery from providing them. As the Bank and IMF often give indebted countries a very short time period in which to construct a "viable" water action plan of their own that can meet these institutions' rarefied requirements, the transnational water policy network's expertise and action plans are the ones most likely to get invoked by borrowers to satisfy the Bank and IMF's pressure for water policy reform.

Beyond loans specifically targeting water and sanitation services, the Bank also imposes stringent conditions on its large structural adjustment loans, the Poverty Reduction Support Credits. The selling-off of state owned enterprises, utilities, and public services (including water and sanitation) has become a prerequisite for continued access to Bank and IMF loans (Grusky 2002).[33] In 2000 alone, the governments of Benin, Honduras, Nicaragua,

Niger, Panama, Rwanda, São Tomé and Principe, Senegal, Tanzania, and Yemen agreed to conditions placed on IMF Poverty Reduction and Growth Facility loans before receiving much-needed capital and/or debt reorganization. These loans and debt renegotiations had water privatization and cost recovery as key conditions. The IMF's Emergency Post-Conflict Policy Loan to Guinea-Bissau, and Tanzania's acceptance of its Poverty Reduction loan, were predicated on privatization of public water services. Indeed, in order for most "Highly Indebted Poor Countries" (or HIPCs, as the Bank refers to them) to receive debt relief, it has been necessary to lease their water services to private—and invariably Northern—firms.[34]

At the end of 2001, the Bank had outstanding loan commitments in water-related sectors of nearly $20 billion (World Bank 2002). Most of the Bank's water service loans have started out with cost-recovery mandates, only to be ratcheted up to partial or full privatization when governments prove themselves unable to comply with the Bank's requirements for cost recovery, and when few communities are willing or able to afford the associated price increases (Grusky 2002; World Bank 2002). Without compliance, the public sector choice is judged as inadequate, and private alternatives are introduced. By 2002, most of the Bank's cost-recovery agreements had led to some form of privatization, and were presented as a bail-out of sorts by foreign firms "willing to help" indebted and floundering public agencies meet World Bank- and IMF-set targets. In effect, corporations are placed in the role of charitable trusts that are offering a helping hand, technology transfer, and expertise where it is needed the most.

If, however, we shift the analytical frame and see the problem in terms of the two-decade-long process of structural adjustment in which many Southern borrowers have been spending much more on interest repayments to the World Bank and the IMF than on public infrastructure and basic services, then the way in which we judge the roots of ineffectual public service changes. If the "global community" of actors articulating the rationality of privatization comprises the same actors who pressured states to dramatically reduce spending on public infrastructure and services—including the water sector— then the network's "at-a-distance" objective standpoint becomes subject to question.

Indeed, there is good reason to critically question the "global water scarcity" and "crisis" discourses of the transnational water policy network, and to examine the very real political-economic interests that lie behind it. First, as noted above, these practices are a product of a particular agenda of the IFIs and the global water industry and have not arisen as the direct result of demands made by water-deprived poor communities. (This is not to deny, of course, that 40 percent of the world's population lacks access to clean water and sanitation.) But this particular policy initiative has come "from above" and is part of the *green-neoliberal* capitalist transformation being promulgated by the IFIs and their development partners. Since 1990, the World Bank has not only helped finance the birth of these transnational policy networks, but has also financed the widespread privatization of other public utilities, industries, and goods (Goldman 2005). In the realm of water alone, the World Bank awarded 276 water supply loans between 1990 and 2002, one third of which require the borrowing country to privatize some aspect of its water operations in order to receive these funds.[35] Indeed, the number of loans requiring privatization as a precondition has tripled since 1996 (International Consortium of Investigative Journalists 2002: 16). Of the 193 structural adjustment loans approved between 1996 and 1999, nearly 60 percent required privatization as a condition.

In Africa, there has been a marked trend toward privatization. Up until 1997, privatization of water services had occurred in only a few West African countries, but in 1999 the number of contracts with private firms rose sharply. By May 2002, more than eighteen water privatization contracts had been signed between European firms and African governments, five in South Africa alone, with eight more countries in the process of negotiation. Vivendi (now Veolia Water, France), Saur (France), Biwater (England), Aguas de Portugal, and Northumbrian Water (England), are the most frequent lead companies; the contracts' duration ranges from 5 years to 50 years, and sometimes combines control over both electricity and water. By 2002, more than 460 million people worldwide were purchasing their drinking water from European-based companies. The six largest companies work in more than fifty-six countries, and their revenues have grown dramatically between the mid-1990s and 2002 (Global Water Report 1996; Barlow and Clarke 2002; Grusky 2002; International Consortium of Investigative Journalists 2002; Shrybman 2002). In sum, this remarkable shift from "public" to "private" serves a particular set of economic interests, with the world's largest firms and dispersed comprador classes eager to be part of this new wave of development capital investment.

Cracks in the pipes

Amidst the recent wave of privatization, two main actors are balking: firms and consumers (Vidal 2006). In February 2002, John Talbot, the chief executive of Saur International, the world's fourth largest water company, spoke before a World Bank audience, arguing that the needs of the Bank's clients are so great that although extending water to all made good sense in terms of "sustainable development," he had to ask whether this "is [a] good and attractive business."[36] Cost recovery from the poor majority is not feasible, Talbot suggested, and the private sector may not be the place to tap for investments in these sectors. In his words, it was "simply unrealistic" to believe "that *any* business must be *good* business and that the private sector has unlimited funds ... The scale of the need far out-reaches the financial and risk taking capacities of the private sector." As a result, subsidies and soft loans would be necessary to make the endeavor worthwhile. "Even Europe and U.S. subsidize services," Talbot coyly noted. "If [subsidization] does not happen, the international water companies will end up being forced to stay at home."[37] Talbot's proposed solution is particularly ironic because it turns dominant logic on its head: rather than provide subsidies to consumers (which many actors in the network believe is wastefully wrong), the World Bank and other development funders should provide government subsidies, soft loans, and guarantees *directly to private firms* that know how to use them most efficiently and prosperously.

To wriggle out of their existing contractual (and ethical) commitments to provide water for all, water service companies are redefining the language in their legal contracts. For instance, in Suez's contract with the city of La Paz, Bolivia to connect the major shanty town of El Alto to the water system, Suez argued that "connection" would no longer mean a "piped connection" but "access to a standpipe or tanker"—precisely the condition that CEOs and elite transnational policy networks once called deplorable under public regimes.[38] Water companies are also demanding that poor communities dedicate free labor to help build the supply system in exchange for water supply. In essence, these firms are creating a non-monetary barter system (which rests on self-exploitation by the poor with few options) so that they can live up to their agreements and shore up their profit rates.

In Ghana, privatization ended abruptly when the World Bank withdrew funding because of public outcries about corruption on the part of the parent company, Enron. In Gambia, Guinea, Kenya, Mozambique, South Africa (Fort Beaufort), and Zimbabwe, either the government or the water company pulled out amidst controversies raised by mobilized and angry communities. In some places, firms have withdrawn because they were unable to make their expected profits without substantially changing the rules or interpretation of the contract. The response by poor "customers" has been a vociferous refusal to accept dramatic increases in price and no improvement in service, pressing elected officials to demand equitable service and lower prices from foreign firms. Tellingly, in Grenoble, France (the home of Suez, the firm that promises to bring Africa its "European services"), the people of Grenoble kicked out the Suez subsidiary, Lyonnaise des Eaux, for gross violations of over-charging, theft and corruption in its water and sewage services (Lobina 2000; Barlow and Clarke 2002). The irony of this event, of course, is not lost on Ghanaian water consumers. It is the flip side to the neocolonial discourse that deems corruption, theft, and collusion as attributes of Third World public sectors, and not of France or French firms. It flies in the face of the old European tune of good Western "conduct" and "governance" that the World Bank and its transnational policy networks sing to non-Western borrowers.

In 2002, a controversial lawsuit was filed with the World Bank-run International Centre for Settlement of Investment Disputes (ICSID) by the California-based Bechtel corporation. Throughout the month of April 2000, tens of thousands of Bolivians gathered in the streets of Cochabamba to reject the water privatization policy of the government negotiated by the Bank, and its sell-out to Bechtel. After 8 days of continuous protest, the local government relented, repealed the contract, and expelled a Dutch subsidiary of the US company. In February 2002, Bechtel filed a $25 million lawsuit with ICSID against Bolivia for the loss of future profits. "We could use that money," reported a Bolivian community leader Oscar Olivera speaking in Johannesburg at a World Summit forum, "to pay 25,000 teachers or to build 120,000 water-gathering structures in Cochabamba. Instead, we must hire lawyers and fight a company whose annual revenues are $14 billion, or double Bolivia's gross national product." Olivera continued: "The problem is that the World Bank, who supported the privatization deal in Bolivia, is now also the judge of this case. And to whom is the Bank accountable?"[39] As the ICSID is under the auspices of the World Bank and is the legal arbiter of disputes for the Bank's aid and loan agreements, it has become the preferred site for arbitration by large multinational firms filing suits against Bank borrowers.[40]

The motive for these protests and contract nullifications is the steep rise of water prices for the poor. For poor urban and rural households, water fees now consume a substantial percentage of household income, sometimes as much as one third. In Cochabamba, the cost of water came to equal one fourth of a typical family's income after the Bechtel subsidiary increased its prices to reflect water's "true cost."[41] For some groups, the price of water spiked more than 200 percent (Laurie and Crespo 2003). Bechtel also insisted on charging communities for their consumption of water from people's own handmade rain-catchment systems, the pre-existing water conservation technologies that pre-date unreliable government taps. It best exemplified the attack on enduring local ecological practices and fundamental community rights, and produced the rally cry that Bechtel was even charging the poor for their use of the rain (Finnegan 2002).

In the Black townships of Johannesburg, South Africa, where most water consumers are under- or unemployed, the price of water rose over 50 percent after the public water system was privatized. These township communities have experienced a proportionally greater price hike than that experienced by middle-class consumers in neighboring white suburbs, and by large industrial and mining firms (Bond 2003), which critics called the *neoliberalization of apartheid*. In Guinea, water prices rose more than five-fold after privatization, resulting in a steep drop in bill collections and a steep rise in inactive connections. By 2006, the "Water for All" campaign all but collapsed from social movement pressure: 80 percent of the privatization projects in Africa had either been nullified or were under serious renegotiation; throughout South Asia, not a single private contract had led to an extension of water service to poor communities; and throughout Africa and Asia between 1997 and 2005, only 600,000 new water connections were built under these private contracts.[42] The UN Millennium Development Goal of supplying water to hundreds of millions of deprived people had failed. Instead, a number of significant political regime changes had occurred due to mass-based mobilizations and democratic elections, especially throughout Latin America, based on campaigns that were explicitly anti-World Bank, IMF, and resource privatization.[43] In the face of this enormous wave of discontent, the authority and expertise of the transnational policy networks were temporarily muted.

Conclusion: destabilizing the network

In today's dominant discourse, the distinction between public and private is assumed to be sharp and clear, such that one can make the sweeping generalization that the world's past and present water problems are due to the public sector. Yet even the most conventional historical readings of the world's largest water projects—e.g. the Hoover Dam, Suez Canal, Indus river waters projects—reveal that this distinction is a specious one, and that in fact, the public–private distinction in practice has always been blurred. Most of the world's largest water projects have been joint public–private ventures in which states have typically been the lead investors and movers behind them, while private capitalist firms have done the infrastructural and contract work, and received most of the benefits they provide. Whether they are feeding industrial farming, mining, or energy production, most grand water schemes have had highly subsidized state support in order that a minority elite could profit and often become an enriched class of their own (Worster 1985; Cronon 1991; McCully 1996; Scott 1998). In some cases, the same actors who are generating and awarding the contracts in their roles as state officials are also benefiting from these decisions in their roles as goods and services providers, investors, or landowners. So, why is the "public" always presented as corrupt and inefficient when discussing governance in the global South?

Under colonial rule, vast amounts of valuable "public" natural resources (including water, watersheds, and river systems) were controlled by "private" trading companies awarded contracts by "public" European royalty and imperial states. Zambia, for example, was colonized by the British South Africa Company, a private multinational corporation led by Cecil Rhodes (Ferguson and Gupta 2002: 992). Today, Zambia along with many other African nations are ruled "in significant part, by transnational organizations that are not in themselves governments, but work together with powerful First World states within a global system of nation-states that Frederick Cooper has characterized as 'internationalized imperialism'" (Ferguson and Gupta 2002). So, how can we say without batting an eye that the public has failed such that, now, it is time for the private sector to take over the experiment? It requires the violence of abstraction and the denial of colonial-imperial history to derive such a simplified narrative (Scott 1995).

Where do these transnational knowledge and expertise networks fall on this private/public divide? As this chapter tries to demonstrate, the relationship and identities of global panels of experts, scientific advisory boards, NGO and business councils, and international aid agencies should not be taken for granted; their genealogies and biographies *do* matter. Who is billed as scientific or political, public or private, global or local, and inside or outside of civil society has its consequences. We need to do a better job of interrogating this self-proclaimed a-political realm of global civil society, where most of the players are on first-name basis with each other, and comparing it to the more disparate and disagreeable "uncivil" societies challenging them.

Global networks of knowledge and expertise are believed to be central to the globalization project, and they receive tremendous philanthropic (and scholarly) support for being highly participatory and avowedly "above politics." Why and how has this discourse become common sense? Why has this particular process of networking become the privileged site to direct civil society activity (Riles 2000)? What types of political processes become erased, undermined, and subordinated in the process? Elite transnational policy networkers are supposedly best able to generate and work in spaces of just-in-time, flexible, deterritorialized, and depoliticized expert realms. But, the instant expertise certification one earns as a member of the jet-setting transnational class of networkers suggests we need to give greater attention to this power/knowledge nexus. The World Bank and an array of eminent panels and commissions are constantly being invoked to arbitrate for the world of nations the critical issues of AIDs, SARS, climate change, civil war, reconstruction of Afghanistan, and more. The fact that we rely upon these elite class networks and are unable to find alternatives to the process suggests the enormous success of World Bank hegemony in the realm of global policy.

This chapter has focused on the remarkable rise and legitimacy since the mid-1990s of powerful transnational networks promoting global water reform, in order to help shed light on the increasingly significant phenomenon of this type of elite policy networking and its basis in the World Bank's expanding power/knowledge regime of green neoliberalism. Although Northern media repeatedly question the "accountability" of the green-haired anarchists who demonstrate at major international finance meetings, our attention needs to turn to the question of who comprises the "official" transnational expert networks, interrogate from where their authority derives, what the institutional effects of their extraordinary rise and influence in the global political economy are, and finally, the processes by which this enormous global influence of the World Bank gets (re)produced. The political stakes in such inquiries have never been higher, and the immanent possibilities never as grand.

Notes

1 A revised version of this chapter has come out in a 2007 special issue on "pro-poor water politics" in *Geoforum*, and borrows substantially from chapter 6 in my book, *Imperial Nature: The World Bank and Struggles for Social Justice in the Age of Globalization* (New Haven, CT: Yale University Press, 2005).
2 I thank Yildirim Senturk and Wes Longhofer for their excellent research assistance.
3 For the report, see www.queensu.ca/msp

4 A senior vice-president of the World Bank acknowledged the Bank's role in the Southern African famine at a major press conference at the start of the World Summit in Johannesburg. Caught in a confessional moment, this senior Bank official admitted that had the Northern subsidies been eliminated prior to Africa's, the famine might not have taken so many lives.

5 See also Global Water Archive at www.platts.com/gwr/081902.shtml

6 This report was released during the 2nd World Water Forum at The Hague, March 2000.

7 See www.worldwatercouncil.org/forum.shtml

8 See ibid.

9 The terminology here may be confusing, in that the commissions, councils, partnerships and forums discussed in this paper are at once networks in and of themselves, as well as forming part of a larger network in which these smaller networks interact.

10 See www.worldwatercouncil.org/vision.html

11 World Bank president Wolfensohn was a founding member of the WBSCD.

12 See www.iccwbo.org. These 160 members of the WBCSD are drawn from more than thirty countries and twenty major industrial sectors. See World Business Council for Sustainable Development (2002) "Water for the Poor," vol. 2003: World Business Council for Sustainable Development (WBCSD). Downloaded from www.gm-unccd.org/FIELD/Private/WBCSD/Pub1.pdf

13 In this context, the "new millenium development goals" refer to the goals established at the Millennium Session of the UN General Assembly in 2000 for addressing problems of water access. See ibid.

14 Quoted from WaterAid website, "Private Sector Participation," www.wateraid. org/site/in_depth/current_research/157.asp (accessed February 13, 2003).

15 Just like so many organizations described here, WaterAid has circulated reports that question the argument that privatization is the only or best way to help the poor. Indeed, disagreement and dissensus is a critical element to the making of hegemony. See, for example, the report, "New Rules, New Roles: Does PSP (Private Sector Participation) Benefit the Poor?" (WaterAid and Tearfund, March 2003).

16 See www.wateraid.org/site/in_depth/current_research/400.asp (accessed February 13, 2003). Emphasis added.

17 This information is drawn from WaterAid's website, www.wateraid.org (accessed February 13, 2003).

18 From www.wateraid.org (accessed February 13, 2003).

19 Other major funders of these transnational policy actor networks include the bilateral aid agencies of the countries in which the world's largest water-service firms reside: DFID, the British Aid Agency, SIDA, the Swedish Aid Agency, the French Ministry of Foreign Affairs, the Netherlands Ministry of Foreign Affairs, and US AID. Most of these policy actors have emerged since 1996 and their agendas hew closely to the Bank's water privatization agenda.

20 See www.worldwaterforum.org/eng/wwf02.html

21 See www.symposium-h2o.com/symposium.html

22 See www.worldwatercouncil.org/download/FinPan.Washington.pdf

23 See www.worldbank.org/wbi/sdwatermedianetwork/

24 See www.wupafrica.org/what.html

25 Journalists are trained and paid to attend world water forums and world summits, taking courses in topics relevant to their experiences at World Bank events, such as (the World Bank perspective) on human rights, privatization, and development economics. See WBI's annual report 2002.

26 See www.iccwbo.org

27 "The water crisis is a governance crisis, characterized by a failure to value water properly and by a lack of transparency and accountability in the management of

water," argues a Global Water Partnership report, for example. "Reform of the water sector, where water tariffs and prices play essential parts, is expected to make stakeholders recognize the true costs of water and to act thereafter" (International Consortium of Investigative Journalists (2002).

28 Most of the WSSD updates and reporting comes from websites that are no longer functioning.

29 At the same time, the global water lords were repeating, in the most Victorian-colonial phrasing, that the Black poor were victims of their own bad habits. South African and UN dignitaries exhorted "Wash Your Hands!" as the water campaign's rallying cry during the Summit and at the WaterDome.

30 The exceptions are in the USA and Western Europe; however, it could be argued that the world's largest firms can expand into the Northern markets largely because of the heavy World Bank/IMF subsidization of the firms' deals in the South.

31 Of course, large borrowers such as Brazil, Mexico, India, and China can exert some counter-pressure on the Bank since their withdrawal could have devastating effects. Hence, Bank staff act, first and foremost, to avoid such conflict.

32 Debt relief without conditionalities and debt reparations were the most common political demand from African activists at the "anti-Summit" forums in Johannesburg during the World Summit meetings. (Author's personal notes.)

33 For the Bank's latest innovation, Poverty Reduction Support Credits, the first two of the three credits awarded (to Uganda and Burkina Faso) included water privatization as a priority. See World Bank, "Poverty Reduction Support Credits for Uganda and Burkina Faso," at www.worldbank.org

34 Since structural adjustment loan agreements are often outside of the public domain, the information on other Bank/IMF privatization conditionalities in their SAP loans comes through public circulation of "confidential" papers as well as discussions that leak within borrowing countries (see Grusky 2002). See also Letters of Intent and Memoranda of Economic and Financial Policies prepared by government authorities with the IMF/WB; documentation is available at the IMF website: www.imf.org

35 When these numbers are broken down by year, one finds a continuous increase in privatization as a requirement for access to capital, starting at fewer than 20 percent in 1990 to more than 80 per cent in 2002 (International Consortium of Investigative Journalists 2002).

36 "Is the Water Business Really a Business?" J. F. Talbot, CESO Saur International, World Bank Water and Sanitation Lecture Series, February 13, 2002, www.world bank.org/wbi/B-Span/docs/SAURD.pdf

37 This about-face, of course, has important repercussions on World Bank and IMF lending practices, since it becomes more difficult for these institutions to demand privatization if no firms are willing to provide the services.

38 See also Laurie and Crespo 2003.

39 Author's notes from Johannesburg, August-September 2002.

40 In February 2003, lawyers representing the people of Cochabamba requested that the ICSID open its doors to the public and the media, but the ICSID judges refused. See "Secretive World Bank Tribunal Bans Public and Media Participation in Bechtel Lawsuit over Access to Water," Earthjustice press release, February 12, 2003.

41 Frontline PBS website, Multinational Monitor interview, January 2000, and a presentation by Cochabamba machinist Oscar Olivera, of the Coordiadora de defense de Agua y la Vida (the Coalition in Defense of Water and Life), at the International Forum on Globalization, August 2002, Johannesburg.

42 Hall and Lobina 2006.

43 Recently, political parties have been voted out because of their relations with the World Bank and IMF and questions of privatization of basic public goods (e.g.

Bolivia, Ecuador, Venezuela, Uruguay, and Argentina). In October 2004, by popular referendum, the people of Uruguay voted for a new constitutional reform that declared water as a public right and prevents the government from privatizing it, despite strenuous pressure from the international finance institutions (see Public Citizen website, www.citizen.org/cmep/Water/).

References

Cosgrove, W. J. and Rijsberman, F. R. (2000) "World Water Vision: Making Water Everybody's Business," London: World Water Council (WWC).

Alliance, Conservation Finance (2002) Online. Available at www.conservationfinance.org

Babb, S. (2005) "Social Consequences of Structrual Adjustment: Recent Evidence and Current Debates," *Annual Review of Sociology* 31: 11.

Barlow, M. and Clarke, T. (2002) *Blue Gold: The Fight to Stop the Corporate Theft of the World's Water*, New York: New Press.

Bayliss, K. and Hall, D. (2002) "Unsustainable Conditions: The World Bank, Privatisation, Water and Energy," vol. 2003, London: Public Services International Research Unit (PSIRU), University of Greenwich.

Berry, S. (2003) "Claiming Patrimonial Territories In the Era of Privatization: Examples from Ghana," in *29th Annual Spring Symposium, African Studies*, University of Illinois at Urbana-Champaign.

Block, F. L. (1977) *The Origins of International Economic Disorder: A Study of United States International Monetary Policy from World War II to the Present*, Berkeley: University of California Press.

Bonanno, A., Busch, L., Friedland, W. H., Gouveia, L., and Mingione, E. (eds.) (1994) *From Columbus to ConAgra: The Globalization of Agriculture and Food*, Lawrence: University Press of Kansas.

Bond, P. (2003) *Against Global Apartheid: South Africa Meets the World Bank, IMF and International Finance*, Cape Town: University of Cape Town Press.

———(2003) "The Politicisation of South African Water Narratives," Paper presented at the forum of the Heinrich Böll Stiftung and the Free University of Berlin, August 7.

———(2004) "Water Commodification and Decommodification: South African Narratives from Johannesburg to Kyoto to Cancun and back," *Capitalism, Nature, Socialism* 15(1): 7–25.

Carty, B. (2002) "Interview with Peter Spillet (Head of the Environment, Quality and Sustainability for Thames Water), Dec. 6, 2002," Canadian Broadcasting Corporation (CBC).

Cronon, W. (1991) *Nature's Metropolis: Chicago and the Great West*, New York: W.W. Norton.

Dezalay, Y. and Garth, B. G. (2002) *The Internationalization of Palace Wars: Lawyers, Economists, and the Contest to Transform Latin American States*, Chicago: University of Chicago Press.

Ferguson, J. and Gupta, A. (2002) "Spatializing States: Toward an Ethnography of Neoliberal Governmentality," *American Ethnologist* 2: 981–1002.

Financial Times (2000) "Poor Countries 'Must Raise Water Prices': World Commission Warning on Shortages of Vital Resources," *Financial Times*, March 12.

Finnegan, W. (2002) "Leasing the Rain: The Race to Control Water Turns Violent," *New Yorker*, April 8.

Foucault, M. (1994) "Two Lectures," in N. B. Dirks, G. Eley, and S. B. Ortner (eds.) *Culture/Power/History*, Princeton, NJ: Princeton University Press.

Gelb, A. H. and World Bank (2000) *Can Africa Claim the 21st Century?* Washington, DC: World Bank.

George, S. and Sabelli, F. (1994) *Faith and Credit: The World Bank's Secular Empire*, London and New York: Penguin Books.

Global Water Report (1996) "Privatisation, a Question that Just Won't Go Away: Interview with Pierre Giacasso, Director of Water Service of the Service Industriels de Geneve, Uncovers Trends in World Water Supply."

Goldman, M. (1998) *Privatizing Nature: Political Struggles for the Global Commons*, New Brunswick, NJ: Rutgers University Press.

——(2001a) "The Birth of a Discipline: Producing Authoritative Green Knowledge, World Bank-style," *Ethnography* 2: 191–217.

——(2001b) "Constructing an Environmental State: Eco-governmentality and Other Transnational Practices of a 'Green' World Bank," *Social Problems* 48: 499–523.

——(2005) *Imperial Nature: The World Bank and Struggles for Social Justice in the Age of Globalization*, New Haven, CT: Yale University Press.

Gramsci, A., Hoare, Q., and Nowell-Smith, G. (1971) *Selections from the Prison Notebooks of Antonio Gramsci*, New York: International Publishers.

Grusky, S. (2002) "Profit Streams: The World Bank and Greedy Global Water Companies," *Public Citizen*, Washington, DC.

Halberstam, D. (1972) *The Best and the Brightest*, New York: Random House.

Hall, D. (2003) "Financing Water for the World: An Alternative to Guaranteed Profits," vol. 2003, London: Public Services International Research Unit (PSIRU), University of Greenwich.

Hall, D. and Lobina, E. (2006) "Pipe Dreams. The Failure of the Private Sector to Invest in Water Services in Developing Countries," London: Public Services International Research Unit (PSIRU), University of Greenwich.

Hall, D., Bayliss, K., and Lobina, E. (2002) "Water Privatisation in Africa," in *Municipal Services Project Conference*, Witwatersrand University, Johannesburg.

Hall, D. and de la Motte, R. (2005) *Dogmatic Development: Privatisation and Conditionalities in Six Countries*, London: Public Services International Research Unit (PSIRU), University of Greenwich.

Helleiner, E. (1994) *States and the Reemergence of Global Finance: From Bretton Woods to the 1990s*, Ithaca, NY: Cornell University Press.

Institutional Investor (1988) *The Way It Was: An Oral History of Finance, 1967–1987*, 1st ed., New York: Morrow.

International Consortium of Investigative Journalists (2002) *The Water Barons: How a Few Powerful Companies are Privatizing Your Water*, Washington, DC: Public Integrity Books.

Jessop, B. (2002) "Liberalism, Neoliberalism, and Urban Governance: A State-theoretical Perspective," *Antipode* 34(3): 473–94.

Kapur, D., Webb, R. C., and Lewis, J. P. (1997) *The World Bank : Its First Half Century*, 2 vols., Washington, DC: Brookings Institution Press.

Kapstein, Ethan (1994) *Governing the Global Economy: International Finance and the State*, Cambridge, MA: Harvard University Press.

Laurie, N. and Marvin, S. (1999) "Globalisation, Neo-liberalism and Negotiated Development in the Andes: Bolivian Water and the Misicuni Dream," *Environment and Planning A* 31: 1401–15.

Laurie, N. and Crespo, C. (2003) "An Examination of the Changing Contexts for Developing Pro-Poor Water Initiatives Via Concessions," SSR Project, University of Newcastle, UK, Geography Department.

Li, T. (2007) "Government Through Community in the Age of Neoliberalism," in *The Will to Improve*, Durham, NC: Duke University Press.

Lobina, E. (2000) "Grenoble–Water Re-municipalised," London: Public Services International Research Unit (PSIRU), University of Greenwich.

McCully, P. (1996) *Silenced Rivers: The Ecology and Politics of Large Dams*, London: Zed Books.

McMichael, P. (2000) *Development and Social Change: A Global Perspective*, 2nd ed., Thousand Oaks, CA: Pine Forge Press.

Mestrallet, G. (2001) "The War for Water: Open Letter," vol. 2003: Water Observatory (published first in Le Monde). www.waterobservatory.org

Ngwane, T. (2003) "Sparks in the Township," *New Left Review* 22, July-August.

Owen, D. (2001) "Second Chance for Private Water?" *Privatisation International*, February 14.

Peck, J. and Tickell, A. (2002) "Neoliberalizing Space," *Antipode* 34(3): 380–404.

Pincus, J. (2002) "State Simplification and Institution Building in a World Bank-Financed Development Project," in Pincus, J. and Winters, J. (eds.) *Reinventing the World Bank*, Ithaca, NY: Cornell University Press, 76–100.

Pincus, J. and Winters, J. (2002) *Reinventing the World Bank*, Ithaca, NJ: Cornell University Press.

Pitman, G. K. (2002) "Bridging Troubled Waters: Assessing the World Bank Resources Strategy," Washington DC: World Bank Operations Evaluation Department.

Public Citizen (2005) *Veolia Environnement: A Corporate Profile*, Public Citizen's Water for All Campaign, Washington, DC, February.

Riles, A. (2000) *The Network Inside Out*, Ann Arbor: University of Michigan Press.

Roberts, J. (2002) "The Role of the Media in Reporting on Water Issues in the Middle East and North Africa," in *4th International Symposium on Water, Session on Implementing Public Communications Programmes and the Role of the Media*. Cannes, France.

Saad-Filho, A. and Johnston, D. (eds.) (2005) *Neoliberalism: A Critical Reader*, London: Pluto Press.

Scott, D. (1995) "Colonial Governmentality," *Social Text*, 191–220.

Scott, J. C. (1998) *Seeing Like a State: How Certain Schemes to Improve the Human Condition Have Failed*, New Haven, CT: Yale University Press.

Shapley, D. (1993) *Promise and Power: The Life and Times of Robert McNamara*, 1st ed., Boston, MA: Little, Brown.

Shrybman, S. (2002) "Thirst For Control: New Rules in the Global Water Grab (Prepared for the Council of Canadians)," Ottawa: The Blue Planet Project.

Vidal, J. (2006) "Big Water Companies Quit Poor Countries," *Guardian*, London, March 22.

Wade, R. (1997) "Greening the Bank: The Struggle over the Environment 1970–95," in D. Kapur, J. P. Lewis, and R. Webb (eds.) *The World Bank: Its First Half Century*, Washington, DC: Brookings Institution Press, 611–734.

Water Aid and Tearfund (2003) "New Rules, New Roles: Does PSP (Private Sector Participation) Benefit the Poor?" Report by E. Gutierrez, B. Calaguas, J. Green, and V. Roaf. www.tearfund.org/webdocs/

World Bank (1990) "The World Bank and the Environment: Annual Report," Washington, D.C.: World Bank.

———(1991) "Agricultural Biotechnology: The Next 'Green Revolution'?" in Agricultural and Rural Development Department (ed.) *World Bank Technical Paper no. 133*, Washington, DC: World Bank, pp. x, 51.

———(Environment Department) (1994) "Making Development Sustainable," Washington, DC: World Bank.

———(1995a) "Mainstreaming the Environment," Washington, DC: World Bank.

———(1995b) *Annual Report 1995*, Washington, DC: World Bank.

———(1998) *World Development Report, 1998/99: Knowledge for Development*, New York: Oxford University Press.

———(1999a) *Annual Report*, Washington, DC: World Bank.

———(1999b) *World Development Report*, Washington, DC: World Bank.

———(2002) *Annual Report*, Washington, DC: World Bank.

———(2003a) "Public Communications Programs for Privatization Projects: A Toolkit for World Bank Task Team Leaders and Clients 2003, Development Communications Unit," Washington, DC: World Bank.

———(2003b) *World Development Report*, Washington, DC: World Bank.

———(2003c) "World Bank Group Private Sector Development Strategy Implementation Progress report, June 20, 2003," Washington, DC: World Bank. Online. Available at http://rru.worldbank.org/Documents/WBG_PSD_Implementation_Progress_Report_June_2003.pdf

World Business Council for Sustainable Development (2002) *Water for the Poor*. Online. Available at http://www.gm-unccd.org/FIELD/Private/WBCSD/Publ.pdf

World Commission on Dams (2000) *Dams and Development*, London: Earthscan.

World Commission on Water for the 21st Century (WCW) (2000) 'The Africa Water Vision for 2025: Equitable and Sustainable Use of Water for Socioeconomic Development.' Online. Available at www.worldwatercouncil.org/

Worster, D. (1985) *Rivers of Empire: Water, Aridity, and the Growth of the American West*, New York: Pantheon Books.

9 Democratizing environmental expertise about forests and climate

Tim Forsyth

This book started with the question: "Who knew and when did they know it?" (Kütting and Lipschutz, Chapter 1). It is a shame that so much global environmental policy is being written today without asking this question. The knowledge underpinning environmental policy is usually assumed to be accurate, authoritative and urgent. Yet the politics of who makes this knowledge—with whose participation and assumptions—is often less apparent. There is a need to ask about how environmental expertise came into being in order to assess who shaped our understandings of the world and what the implications of these worldviews are.

In recent years, discussions about the expertise underlying new environmental agreements have frequently focused on the concept of epistemic communities. In Peter Haas' terms, an epistemic community

> is a network of professionals with recognized experience and competence in a particular domain and an authoritative claim to policy-relevant knowledge within that domain ... What bonds members of an epistemic community is their shared belief or faith in the verity and the applicability of particular forms of knowledge or specific truths.
>
> (Haas 1992: 3)

This concept of epistemic communities has been used to define the role of expertise in shaping international agreements on ozone, climate change, and other topics (Young 1999; Dimitrov 2006). For climate change policy, the Intergovernmental Panel on Climate Change (IPCC), and the associated technical bodies of the United Nations Framework Convention on Climate Change (UNFCCC) are the main formal expert bodies.

But against this view, social science analysts have proposed that this approach to expertise overlooks important concerns about how expertise is created and defined.

First, how far does membership and transparency of expert networks influence the nature and ultimate success of policy guidelines? For example, Stephen Turner (2003) has argued that political analysis has not yet understood the social dynamics in which expertise can be met with trust. Historic state-based agencies are frequently mistrusted. Civil society advocacies are too diverse to indicate authority. And modern expert networks such as the Intergovernmental Panel on Climate Change (IPCC) are democratically unaccountable. How can the rules of expert networks be made more inclusive and transparent?

Second, what is expertise? Increasingly, environmental discourses and beliefs are adopted by various organizations and individuals as guidelines for policy, but these actors are very different and more diffuse than the specific experts identified by Haas. For example, Princen et al. (1994: 226) commented, "NGOs are increasingly prominent forces in framing environmental issues. They help establish a common language and, sometimes, common world views." Is expertise only restricted to "experts"? And are these views "expertise"?

And third, what are the social norms underlying expertise? Sheila Jasanoff (1996), for example, has argued that making a "common" or "world" view begs the question of whose world are we recreating? Tim Luke (in this volume) also noted: "'the global' of globalization is a polyfocal cluster of many different knowledge strategies." Whose strategies are being adopted? How is "authoritative" knowledge shaped by social norms?

These questions are particularly pertinent in relation to climate and forests. Increasingly, policies about forests and climate change are being linked because of the ability for vegetation to sequester carbon dioxide, produce biofuels, or reduce other greenhouse gas emissions. But the nature of forests, the uses to which they are put, and their various stakeholders are extremely diverse. What are the implications for authoritative expertise? Or for representing diverse viewpoints within environmental policy?

This chapter argues that there are still very important questions to ask about the emergence of environmental expertise linking climate change to forests within global environmental policy. This is particularly the case concerning poor people living around forest zones in developing countries. The chapter reviews some of the policy initiatives and underlying notions of current expertise about forests and climate. It then discusses ways these may be linked to social norms and limited participation.

The chapter's final points are that reforming environmental expertise is not simply changing the membership of international expert networks or epistemic communities. Rather, there is a need to rethink how social norms and authoritative knowledge interconnect, and—particularly—how current networks create expertise to legitimize social norms. These conclusions form a slight counterpoint to Karvonen and Brand's chapter in this volume by arguing that we should not see "expertise" only in terms of how technical bodies are defined and composed, but in terms of how and why "knowledge" becomes authoritative.

International knowledge regimes on forests and climate

Forests occupy a curious position within global environmental problems. At one level, they contribute to global climate change by sequestering large totals of carbon in biomass and underlying soils, and because removing or burning forests releases these gases. Yet, at another level, forests are also sources of livelihoods for many poor people, who stand to lose if forestland is protected or increased without paying attention to how they make their livelihoods.

In academic terms, such tensions in forest use may be discussed using Billy Lee Turner's (1990) classification of "systemic" and "cumulative" global environmental problems. Under this scheme, "systemic" environmental problems relate to a global system where environmental change in one location may affect the globe as a whole. Forest clearance—or afforestation and reforestation—may therefore be both causes of and solutions to global climate change no matter where they occur.

However, in contrast to "systemic" problems, there may also be "cumulative" global problems if environmental change is creating problems in various locations worldwide, regardless of whether this change is connected to a world system. Forest loss may contribute to cumulative problems if deforestation is resulting in overall biodiversity decline, or loss of habitats for species. Moreover, forest loss (and associated forest activities such as the creation of national parks or reforestation) impacts in various cumulative ways on the livelihoods of people living in and around forests.

This multiple relevance of forests for discussions about environmental policies has resulted in repeated clashes between expert networks calling for forests to be integrated into climate change policy in ways that either enhance the "systemic" or "cumulative" ways.

Various uses for forests have been proposed under the climate change negotiations (IPCC 2000; Griffiths 2007). At the simplest level, forests provide "sinks" for carbon dioxide and therefore need to be incorporated into any national or international inventory about stocks and flows of carbon. More complexly, the so-called "flexible mechanisms" of the Kyoto Protocol allow investors to claim credits or tradable certificates if they can invest in climate-friendly activities such as reforestation. Carbon-offset forestry is reforestation or afforestation specifically designed to compensate for greenhouse gas emissions elsewhere. Forestry in this fashion is justified on the global systemic principle that emissions in one location may be offset by sequestration in another, and because it is usually assumed that planting fast-growing trees is relatively inexpensive in the tropics. Using forests to offset industrial emissions has been debated under the climate change negotiations since the 1995 First Conference to the Parties of the United Nations Framework Convention on Climate Change (UNFCCC) in Berlin.

In addition to offset forestry, so-called "avoided deforestation" was introduced in 2005 as a way to mitigate climate change by reducing or preventing deforestation. This concept was proposed by the Coalition of Rainforest Nations (comprising thirty-three countries) led by Costa Rica and Papua New Guinea, but at present is not permitted as creditable under the Kyoto Protocol. In 2006–7, however, both carbon-offset forestry and avoided deforestation gained support when the World Bank led discussions for a "Global Forest Alliance" and "Forest Carbon Partnership Facility" in collaboration with conservation NGOs such as the Nature Conservancy, Conservation International, WWF, and private sector investors.

But proposals like these are also controversial and contain hidden controversies about expertise.

Historic disputes and the role of history

Perhaps the most archetypal controversy concerning the role of forests in climate change policies emerged during the early 1990s between the Washington, DC-based think tank, the World Resources Institute (WRI), and the Indian NGO, the Centre for Science and Environment (CSE). In 1990, WRI published one of the first reports that allocated potential national responsibilities for greenhouse gas emissions, in the build-up to the Rio Earth Summit (WRI 1990). WRI used an index later published in 1991 (Hammond et al. 1991). The index gave substantial weight to current deforestation rates and to the predicted release of methane from wet rice and livestock, and put three developing countries of Brazil, India, and China among the top six emitting countries.

This report, however, attracted criticism from CSE on various grounds (Agarwal and Narain 1991). First, the report focused primarily on national and not per capita emissions, which, of course, were much smaller in developing countries than in developed countries. Second, the index simplified and did not differentiate between different forms of deforestation (such as, for example, between commercial logging and expansion of agricultural land by poor farmers) and did not address the potential recovery of secondary forest or replacement land cover. And third, the index looked only at current tropical deforestation. Critics suggested that historic deforestation in developed countries should also be included (as greenhouse gases have lives of many years) (Brookfield et al. 1995: 144–46).

A related dispute emerged in 1997 in the approach to signing the Kyoto Protocol. The government of Brazil issued a proposal that targets for reducing greenhouse gas emissions should reflect the historic importance of past deforestation and past industrial emissions (Brazilian Proposal 1997). According to this proposal, the past contributions from developed countries represent about 84 percent of energy system emissions and, accordingly, the targets for each developed country should be calculated using a historic index of industrialization. The proposal calculated various levels of historic responsibility for individual countries and eventually proposed that—for example—the United Kingdom should have a target of reducing emissions by close to 63 percent of 1990 levels by 2010; Germany by 27 percent; and the USA of 24 percent. The proposal did not calculate totals for developing countries. It also calculated different levels of need for distributing funds from a "Clean Development Fund" from developed to developing countries in order to enhance clean industrialization.

Clearly, this proposal was not adopted at Kyoto. Shortly after this proposal, the US Senate voted 95–0 to reject any policy for climate change that did not include targets for developing countries (although it is not clear if this vote was a direct response to the Brazilian proposal). In addition, the "Clean Development Fund" was not adopted as a form of transferring resources from developed to developing countries, but became the "Clean Development Mechanism" (CDM) as a way for developed countries to achieve their targets.

But the CDM also became a source of controversy for forests in disputes during the early 2000s. The specific text of Article 12 of the Kyoto Protocol in 1997 did not use the word "sinks" or "forests" and the CDM was intended to "to assist Parties not included in Annex I in achieving sustainable development and in contributing to the ultimate objective of the [Climate Change] Convention." Some developing countries such as Brazil, India, and China strongly opposed the inclusion of forests-based projects in the CDM on the grounds that the benefits were difficult to measure and undermined other, arguably more technological or adaptation-oriented, forms of investment. Other countries, notably Peru, Chile, Colombia, Costa Rica, Bolivia, and Uruguay, argued in favor of the benefits of sinks-based investments. As a result, the 2001 Marrakech Accords and earlier Bonn Agreements specified rules for what levels of forests-based investments were allowed under the CDM or for national targets (Bäckstrand and Lövbrand 2006).

Forests and the "restoration of nature"

Clearly, protecting forests, reforestation, and afforestation can increase the available sinks to sequester carbon dioxide and to prevent the release of greenhouse gases through burning and land disturbance. But the benefits of planting trees to address climate change, and the norms which drive these activities, may also be questioned.

At a general level, some comments about restoring forests for climate change policy have been inspired by the aesthetics of tropical forests and notions of lost wilderness. For example, the British explorer and popular writer, Robin Hanbury-Tenison (2001) wrote a newspaper article in which he urged readers to see climate change and forests as linked. "Carbon sinks," he urged, "are exactly the elements of the Kyoto protocol that offer our last hope of saving the rain forests."

Social scientists have discussed this kind of link for years. Some 9 years before, the sociologists, Taylor and Buttel wrote,

> [the] rainforest connection has … been central in the scientific and popular construction of global change knowledge. At the level of environmental science, it has led to greater stress on the conservation biology of rainforest biodiversity, not only as a subordinate theme within the global environmental change framework, but also as a glamour topic in its own right.
>
> (Taylor and Buttel 1992: 411)

Yet, other writers have also suggested that even large-scale plantation forestry—with little resemblance to rainforests—can also serve important restorations of nature. Lester Brown, the long-standing environmentalist, and co-founder of the Worldwatch Institute, wrote:

> Restoring forests ... means reversing decades of tree cutting and land clearing with forest restoration, an activity that will require millions of people planting billions of trees ... A small area devoted to plantations may be essential to protecting forests at the global level.
>
> (Brown 2001: 82, 85)

Furthermore, carbon offset forestry has also been welcomed by other environmentalists who have considered reforestation to be somewhat of a "magic bullet" to address a range of environmental problems comprising climate change; declining biodiversity; and, soil erosion and water shortages. Yet, these statements have also been questioned:

> The mindset created by the paradigm which links the absence of forests with "degradation" of water resources, and "more forest" with improved water resources, has not yet been destroyed. Until it is replaced it will continue to cause governments, development agencies and UN organizations to commit and waste funds on afforestation or reforestation programs in the belief that this is the best way to improve water resources.
>
> (Calder 1999: 37)

Moreover, the ability for forests to sequester carbon at high rates depends on many physical and socio-economic factors. Clearly, demonstrating "additionality"—or the proven benefits of afforestation/reforestation on carbon absorption—depends on establishing clear baselines, and on ensuring "leakage"—the displacement of deforestation from one location to another—does not occur. Some critics have overtly accused forestry projects of overstating the climate change mitigation impacts of reforestation (Cullet and Kameri-Mbote 1998). In some circumstances, perverse incentives exist to cut down existing forests in order to replant land with plantation monoculture because these have higher resale value and faster rates of sequestration (Stern 2007: 549).

Expertise and the interests in the carbon offset market

And the actual projects involving forests for climate change policies have also been controversial. Much discussion has focused on whether forests-based projects are designed to enhance overall environmental quality, or simply allow emitters to continue emitting in the short term. One official at the US Department of Energy was quoted as saying in 1994 that, "tree planting will allow US energy policy to go on with business as usual out to 2015" (in Lohmann 1999: 2).

Different visions of forests and nature have led to clashes. Not all nationalities or forest users in developing countries share the vision of lost wilderness. At one meeting in Chatham House in the late 1990s, an African climate change negotiator shouted, "our countries are not toilets for your emissions!" Other specialist agencies have argued that much discussion of carbon-offset forestry and avoided deforestation focuses too much on forests of existing quality, rather than degraded forests (which are used by local people for various functions such as collecting products or grazing livestock), and that these schemes overlook economically productive forest crops such as rubber or oil palm, which may provide important livelihood opportunities for poor people, but which do not match many outsiders' visions of "rainforest" or pristine nature (Boyd 2005; World Agroforestry Centre 2007).

Yet, despite these calls to consider the role of livelihoods within climate change policies, much discussion of forests-based climate change policies have championed monoculture tree plantations because these offer fast rates of carbon sequestration. In addition, they also appeal to controversial notions of replacing "lost wilderness" or the "magic bullet" of reforestation. Indeed, these activities are also related to investment opportunities. Lester Brown, for example, wrote:

> At present tree plantations cover some 113 million hectares. An expansion of these by at least half, along with a continuing rise in productivity, is likely to be needed both to satisfy future demand and to eliminate one of the pressures that are shrinking forests. This, too, presents a huge opportunity for investment.
>
> (Brown 2001: 95)

But this focus on investment has also created a controversy of its own. In 2000, the IPCC published a "Special Report on Land Use, Land Use Change and Forestry" (LULUCF) (IPCC 2000), which summarized the scientific disputes concerning forests-based climate change policies, and offered some advice on achieving these projects successfully. But against this, the Uruguay-based NGO, the World Rainforest Movement (WRM), published a damning rebuke of this report. In particular, the WRM alleged a conflict of interest from the IPCC because lead authors of the report also had stakes in private-sector consultancies seeking to promote carbon offset forestry (WRM 2000). The online journal, the *Multinational Monitor* (2000) wrote:

> The WRM's charge of conflict of interest is particularly stinging since the Intergovernmental Panel on Climate Change responsible for the report prides itself on being an independent body providing "neutral" scientific, technical and economic information to the parties to the Framework Convention on Climate Change and the Kyoto Protocol.

The difficulties of afforestation/reforestation, in terms of establishing baselines, avoiding leakage, and measuring additional benefits for climate change mitigation are now well recorded in IPCC and UNFCCC meetings. But there is still continued concern about how far forests-based climate change policies are either effective (in global climate change terms); locally equitable (in terms of affording rights to local people); or politically acceptable to either citizens interested in offsetting carbon this way, or within the international climate change negotiations. For example, the UK-based Carbon Neutral Company has publicly stated that it will not engage in carbon offsets through forestry, and instead seeks to invest in projects advancing renewable energy in developing countries. Much of the ethical concern affecting offset projects was expressed by Lohmann (1999: 6), who wrote: "Pretty soon, it may be expected, every time you turn an ignition key, flip a switch, take a holiday, or cook some food, you will not only be using up fossil fuels but also planting trees on someone else's land." And meanwhile, discussions of climate change policies being "CO_2lonialism" continue. In 2000, for example, a number of NGO activists, including representatives from Greenpeace and the Rainforest Action Network, signed the "Mount Tamalpais Declaration" (after the site in California) to oppose the use of the CDM for supporting plantations and to urge greater consultation of local users of forests in decisions about climate change policy.

Such concerns may still continue under proposals for avoided deforestation. Sir Nicholas Stern's report on climate change suggested that avoided deforestation was a "highly cost-effective option" because it benefited climate change and forest policies simultaneously (Stern 2007: 537). Yet, this statement does not consider who might bear costs. Critical NGOs such as the Forest People's Programme (Griffiths 2007) and Bretton Woods Project (2007) have expressed concerns that the proposals to protect forests for climate change mitigation may support forest conservation models that lead to evictions or the inappropriate portrayal of marginal people (such as those who used to practice shifting cultivation) as drivers of deforestation. Accordingly, these groups ask if avoided deforestation may violate local human and property rights in forest zones. A further report by Greenpeace (2007) has focused on the Democratic Republic of Congo and has argued that the World Bank's strategies there are to increase, rather than avoid deforestation, by using logging as a form of economic development—and that logging titles have frequently been allocated without acknowledging local land rights. Indeed, this report claims payments of just salt and beer have been made to community leaders in return for logging rights. Stern (2007: 541) adds about avoided deforestation: "clarity over boundaries and ownership, and the allocation of property rights regarded as just by local communities, will enhance the effectiveness of property rights in practice and strengthen the institutions required to support and enforce them." But the Stern Review proposes few measures to achieve these steps.

Expertise and democracy in forests and climate change

Clearly, this summary is brief, but it offers some indication of the disputes about expertise concerning forests-based climate change policy. How can we assess these conflicting knowledge claims?

Perhaps the most important questions are whether, and what kind of, epistemic communities exist in the debate about forests and climate change policies. At one level, the official expertise published through the IPCC and UNFCCC, such as the "Special Report on Land Use, Land Use Change and Forestry" (IPCC 2000) constitute formal expertise in the terms of an epistemic community defined by Haas (1992: 3). As such, these are "a network of professionals with recognized experience and competence in a particular domain and an authoritative claim to policy-relevant knowledge within that domain." Yet, it is also clear that these claims are also considered illegitimate by many critics outside these organizations, who have also formed competing critical networks such as the alliance of NGOs and activists in the Tamalpais Declaration. Consequently, the most likely epistemic community linked to forests and climate change policies has—so far—lacked legitimacy, and, arguably, there are various epistemic communities existing simultaneously with different agendas and obviously alternative ways of viewing these issues.

The three questions posed at the start of this chapter are relevant. First, how far does membership and transparency of expert networks influence the nature and ultimate success of policy guidelines? Clearly, some of the authors and experts involved in the IPCC Special Report may be considered both legitimate and illegitimate because they have recognized experience in forestry and carbon sequestration, but also personal profit motives for issuing advice. More generally, much discussion about forests and climate change have focused on the definition of the problem in global, "systemic" terms of how far forests-based interventions can address global atmospheric concentrations of greenhouse gases, rather than more local dilemmas such as access to resources and livelihoods. Similarly, at the same time, many of the critics of this expertise, and members of informal expert networks, such as the World Rainforest Movement, are defined by their agendas to prioritize smaller landholders and farmers above other actors, or global environmental concerns. Consequently, much of the claims to expertise on forests and climate change are currently defined more by interest groups than an attempt to bring these groups together to create some shared vision of integrating forest zones into climate change policies.

Second, what is expertise? In Haas' terms, the expertise coming from an epistemic community is inherently rooted in the professional standing of the community members, and their demonstrable reputation for knowledge in this field. Yet, increasingly, the field of carbon-offset forestry and climate change policy is guided by general discourses that are adopted by members of the public, or people without such specialist and historic experience. It is one thing, for example, to "know" that mitigating climate change requires reducing emissions and increasing the ability of some zones to sequester carbon. Yet, it is another to assume—as Lester Brown or Robin Hanbury-Tenison do—that simply planting trees is a cure-all for various ecological ills, or the restoration of "lost wilderness." As discussed, such statements are certainly controversial and are more open to scientific query than commonly acknowledged.

Much of these claims, however, are based on popular imaginary that deforestation has threatened the stability of the earth, or that a tree-covered landscape is inherently better than one without trees. These are not new themes in environmental discussion. For example, in a book romantically entitled, *The Power of Trees: The Reforesting of the Soul*, Michael Perlman writes:

> Our relationships, human and nonhuman, whatever their quality, inevitably involve combinations of similarity, sameness, and intimacy on the one hand; and of difference, distinction and more radical alienation and estrangement on the other. In exploring what trees tell us about these combinations, we explore what they can mean for the nature of ecological relationship in its fullest sense—for Eros in its fullest sense ... a dangerous alienation from our natural, ultimately our *forest* roots, lay at the heart of the global ecological crisis ...
>
> (Perlman 1994: 4)

Similarly, in another popular book, *The Dying of the Trees*, Charles Little reinforces images of environmental equilibrium, ecological fragility, and threatened wilderness by describing the impacts on trees alone:

> What has this got to do with trees? The answer is, it has everything to do with trees ... the more trees die, the more trees will die. Could, perhaps, the whole of the global ecosystem go spinning out of control?
>
> (Little 1995: 226–28)

Little goes on to quote a meteorologist colleague as saying, "Forests may be God's strategy in the way they mediate climate change" in performing a "divine balancing act in nature" (Little 1995: 96–97, quoting Douglas G. Fox).

Clearly, trees and forests are important for various reasons, for a range of different actors. Yet, the suggestion that maintaining large areas of forest land is somehow important to restore a balance of nature is not matched by the diverse debates about the dynamic impacts of deforestation and reforestation (e.g. Calder 1999; Bonell and Bruijnzeel 2004). Moreover, there is a need to discuss what kinds of trees and forests are being planted (whether these include monoculture plantation forestry, rubber and oil palm). Plus, the historical reality is that many trees were removed by developed countries but these historic acts of deforestation are not being accounted for under current approaches to climate change policy.

The sociologist Anthony Giddens has noted,

> the ecological crisis is a crisis brought about by the dissolution of nature—where "nature" is defined in its most obvious sense as any object or process given independently of human intervention.
>
> (Giddens 1994: 206)

Under these circumstances, it is not surprising that common-day, but simplistic, discourses about nature and forests are now claimed to be expertise to justify policy. But there seems little acknowledgement of how far "expertise" about forests and climate change are affected by, or indeed are constituted by, popular discourses that are also challenged by other networks of expertise.

And, third, what are the social norms underlying expertise? Perhaps this is the most important question for governing environmental expertise. Social norms control the generation of knowledge in the context of what is considered meaningful and important. But also, norms control the manner in which different actors or networks are considered authoritative and legitimate. Indeed, this is one of the tensions contained within Haas' early definition of epistemic communities (1992: 3), where he states: "What bonds members of an epistemic community is their shared belief or faith in the verity and the applicability of particular forms of knowledge or specific truths." This statement indicates the difficulty of building scientific expertise outside of an ethical framework, or the values by which "experts" generate knowledge.

Jasanoff (1996; 2004) elaborates the concept of "coproduction" as a means of understanding how such social norms (or visions of how the world should be) co-evolve with knowledge claims. She (2004: 2) defines coproduction as "shorthand for the proposition that the ways in which we know and represent the world (both nature and society) are inseparable from the ways in which we choose to live in it." Consequently, a coproductionist approach to forests and climate change policies might ask which social norms govern how we would like the world to be, and which kinds of society(ies) do we want to empower, or define it?

Clearly, an analytical approach inspired by coproduction might indicate how—for example—conservationist NGOs in relatively richer countries might propose global "systemic" framings for forests and climate change that restore images of lost wilderness and allow greater leeway for industrial emissions in the short term. Similarly, it is unsurprising that pro-development NGOs in the Global South might propose forests should be used for maximizing livelihoods for poor farmers rather than being sealed off to provide sinks for richer countries' emissions.

More importantly, however, a coproductionist approach also acknowledges that "facts" and "norms" have to be evaluated simultaneously. Rather than seeking "the" correct answer to whether forests can, indeed, sequester carbon, or provide additional ecosystem benefits that outweigh short-term commercial or livelihood benefits, we should ask what kind of norms should give rise to what kind of environmental expertise. Second, we should also ask what social norms are already embedded in certain notions of environmental causality or environmental values that are currently seen to be fixed and beyond negotiation. For example, the belief that restoring "lost wilderness" may help stabilize the global system may be destabilized by reviewing both the factual evidence to support such claims at the same time as the partiality of the social norms underlying it. Yet, an inclusive and flexible form of environmental governance based on coproduction would not suggest rejecting these norms or desires about nature in total, but instead on locating them as just one vision among many that can guide environmental policy.

At present, much general discussion about the role of forests in climate change policy is inspired by the vision that they fit into a global "systemic" representation of climate change. The ability to absorb carbon, and to achieve this simultaneously with additional benefits such as biodiversity and habitat conservation, should not be denied. But the consideration of alternative framings—such as the role of forests in local livelihoods, or how effective livelihoods may reduce vulnerability to oncoming climate change—is less present in discussions about global climate change. Or, when it does occur, it takes place in rival networks, which frequently are represented as in conflict with, and hence less authoritative than, the formal expert networks associated with the IPCC or UNFCCC.

Already, some indications of change are occurring. For example, the 2001 Marrakech Accords (and earlier Bonn agreements) have placed important restrictions on how far forests are to be integrated into achieving national targets for greenhouse gas reductions. Climate-friendly investment programs such as the World Bank's Prototype Carbon Fund have gradually moved to enhance investment in renewable energy or energy efficiency projects rather than forests-based investment. The Stern Review (Stern 2007: 538) also distinguished between international action to protect existing forests versus establish new forests, which Stern states offer varied benefits, although still seeing forests generally in terms of their contribution to systemic global environmental change.

Yet, the emerging situation for "global" expertise on forests and climate change seems to be leading toward a consensus of agreed principles and practices, rather than a more diverse and flexibly governed approach based on diversity of norms. There is a need to acknowledge that different claims for expertise on forests and climate change do not simply reflect the membership of expert bodies and whose interests they represent, but rather a deeper and more historically embedded influence of how societies see forests as crucial to their existence. Making forests-based climate change policies more democratic does not simply mean explaining the potential benefits of forest conservation for climate change mitigation, but re-evaluating how and why so many of us value forests so much, and how these framings have influenced what we think is factual about the environment.

Conclusion

This chapter has provided a brief discussion about approaches to forests under climate change policies in order to assess the evolution of expertise in international environmental agreements, and especially the view that epistemic communities provide neutral and vital assistance about policy. This chapter argues that this view needs to be considered more critically.

While it is undeniable that we need to have expertise to guide us about environmental problems, there needs to be more discussion about how we achieve this expertise, and the political implications of defining it closely.

Moreover, there is a need to see "expertise" as more than simply the composition and objective of formal, technical bodies, but instead see expertise as knowledge claims that have somehow become stabilized (i.e. seen as natural) or considered socially legitimate.

In terms of policy discussions, Haas' (1992: 3) definition of epistemic communities of well intentioned experts with recognized experience needs to be questioned for three key reasons. What are the social controls on membership of such networks? When is expertise contained only within expert bodies, versus being distributed more broadly through environmental discourses? And how do social norms control the generation of knowledge and the identification of expertise?

These questions are crucial for addressing both climate change and parallel concerns about forest livelihoods, biodiversity, and multifaceted additional ecological impacts of forest clearance and restoration. Seeing forests only in terms of either global "systemic" change or more localized "cumulative" changes (B. L. Turner 1990) is too simplistic. We need to approach forest policies while acknowledging diverse purposes and valuations, while seeing the historic influence of specific social norms in creating the rather romantic Western images that somehow planting large areas of monoculture tree plantations will restore a lost wilderness, or will be a magic bullet to cure diverse additional ecological problems.

In turn, this also means we should not see discussions about governing expertise about climate and forests as simply diversifying membership of technical advisory bodies. For example, Brand and Kavonen (in this volume) ask: Why should expert bodies diversify membership? How can technical bodies become more accessible to different disciplines?

Clearly, we need to consider the membership and rules of conduct of expert bodies, and the ways in which technical expertise can be diversified. But democratizing environmental expertise is not just about the expert bodies but also about the underlying assumptions of underlying environmental beliefs. There is little point—from a perspective of representing wider social groups—to diversify membership of expert bodies if the underlying assumptions and problem framings are left unchanged.

There are many good reasons to protect forests, or integrate climate change policies with forest protection and re/afforestation. But too often, forest policies are connected to climate change on the basis of romantic visions about lost wilderness, or outdated and inaccurate statements about the hydrological or geomorphological impacts of reforestation. Neither of these trends helps development programs that can help poor people who live in or around forest zones, and even may make their lives worse by restricting livelihoods. Yet, sometimes, people active in climate change policy debates suggest that some forms of climate offset forestry is justified because some developing countries such as Costa Rica and Papua New Guinea have proposed forests-based climate change policies. These countries see attractive opportunities for integrating climate change policies with local forest protection. But it is important to allow discussions about these policies to develop without seeing the underlying scientific justifications for forest policies as fixed or universally applicable across borders.

Seeing environmental expertise and social norms about society and nature as coproduced is an important step to acknowledging the diverse ways that forests-based climate change policies can emerge. Giving more space to less established experts—or seeking to integrate "systemic" approaches with more localized livelihood concerns—may be a more politically sustainable, and socially just, means of achieving forests-based climate change policies.

References

Agarwal, A. and Narain, S. (1991) *Global Warming in an Unequal World*, New Delhi: Center for Science and Environment.

Bäckstrand, K. and Lövbrand, E. (2006) "Planting Trees to Mitigate Climate Change: Contested Discourses of Ecological Modernization, Green Governmentality and Civic Environmentalism," *Global Environmental Politics*, 6:1, 50–75.

Bonell, M. and Bruijnzeel, L. S. (2004) *Forests, Water, and People in the Humid Tropics: Past, Present, and Future Hydrological Research for Integrated Land and Water Management*, New York: Cambridge University Press.

Boyd, E. (2005) "Emissions Trading Cannot Solve Amazon Deforestation," *Science and Development Network*, November 25, 2005. Online. Available at www.scidev.net/Opinions/index.cfm?fuseaction=readopinions&itemid=450&language=1

Brazilian Proposal (1997) "Proposed Elements of a Protocol to the United Nations Framework Convention on Climate Change," Presented by Brazil in Response to the Berlin Mandate (FCCC/AGBM/1997/MISC 1/ADD.3). Online. Available at www.mct.gov.br/index.php/content/view/22139.html

Bretton Woods Project (2007) "Avoiding Deforestation but Violating Rights?" *Bretton Woods Update*, 56:4.

Brookfield, H., Potter, L., and Byron, Y. (1995) *In Place of the Forest: Environmental and Socio-Economic Transformation in Borneo and the Eastern Malay Peninsula*, Tokyo, Paris, and New York: United Nations University Press.

Brown, L. (2001) *Eco-Economy: Building an Economy for the Earth*, London and Washington, DC: Earthscan and Earth Policy Institute.

Calder, I. (1999) *The Blue Revolution: Land Use and Integrated Water Resources*, London: Earthscan.

Cullet, P. and Kameri-Mbote, P. (1998) "Joint Implementation and Forestry Projects: Conceptual and Operational Fallacies," *International Affairs*, 74:2, 393–408.

Dimitrov, R. (2006) *Science and International Environmental Policy: Regimes and Nonregimes in Global Governance*, Lanham, MD: Rowman & Littlefield.

Giddens, A. (1994) *Beyond Left and Right: The Future of Radical Politics*, Cambridge: Polity.

Greenpeace (2007) *Carving up the Congo*, London: Greenpeace. Online. Available at www.greenpeace.org.uk/media/reports/carving-up-the-congo

Griffiths, T. (2007) *Seeing "RED"? "Avoided deforestation" and the Rights of Indigenous Peoples and Local Communities*, Moreton-in-Marsh, UK: Forest Peoples Programme. Online. Available at www.forestpeoples.org/

Haas, P. (1992) "Introduction: Epistemic Communities and International Policy Coordination," *International Organization*, 46:1, 1–35.

Hammond, A., Rodenburg, E., and Moomaw, W. (1991) "Calculating National Accountability for Climate Change," *Environment*, 33:1, 11–15, 33–35.

Hanbury-Tenison, R. (2001) "The Greens Must Not Be Allowed to Ruin Our Planet," *Daily Telegraph*, July 19, p. 26.

IPCC (Intergovernmental Panel on Climate Change) (2000) *IPCC Special Report on Land Use, Land-Use Change and Forestry*, Bonn: IPCC. Online. Available at www.grida.no/climate/ipcc/land_use/index.htm

Jasanoff, S. (1996) "Science and Norms in Global Environmental Regimes," pp. 173–97 in Hampson, F. and Reppy, J. (eds.) *Earthly Goods: Environmental Change and Social Justice*, London and Ithaca, NY: Cornell University Press.

Jasanoff, S. (ed.) (2004) *States of Knowledge: The Co-Production of Science and Social Order*, London and New York: Routledge.

Little, C. (1995) *The Dying of the Trees: The Pandemic in America's Forests*, New York: Penguin.

Lohmann, L. (1999) *The Dyson Effect: Carbon "Offset" Forestry and the Privatisation of the Atmosphere*, Briefing number 15, Sturminster Newton, UK: The Corner House.

Miller, C. and Edwards, P. (eds.) (2001) *Changing the Atmosphere: Expert Knowledge and Environmental Governance*, Cambridge, MA: MIT Press.

Multinational Monitor (2000) (periodical) Online. Available at www.essential.org/monitor/monitor.html

Perlman, M. (1994) *The Power of Trees: The Reforesting of the Soul*, Dallas, TX: Spring Publications.

Princen, T., Finger, M., and Manro, J. (1994) "Translational Linkages," pp. 217–36 in Princen, T. and Finger, M., *Environmental NGOs in World Politics: Linking the Local and the Global*, London: Routledge.

Rosa, L., Ribeiro, S., Muylaert, M., and Pires de Campos, C. (2004) "Comments on the Brazilian Proposal and Contributions to Global Temperature Increase with Different Climate Responses—CO_2 Emissions Due to Fossil Fuels, Co_2 Emissions Due to Land Use Change," *Energy Policy*, 32:13, 1499–1510.

Stern, N. (2007) *The Stern Review on the Economics of Climate Change*, London: HMSO.

Taylor, P. and Buttel, F. (1992) "How Do We Know We Have Global Environmental Problems? Science and the Globalization of Environmental Discourse," *Geoforum*, 23:3, 405–16.

Turner, B. L. II (1990) "Two Types of Global Environmental Change: Definitional and Spatial Scale Issues in Their Human Dimensions," *Global Environmental Change*, 12, pp. 14–22.

Turner, S. (2003) *Liberal Democracy 3.0. Civil Society in an Age of Experts*, Thousand Oaks, CA: Sage.

World Agroforestry Centre (2007) *Avoided Deforestation With Sustainable Benefits*, Bogor: ICRAF. Online. Available at www.worldagroforestrycentre.org/downloads/publications/PDFs/pp07044.pdf

WRI (World Resources Institute) (1990) *World Resources 1990–91*, New York: Oxford University Press.

WRM (World Rainforest Movement) (2000) "Sinks That Stink," *WRM Bulletin*, June 2000. www.wrm.org.uy/actors/CCC/sinks.html

Young, O. R. (ed.) (1999) *The Effectiveness of International Environmental Regimes; Causal Connections and Behavioral Mechanisms*, Cambridge, MA: MIT Press.

10 Global assistance for local environmental movements

Capacity-building in Bosnia-Herzegovina

Adam Fagan

Introduction

The academic literature on environmental politics in post-socialist Europe has adopted the discursive and conceptual framework of capacity-building to assess and analyze socio-economic change and development (Baker and Jehlicka 1998). From the perspective of the Bosnian environmental movement it is argued here that while the capacity-building initiatives of foreign donors (most notably the EU) may succeed in developing the provision of services such as recycling, building the professionalism of NGOs and enabling them to undertake, often in lieu of the state, certain regulatory, research and policy-related functions, such intervention does little to augment the political influence of NGOs. Moreover, despite the "good governance" rhetoric that accompanies this manifestation of global–local intervention, capacity-building assistance fails to construct "self-organizing" governance networks able to hold the market and political hierarchies to account (Rhodes 1996). The main reason for this is that legacies of ethnic conflict, state collapse and political and institutional instability condition and at times invalidate the impact of what amount to incremental and piecemeal measures delivered by foreign donors with little regard for local realities. This chapter contributes further evidence to endorse the claim that, despite harnessing their intervention to concepts such as civil society and democracy promotion, the capacity-building assistance offered by the EU, USAID, the World Bank and a host of multilateral and bilateral donors does little to empower marginalized communities and those wishing to contest the decisions of elites (Cellarius and Staddon 2002; Wedel 2001; Quigley 2000; Sampson 1996).

The chapter begins with a critical examination of various aspects of "capacity-building," focusing in particular on embedded assumptions regarding the transferability of knowledge, the framing of assistance as technical aid rather than political intervention, and the apparent absence of a sequential logic with regard to the delivery of assistance. Beyond a theoretical and conceptual critique, the remainder of the chapter will focus on the deployment of capacity-assistance measures in the context of strengthening environmental

NGOs, governance and civil society in post-conflict Bosnia-Herzegovina (Assetto et al. 2003; Grindle 1997).

Environmental capacity-building

Capacity-building has been a core component of the development studies literature since the 1950s and the post-war wave of decolonization in Africa. As a conceptual framework, it provides those studying post-authoritarian states with a set of benchmarks for monitoring change and progress and for building institutional and policy frameworks, while at the same time acknowledging the impact of constraining legacies from the immediate past. Capacity-building has become, since the mid-1990s, intrinsically linked to efforts by the World Bank, the IMF and other international financial institutions (IFIs) to develop "good governance" as part of poverty reduction strategies (PRSP) in the poorest states across the world. The various aspects of capacity, as defined by international donors, have become an extensive and ever lengthening list, including the building of institutions, development of state functions and the interactions between state, market and civil society (Grindle 2004: 526). Although the more specific notion of "environmental capacity-building" gained momentum at the UN Conference on Environment and Development held at Rio in 1992, and is deployed more generally around discussions of sustainability and globalization, donor-driven capacity-building and development initiatives tend to be all embracing and focus on environmental reforms as part of PRSP or in the broader context of institutional and state reform (Grindle 1997).

Nevertheless, the OECD defines environmental capacity specifically as "a society's ability to identify and solve environmental problems" (OECD 1994: 2). Accidents and natural resource endowment notwithstanding, capacity is determined and shaped by political actors and their decisions, the dimensions and appropriateness of policy, and the availability of technical knowledge and expertise. In his discussion of the factors limiting a state's environmental capacity, Jänicke (1997: 1) includes "lack of ecological, technological or administrative knowledge, lack of material or legal resources, the weakness of environmental organizations or institutions in relation to vested interests ..." Analyses of a state's capacity tend to focus on the quality of public sector human resources, non-governmental organizations and state or quasi-state institutions (VanDeveer and Dabelko 2001: 20). The environmental capacity of a particular country is not static: new issues and problems plus the availability of new technology and approaches can alter the assessment of a country's ability and success in dealing with environmental issues. Moreover, the focus of capacity-building can shift from one "site" to another, with a country deemed to have developed sufficient capacity in some aspects of environmental management and yet not in others.

Proponents argue that it is important not to reduce the dimensions of the concept to the formal policy process, legislation and the role of governments.

The OECD has cautioned against trying to explain the failure of environmental policy solely in terms of the wrong policy or the use of inappropriate regulatory instruments (OECD 1992: 3). Indeed, by far the greatest virtue of the capacity concept is the stress placed on the objective limitations to successful environmental intervention. The approach places emphasis on the "complex interaction of influences" rather than on "a single isolated factor, or a favorite instrument ... or a single type of actor, condition or institution" (Jänicke 1997: 5). In other words, analysis of capacity must look not just at the weaknesses of institutions, but at the causes of incapacity that may include the absence of shared objectives, or economic and social constraints on individuals within key organizations. Capacity is therefore determined not so much by the actors themselves, but by the structural context in which they operate. Similarly, capacity-building should not be about installing policies that may have worked elsewhere and are deemed to be best practice in Western Europe or the USA without considering the context to which they are being transferred. As VanDeveer and Dabelko (2001: 20) observe,

> when efforts to build capacity fail, they often do so because of a lack of domestic concern in the recipient country about the policy objective ... If technical assistance programs fail, it is likely to be the fault of program design, not the fault of recipients.

By paying heed to both structure and agency, the capacity-building framework offers an extensive and far-reaching set of criteria for explaining the constraints on successful environmental management and sustainable development, as well as providing a theoretical basis for mapping change across a wide spectrum of variables.

Despite such rhetoric, the reality of environmental capacity-building initiatives "on the ground" tends to be a disregard for long-term impact and sustainable solutions in favor of short-term and rather haphazard interventions, couched in somewhat technocratic language. As VanDeveer and Sagar (2005: 3) observe, what is invariably absent from discussions of capacity-building is a sense of strengthening a society's "capacity to recognize, analyze and define environmental problems and their causes." They conclude that "activities targeted purely towards assisting countries in the completion of specific tasks, or moving towards short-term goals, may not only fail to build local capacity, but may actually be counter-productive" (VanDeveer and Sagar 2005: 3). Insofar as capacity-building invariably becomes conflated with notions of building "good governance," the reality for developing states tends to be a plethora of donor-driven initiatives focusing on tangible outcomes and short-term objectives that reflect "multiple priorities [and] an unrealistically long agenda" (Grindle 2004: 526).

In practice, most capacity-development programs involve either building the capacity of donor agencies to help in the implementation of environmental programs abroad, or funding projects to build capacity in recipient countries. In the first case, this involves integrating environmental considerations into donor programs and developing the skills base of the staff in the agency. In terms of assistance to recipient countries, emphasis is placed on building expertise in the fields of environmental economics and law and developing monitoring tools. This tends to be top-down assistance, such as building planning and administrative capacity in ministries. It also places great emphasis on developing the role of NGOs in policy forums, as providers of scientific knowledge, and as institutions for the collection of data collection and research.

In its 1999 review of capacity-development for the environment (CDE) efforts, the OECD observed that most programs had realized only limited success (OECD 1995: 10). It was suggested that the reasons for this had largely to do with the conceptualization of capacity held by donor agencies. Rather than top-down initiatives based around discrete projects decided on by development agencies, the OECD urged donors to:

1 Recognize, analyze and help define environmental problems and their causes;
2 Encourage joint decision and management processes (i.e. not imposed by donors);
3 To locate local initiatives in the context of global implementation capacity.

In an attempt to emphasize the importance of the social processes that need to occur for successful implementation, as well as the need for problems and solutions to be defined and identified locally, and also to shift the focus of capacity development away from recipient states simply being trained to implement internationally established environmental policy objectives, Van-Deveer and Sagar (2005: 3) define capacity as consisting of three overlapping categories:

1 Capacity to recognize, analyze and help define environmental problems and their causes;
2 Capacity to jointly decide on appropriate management processes;
3 Implementation capacity.

The concern being expressed here is that in the context of Southern states, and no less so in post-socialist states, capacity initiatives have invariably meant little more than funding local NGO representatives to attend international meetings, or to finance technocratic training programmes with little regard to how such knowledge could then be used effectively on a local basis to deliver sustainable and long-term change. A more fundamental contention, and one that is an inherent problem within development more generally, is that capacity initiatives are based on the tacit assumption that there is no *inca*-pacity in the North, and that Southern states must learn everything from the "successful" Northern experience. Related to this is the embedded assumption that within states receiving capacity-building assistance there is no existing capacity and that everything has to be built from scratch. This is particularly contentious with regard to post-socialist states, in which there are invariably high levels of scientific and technical know-how (Carmin and Jehlicka 2005). The assumption also encourages donors toward a "scatter-gun" approach, whereby a host of capacity-building initiatives are launched simultaneously with little regard for what already exists in a particular state, and what measures should in fact be prioritized. Grindle (2004) has referred to this problem in terms of capacity and good governance programs lacking any sense of sequencing.

Perhaps the most fundamental contention, and one with specific relevance to the role of the EU in post-socialist Europe, is the evident disconnection between the environmental capacity programs that donors advocate and their concurrent commitment to the promotion of growth and consumption. Recent studies of environmental capacity in post-socialist Europe now acknowledge that, a decade and a half since the revolutions of 1989, the massive increase in consumption that has occurred as a consequence of marketization, rather than legacies from the socialist period, is the main, or most significant threat to sustainable development (Andersson 2002: 348; Caddy and Vari 2002; Fagan 2001). Yet, the Commission does not see the concurrence of measures pursued by the EU to promote growth and environmental protection as an anomaly. Rather, professional NGOs are seen as functionaries for mediating the impact of high consumption and as endemic features of Western European states that post-socialist Europe must replicate if they wish to modernize and gain entry to the EU.

Environmental capacity-building in practice: the experiences of post-socialist Europe

Environmental capacity-building initiatives delivered by transnational donor agencies across post-socialist Europe tend to be based on two core assumptions: that no worthy "capacity" existed in, or is salvageable from, the socialist era; and that liberalization and democratization, having been established as a consequence of free elections, will follow a linear course that will deliver improvements in environmental capacity. In other words, the necessary shift from what Jänicke (1997: 10) terms "formal" institutionalization to "substantive" institutionalization, or from "apparent capacity" to "effective capacity," is inextricably tied to the assumption of linear consolidation. Despite the extension of capacity-building programs to the Balkans and Southeastern Europe, donor aid for environmental NGOs remains couched in the language and logic of democratization and transition. Yet the reality of post-socialist Europe beyond the Czech Republic, Slovakia, Poland and Hungary is, at worst, stalled democratizations or, at best, non-linear development. Free and fair elections aside, Serbia, Montenegro, Bosnia-Herzegovina and Albania have yet to fully establish and legally enshrine the procedures and institutions that would enable citizens and organizations to gain information regarding environmental waste, to participate in policy-making processes or seek redress, or to stand a chance of having their interests represented by stable and effective political parties (Batt 2005: 3). In terms of transition and regime change, these states are not at the consolidation stage that, for example, the Czech Republic had reached by the mid-1990s when environmental capacity-building initiatives were introduced by the EU and other donors. In BiH, notions of citizen participation in decision-making processes, the freedom and availability of information, and the notion of officials being both accountable and operating according to a legally enshrined due process have yet to be constitutionally established, let alone procedurally entrenched. Capacity-building initiatives are implicitly, if not explicitly, based on assumptions of a functioning market economy, a state administration equipped and empowered to perform certain regulatory functions, and at least a framework of trilateral governance in which NGOs, the state and the market interact. That such institutional arrangements, legal frameworks, and liberal norms and values are not in place acts as a critical determinant of the success of capacity-building intervention; for example, whether environmental NGOs will be able to exert influence within policy frameworks, or through EIA processes, will depend on both political and legal opportunity structures (Hilson 2002). Aside from the effectiveness or professionalism of the NGOs themselves, a host of variables, including the liberalization of the media, freedom of information, and bureaucratic reforms at the local level will determine the interaction between NGOs and elites. A sense of which reforms are in fact priorities, and whether political and legal changes are indeed a prerequisite, is seemingly absent from donor agendas.

An even more fundamental assumption is that the intervention of multilateral agencies in delivering convergence or harmonization with the practices and norms of the North is entirely enabling and positive for recipient states. For instance, in Weidner and Jänicke's (2002) comparative study of environmental capacity in seventeen countries, multilateral and bilateral support for environmental protection in developing states is accepted uncritically as a positive force. No serious consideration is given to whether the dependency of environmental NGOs on foreign donors is a sustainable development strategy, or if the imposition of legislative frameworks or patterns of institutional behavior borrowed from Western Europe and the US will affect levels of implementation. Indeed, scholars analyzing capacity-building assistance invariably fail to critically engage with the notion that such intervention forms a key part of what critics refer to as "post-conditionality," a less overt, though still contentious, form of intervention that seeks to develop good governance through inter-sectoral partnership rather than by imposing structural adjustment on donor-dependent regimes as was the case in the 1980s and 1990s (Harrison 2004: 71). In the Southeastern European states and the Western Balkan states of the former Yugoslavia (referred to by the

EU as "potential candidate countries"), the emphasis placed by donors on poverty reduction and the discourse of participation, deliberation, and civil society can easily obfuscate the underlying objectives of economic liberalization, growth, and the integration of these states into global markets. Linking capacity-building to security and the need to build regional co-operation in the wake of ethnocide obscures further the economic imperative.

Environmental capacity assistance offered by bilateral donors is a salient manifestation of such contemporary intervention and forms part of the trans-formation of state power in a not dissimilar way to that which has occurred in the developing world, whereby national governments have become inex-tricably linked with networks of transnational actors. Harrison (2004: 23–26) refers to this as the "governance state," where global networks of governance (including international and local NGOs, private companies, donors, and inter-national financial institutions) have become indivisible from nation-states. The impact of such change is, regardless of the political intention or will of individual politicians, the re-configuration of state power and its capacity to regulate and control transnational corporations (TNCs), and to mediate the impact of the conditionality imposed by international financial institutions. There is an extensive literature discussing the disempowerment of Southern states as a consequence of intervention by international financial institutions (Duffield 2001; Hardt and Negri 2000; Clapham 1996). While it might seem somewhat ironic that capacity-building assistance delivered by foreign donors may ultimately weaken the capacity of recipient states by compromising their sovereignty and their ability to regulate the activities of transnational actors, what is at stake here are competing notions of "capacity"—states are being assisted in developing their administrative and regulatory capacity while simultaneously losing, or at least not regaining, their political capacity.

Two further criticisms relating to the practical impact of donor-driven capacity assistance are the lack of sequencing of initiatives and the inbuilt functionalist assumptions regarding what various reforms will achieve. At the core of capacity-building is a structural-functionalist notion that incremental technical and administrative change—better policies, more openness, greater technological and ecological know-how, and communication—will ultimately deliver levels of increase in capacity similar to that witnessed in the industrialized states over the past three decades. Yet changes in institutional structures, new legislation, or the development of expertise do not necessarily reflect nor bring about changes in the underlying structure of power. This is particularly true in the context of post-socialist regime change in Southeastern Europe and the Balkans, where new institutional structures and relations may not be embedded and may have occurred as a consequence of pressure from foreign donors and agencies, and where the legacy of authoritarian rule lingers in terms of the behavior of both officials and social movement actors. On the part of the EU and its various initiatives to develop environmental capacity, there is seemingly little recognition of unintended consequences of introducing new measures and reforms, nor is there any apparent sequencing of initiatives.

But the EU is by no means unique in its approach. Foreign donor agencies operating across post-socialist Europe generally fail to adequately theorize the complex and invariably interlinked nature of the variables identified as *potentially* having an impact on environmental protection. While it is correct to acknowledge that "capacity building efforts can be focused on any number of 'sites': government bodies, NGOs and civil society ... independent unions, scientific and technical communities" (VanDeveer and Dabelko 2001: 20), such segmentation runs the risk of downplaying the interconnected and dependent nature of actors, institutions and organizations in strengthening overall capacity. Organizational capacity, levels of political openness, technological know-how and legislative change are not presented as contingent or dependent variables, but are offered as a sort of check list for measuring change. There is a strong sense of piecemeal and un-coordinated initiatives designed, it is hoped, to kick-start as many of the processes and functions deemed necessary to deliver effective environmental management as quickly as possible.

The criticisms raised above notwithstanding, it must be acknowledged that environmental capacity-building initiatives in the more successful and relatively prosperous CEE states have been successful in terms of establishing new legal and regulatory frameworks in line with EU norms and in developing the professionalism and expertise of environmental non-governmental organizations (ENGOs). However, moving beyond CEE to the Balkans, to states suffering from what Caruthers (2002: 9–10) terms "feckless pluralism," in which "there is significant amounts of political freedom, regular elections, and alternation of power between genuinely different political groupings," but where "democracy remains shallow and troubled," environmental capacity-building initiatives pursued by the EU and other donors encounter a series of additional problems that mitigate their effectiveness.

The perspective of the Bosnian environmental movement highlights the contradictions of using the concept of capacity-building to develop patterns of Western political interaction and associational behavior in the context of a partial democracy in which the authority of the state remains contested and partial. Or, more specifically, where so-called democratic reforms have been pursued in the context of post-conflict reconstruction and what some critics dismiss as "liberal imperialism" (Ignatieff 2003). The remaining sections of this chapter will analyze the Bosnian environmental movement. In any study of contemporary politics in BiH, it is important to begin by outlining briefly the political structure of the country. This is particularly necessary in a study such as this, in which the administrative structure of the state and the delineation of power and responsibility are so intrinsic to understanding the limits of political and social interaction.

Bosnia's political system: the legacy of Dayton

Well over a decade since the Dayton agreement ended the war, and despite recent developments with regard to the role of the High Representative, BiH remains under international administration. The political configuration of BiH is essentially a legacy of the 1992–95 conflict and the peace settlement, agreed at Dayton, which formally ended the war in November 1995. Though de jure a single state, political power and authority rest with the two separate entities: the Bosniak (Muslim)-Croat Federation and Republika Srpska. The Bosnian state has, de facto, virtually no power and does not in any sense function either as a federal or confederal state authority. The recent establishment of a common border police, a unified customs service, a State Court, a single police force, and "significant movement towards an integrated military force" (Caplan 2007: 236) should not detract from the fact that there remains fierce resistance from within both entities for the empowerment and formation of state-level ministries such as education, health and finance. While substantial power still rests in the hands of the entity-level governments, the diffusion within the Federation is more opaque, as the territory is divided further into ten cantons delineated to reflect ethnic divisions within the entity. Each canton elects its own government (and, until recently, its own prime minister), the aim being to allow political representation for the majority ethnic group within a specific territorial area. The fragmentation does not, however, end at cantonal level. Substantial power is then devolved to local municipalities, again in an attempt to maximize political representation of majority ethnic communities. The result is a political quagmire in which responsibility and accountability become blurred and overlap, with much confusion about the validity of legislation across the two entities and the status of state-level decisions versus entity-level laws.

Despite the reforms referred to above, as well as efforts by the EU to build the capacity of state institutions and to transfer authority to state-level institutions, critics and advocates of the Dayton architecture acknowledge that political power and influence in BiH still rests with the international community in the form of the Office of the High Representative, currently Miroslav Lajcak, a Slovak diplomat, who is also the EU Special Representative. The formal role of the OHR is to uphold democratic governance and intervene wherever and whenever the conditions of the peace accord are transgressed. To critics, this represents a colonial power structure, which permanently weakens and infantilizes the Bosnian government at all levels (Belloni 2000: 2). For others, the presence of the OHR and the international community is a transitory period designed to help nurture democratic institutions. However, as Chandler (2005: 308) points out, the reality of power in BiH is that

> in ten years since Dayton, not one piece of substantial legislation has been devised, ratified and implemented by Bosnian politicians and civil servants ... the lack of political autonomy for Bosnian representatives, and of political accountability for Bosnian citizens, is possibly the most remarkable feature of the Dayton settlement.

Perhaps the most significant development in recent years has been the sustained increase in the power and influence of the EU. From initially being involved in the implementation of civilian aspects of the Dayton agreement, the EU has, since 2000, assumed much broader influence. The somewhat vague objectives of Dayton have been largely replaced by the much more specific objectives of the EU accession agenda. In other words, the original aim of gradually transferring power from the OHR to Bosnian politicians and the public has been eclipsed by the transfer of power to the EU via the Directorate for European Integrations (DEI), which has "in effect, become the key executive body in BiH" (Chandler 2005: 343).

The impact on environmental activists and on environmental management of such a power structure is profound. International donors (most notably the EU) place significant emphasis on building environmental governance; getting ENGOs to interact with local municipal officials, and canton and entity-level governments to develop their expertise so that they can make a contribution within the policy process. Though a laudable strategy, any social or political reform that implies bureaucratic or institutional change is immediately constrained by the bifurcation and obliqueness of sovereignty or political responsibility. The political consensus is to accept international trusteeship in the form of the OHR as a compromise solution to the political dilemmas surrounding the existence of a single state and the implications of reforming the Dayton political and constitutional architecture. Beyond merely tinkering with legal frameworks and introducing some minor changes, this reality acts as an unmovable obstacle in the path of significant and wide-ranging policy reform. Of course, a central normative tenet of environmental capacity is integrative capacity and inter-sectoral planning across policy areas. Yet any efforts to ensure that environmental considerations are incorporated within policy and planning decisions in BiH is frustrated by the fact that decision-making for various policy areas takes place across the various tiers of government; for example, planning decisions concerning road building have been devolved to the cantonal level, whereas responsibility for forestry and utilities is divided between municipal, cantonal and state-level governments. While the prospect of dealing with different tiers of government is not in itself an insurmountable problem for ENGOs, the lack of clarity and openness regarding where responsibility lies for decision-making, issuing of permits and licenses, regulation and implementation is identified by all organizations as a serious impediment.

While some municipal officials have come to recognize that ENGOs can provide services and expertise,[1] this has tended to occur only in the Federation and within large urban areas such as Tuzla, Mostar and Sarajevo. In such cases, the relationship is based on mutual weakness and dependency rather than on ENGOs exerting influence over policy and decision-making. Moreover, where municipal leaders have sought to introduce environmental protection and fuse relations with ENGOs, such efforts are undermined by the failure of either the cantonal or federal government to provide regulatory authority or to adequately clarify the division of responsibility.

The relationship between local ENGOs and political elites is further complicated by the absence of financial autonomy at the local level. Raising revenue through taxation is a huge problem in BiH (Pugh 2005: 142), and the notion of local taxation revenue being ploughed back into communities, and into environmental regeneration in particular, is non-existent. In the absence of financial autonomy or revenue, local government and munici-palities rely entirely on either the state or the EU to fund environmental regeneration projects.

An optimistic interpretation sees ENGOs as eventually coaxing govern-ment officials into a relationship based on deliberation and consultation, with environmentalists gradually shifting from apolitical service providers toward performing a more political advocacy role. However, such an out-come is contingent upon power being transferred from the OHR and the EU to domestic political elites. A more negative assessment would see NGOs operating within a power vacuum, becoming quasi-corporatist service pro-viders in the context of a bankrupt and disempowered state (Deacon and Stubbs 1998: 100). It could be argued that there is little long-term benefit in developing the advocacy capacity of NGOs without first dealing with the disempowerment of the elites with whom NGOs are being trained to interact.

The Bosnian environmental movement

In some respects Bosnian ENGOs can broadly be described as being at a similar stage of development as their Central Eastern European counterparts were at the start of the 1990s. Apart from the conservation youth organization Gorans, which was established during the socialist period under the auspices of the Communist Party of Yugoslavia, all the ENGOs in BiH are new, having been established during the war or in the period since 1995.

Organizations tend to be run by a few volunteers, usually university students, who may be involved in several different organizations. Environmentalism has not played a particular role in Bosnian politics and is generally regarded by both politicians and the public as being of low political significance. Indeed, ENGOs have emerged as part of the wider growth in NGOs during the war and the post-war periods, largely as a consequence of the availability of donor money and civil society development projects, rather than as a direct response to specific ecological issues.

Even in cases where an organization has emerged in direct response to a particular local problem, the realities of funding and dependency on foreign donors mean that the issue agenda of the organization quickly shifts away from the local context toward the current issue priorities of the EU, the Regional Environmental Center (REC)[2] or the Heinrich Böll Foundation. This gives rise to a sense of ENGOs as being temporary; many of the orga-nizations listed by ICVA (International Council for Voluntary Associations), a Bosnian-run organization that supports and helps develop the NGO sector, in its 2001/2 directory or on the current REC database, no longer operate or exist. Though according the REC database the number of ENGOs has risen from an estimated twelve in 1997 to over 200 in 2005,[3] many of these are merely registered entities that are not active and may involve only one or two people. Organizations established solely to access project grants, will then disappear once the funding has ended. Of the 200 listed ENGOs, at least half are not exclusively environmental organizations, but have been established by other NGOs working with displaced persons, children's health, or other assistance issues in order to access "green" grants.

Furthermore, of the organizations that are exclusively environmental in their campaign focus, a substantial proportion are not strictly non-governmental insofar as they have been established by employees of government agencies and scientific institutes as a means of accessing foreign funding. A phenomenon observed in other parts of South Eastern Europe and the former USSR (Mandel 2002), this has proven a successful way for cash-starved institutes such as the Hydro-Engineering Institute of the Faculty of Civil Engineering in Sarajevo to access funds. Staff from the Institute have established the Center for Environmentally Sustainable Development (CESD), which operates out of the Institute and has become one of the most successful and prominent environmental organizations in the country. The complex application process for EU projects present less of a challenge for the academics and statisticians involved in CESD than for other ENGOS. Although they work with communities to develop participation in environmental impact assessment, the main focus of CESD is cleaner technology programs and advising government and industry on adapting production to meet environmental standards. Their interpretation of the role of environmental organizations is as technical experts assisting and advising government and industry.[4] CESD has attracted the bulk of donor funding directed toward environmental regeneration in BiH, including money from the Austrian government, the EU, REC, UNDP and various other European and American foundations. Unlike other Bosnian ENGOs, CESD has the capacity to run a number of projects concurrently, drawing on researchers, postgraduate students and other employees of the Institute.

Building the capacity of environmental NGOs in BiH

Any assessment of the Bosnian environmental movement, whether from activists, donors or academics, tends to make immediate reference to a lack of capacity. The environmental sector is seen as particularly weak and undeveloped and significantly below the average for NGOs operating in other sectors.[5]

The Regional Environmental Center (REC), one of the main international organizations supporting the development of ENGOs in BiH, identifies lack of capacity as being the main problem faced by the environmental movement.[6] It is estimated that less than 10 percent of ENGOs have the capacity to stage national-level campaigns, with the majority of organizations only capable of implementing and managing small projects of between €10–20,000. More than 50 percent of organizations lack a computer or access to the internet, and do not have English-speaking staff (seen as critical for applying for grants and dealing with international donor organizations). According to Ekonet, an electronic as well as actual network of ENGOs in BiH, there are probably fewer than ten organizations in the country that could potentially sustain a large national campaign, that have a core permanent staff and a steady flow of funding.[7] Even in such cases the organizations are entirely dependent on project grants and remain small operations.

Perhaps the most successful environmental organization, the Young Researchers of Banja Luka (YRBL), has discovered that despite the lists of ENGOs supposedly operating and in receipt of project grants, "when you come to do something (a joint or national campaign), there are less than 10 organizations ... lots of NGOs don't even have a management team—no structure, no strategic plan, they just work ad hoc, from project to project, or on a particular action."[8] The few NGOs that have developed their campaigning strategies and made progress in developing their internal management structures are then confronted with the problem that they cannot find reliable and equally developed partner organizations with whom to work.[9]

Defined in terms of ability to stage campaigns and to participate in policy debates, there is undoubtedly a lack of capacity amongst Bosnian ENGOs.[10] But whether the sort of capacity-building assistance offered by donors actually enables ENGOs such as YRBL or Ekotim to engage politically, or to challenge environmentally contentious planning decisions, is questionable. While both organizations need more staff and equipment, and would certainly benefit from campaigning know-how and lobbying advice, the conduit for obtaining any such help is project grants, whose focus is decided by donor agencies. One of the reasons that both Ekotim and YRBL were cited for not being able to comment on the motorway proposals was that they were engaged in applying for EU project grants and were tied up with completing other projects for which they had received donor funding. In other words, donor projects and the various funding rounds can act as a political distraction and can serve to totally reorientate the activities and operations of an organization.

Most capacity-building initiatives usually involve enabling organizations to raise revenue and manage a grant project. Indicators of capacity and sustainability are typically whether an organization has the ability to apply for project funding, and whether it has a track record of managing a grant and completing a project.[11] Critics argue that the civil society sector in BiH is not in fact ready or sufficiently developed for the kind of assistance being offered. It is argued that more basic provision and training is required to support local organizations that are barely operative (Sampson 1996). A further claim is that the emphasis on project grants as the basis for developing capacity merely generates growth in the number of organizations that have no roots in civil society or strategic plan for the future. This then leads to further fragmentation of the movement. In the environmental sector, the current reality is that two or three ENGOs who have built up knowledge of how to complete applications in English obtain most of the aid and benefit from the assistance. For instance, YRBL does not have a problem getting EU grants, not because they have particularly developed capacity, but due to the fact that there is hardly any competition from other NGOs. Viktor Bjelic, the organization's spokesperson, argues that such a system also fails to cater for the more established organizations, which require more bespoke training. Dependent on university students as volunteers, lacking a computer, and unable to purchase the required expertise, the majority of registered environmental organizations cannot begin to construct the sort of extensive application for funding required by all the main donors, nor can they demonstrate any kind of successful project history, or hope to obtain the requisite match funding.

EU support for NGOs: developing governance, civil society, or state substitution?

The EU Commission delegation to BiH, which is now the largest donor in BiH and the main source of funding for ENGOs, readily acknowledges that it has difficulty in allocating the resources designated for NGOs and that it ends up awarding projects to the same organizations in each round. The application process for such funds is extremely complicated. It involves the applicant organization having a basic knowledge of project psycho-management tools. NGOs are required to submit a log frame, a logic matrix identifying how the overall objectives of the proposed project would further EU national objectives for BiH. The specific objectives of the project must then be identified with reference to sustainable development of the organization and the methodology for measuring outcomes and identifying indicators of achievement. Applicants are requested to identify quantitative and qualitative baseline assessments against which the EU will measure success on completion of the project.

In 2004 the local delegation launched a call for project proposals on the theme of network-building. The quality of applications was considered to be so poor that out of a potential €7 million, only €1.5 million could be allocated. The local delegation concluded that the process is too complex for most local NGOs and that there was a lack of capacity to develop the kind of projects that the EU wished to support. Subsequent calls have seen the submission of much more sophisticated project proposals, demonstrating a capacity amongst NGOs to master the requirements of project management and logic frameworks. However, such knowledge and expertise is held in the hands of very few organizations, which tend to dominate each call, regardless of the theme or topic. One is forced to conclude that the EU's solution to the absence of quality in 2004 has been to provide more training for NGOs to develop the specific technical skills required to complete grant applications, rather than to reassess the EU's notion of "capacity" and the suitability of this mechanism for delivering aid.[12]

Paolo Scialla, the team co-ordinator for the Democratic Stabilization Programme of the Delegation of the European Commission to BiH in 2004, conceded that the process of applying for short-term project grants on topics and issues identified by Brussels, was "an extremely difficult process." He acknowledged that "[such] complex management tools are not easy for people who have been using them for years." Four years later, and after several calls for projects, research carried out by the author reveals that 80 percent of NGOs receiving EU project grants are based in the main urban areas (Sarajevo, Mostar, Tuzla or Banja Luka). Just under three quarters (73 percent) of successful organizations in 2006–7 had a track record of having secured at least one previous project.[13]

At the core of the EU's capacity-building strategies for BiH lies a perception of NGOs as operating in partnership with government and business, providing expertise and a variety of public and social services, and remaining dependent on foreign donor grants for their existence. First, while the ability of an organization to be financially secure, develop an effective internal management structure and generally become more professional in its dealings with government and business are important skills, is it also vital, in the interests of building democracy and a multi-ethnic liberal civil society, that the capacity of NGOs to act as advocacy or political organizations capable of voicing societal concerns and able to contest policy decisions is developed. What is seemingly being overlooked by donors is that civil society across Western Europe cannot be reduced to the function of professional advocacy organizations operating within the policy process. Nor can the efficacy of civil society be measured solely in terms of professionalism and financial know-how. What gives Western civil society its vibrancy and its capacity to contest and articulate the views of society is, arguably, its diversity, fluidity and the extent to which organizations remain enmeshed within communities.

Second, the interaction between NGOs and government in the context of the one- or two-year EU-funded projects invariably amounts to little more than government agencies either supplying a letter of recommendation as part of the application process, granting permission to work in schools or other public institutions, or providing NGOs with data. The governance vision of partnership between state and NGOs is not the reality.[14]

A more long-term problem concerns the dependency of NGOs on an ever diminishing pool of foreign donor revenue. Capacity-building initiatives in BiH, of which assistance for environmental organizations forms a significant part, are based on the premise that NGOs will obtain the bulk of their income from foreign donors, and therefore need to be skilled in fund-raising and project applications. Yet such a pattern of funding is not sustainable. Donor grants for all NGOs are already in decline in BiH and are likely to be reduced further over the next few years. Donors themselves talk about "Bosnia fatigue" and a sense that they have done as much as they can over the ten years since Dayton.[15] Moreover, the experience of Central and Eastern Europe suggests that to place such emphasis on training NGOs to access foreign donor sources encourages organizations to neglect potential local revenue and to view accountability in terms of meeting the demands of donors rather than the constituencies they claim to represent. For instance, when the foreign donor money dried up in the run-up to EU accession, many Czech NGOs found that despite over a decade of capacity-building training and know-how transfer, they in fact lacked the necessary skills or the contacts to access domestic revenue and as a result faced financial crisis (Fagan 2005).

Capacity-building and local environmental networks

Politically engaged environmental networks that seek to directly challenge planning decisions or the absence of effective regulation, and often with their origins in the socialist period, experience the most difficulty in accessing foreign donor assistance because they either cannot break into the elite of ENGOs that already receive donor assistance and can demonstrate track records, or because the assistance they require is not offered by donors such as USAID, the EU or DFID.

An example of such a grass-roots network is Grupa za podrska (Support Group Green),[16] which emerged during 2004 in response to the construction of an access road through the Rakitnica canyon in southwest Bosnia-Herzegovina.[17] SGG faced several difficulties in its attempts to discover who had made the decision to allow the road to be constructed. Activists were forestalled by the confusion surrounding the political jurisdiction and responsibility of the various tiers of government, and the deliberate flouting of political processes by politicians and officials; neither the cantonal government or the local administration were prepared to take responsibility. Ultimately it required the intervention of the OHR in order to initiate an environmental audit assessment, even though this is a statutory legal requirement.

Most importantly, perhaps, the case of the SGG network also illustrates the extent to which basic campaigning know-how is available locally and can be mobilized on the basis of professional ties, loyalties and connections dating back to the socialist period. Drawing on such personal networks and expertise, SGG activists were able to put together detailed reports and propose an alternative to the canyon road scheme initiated by the construction company and the cantonal ministry. In their quest to challenge the decision and to contest the legality of the construction, SGG required different, more nuanced support from donors. The network did not require training in managerial know-how and coaching on how to complete a grant application form—they did not seek to establish a formal NGO or to professionalize their activities. What they sought were resources to fund a rather conventional campaign based around mobilizing support and publicizing the corrupt practices that had occurred.

Not surprisingly, SGG was unable to access donor assistance, at least not directly. When activists contacted the Regional Environmental Center (REC) and asked for assistance with the campaign, they were refused on the basis that this was a "political campaign" and REC as an international organization has to remain "politically neutral." Yet REC does give money to the federal ministry and has employed the minister and deputy minister of the environment as advisers. REC has also supported other ENGOs—Ekotim and Fondeko—but in the context of less controversial campaigns that involve partnership and cooperation with the authorities rather than direct confrontation.

The political capacity of the SGG network was primarily constrained by corrupt decision-making, a lack of transparency and accountability, and by the absence of legal frameworks governing the availability of information. To an extent, it was less the obfuscation of political responsibility and sovereignty itself and more the use of multiple locations of responsibility as an excuse by officials and elites and a veil to disguise corrupt practices or inactivity that SGG was battling against. Though an EIA process did take place in response to pressure from the OHR (Office of the High Representative), the federation-level ministry responsible for environmental protection decided, in July 2004, to permit the canyon road to be completed, but withheld information regarding his decision for 25 days. Bosnian law states that citizens have 30 days in which to appeal after a decision is announced. This gave SGG only 5 days to lodge an appeal, which they were unable to do.

Conclusion

In contrast to the situation in post-socialist Central and Eastern Europe, the capacity-building initiatives pursued by the EU and other transnational donors are being deployed in BiH in the context of partial democratization, in a weak state in which the constitutional authority of elites is disputed, and where international trusteeship constitutes a bifurcation of sovereignty and authority.

It has been argued in this chapter that the discursive frames of democracy/civil society promotion and good governance, both of which shroud the deployment of capacity-building initiatives in BiH, obfuscate the true impact of this manifestation of global–local linkage. Drawing on recent empirical research on ENGO networks, it can be concluded that the contradiction lies with competing conceptualizations of "capacity": transnational donors promote a very distinct notion of capacity which is deployed with the aim of strengthening professional NGOs to provide services and perform regulatory functions. Support for what might be termed "political" capacity—helping NGOs to develop their advocacy skills and to better represent local issue agendas in political fora—is not on offer. While this somewhat negates the claim made by donors that their intervention is designed to strengthen civil society, it also calls into question the extent to which the donor-supported NGOs are in fact helping to construct "new" governance, based on intersectoral deliberation and a genuine sharing of power. Rather, from the perspective of the Bosnian environmental NGO sector, capacity-building initiatives appear to be about little more than state substitution and the legitimization of external governance and neo-trusteeship.

Notes

1 For example, the ENGO Ekotim helping to provide recycling facilities in Sarajevo municipality.
2 The Regional Environmental Center for CEE is a non-profit organization working to improve the environments of the region. It was established in 1990 by the US and the European Commission. Information on its role in BiH was obtained from interviews with Inka Sehovic, Information and Grant Manager (Sarajevo, February 21, 2005) and Dorde Stefanovic, Banja Luka field office (July 7, 2005).
3 Interview with Inka Sehovic, Sarajevo, February 21, 2005.
4 Interviews with Sanda Midzic and Igor Palandzic, CESD (Center for Environmentally Sustainable Development), Sarajevo, February and July 2005.
5 Interview withViktor Bjelic and Miodrag Dakic, Young Researchers of Banja Luka, Banja Luka, July 7, 2005.
6 Interview with REC, Sarajevo (February 2005), Banja Luka (July 2005).
7 Interview with Viktor Bjelic, Ekonet/Young Researchers of Banja Luka (February 2005).
8 Ibid.
9 Ibid.
10 A stark illustration of the lack of such capacity occurred in July 2005, when several organizations were asked by the state planning authorities to comment on proposals for an extensive and controversial motorway development scheme to run across the country. The two most prominent organizations in the country, YRBL and Ekotim, both felt they lacked the resources to make comments by the required deadline and declined to comment.
11 Criteria used by the OSCE, USAID, EU and the World Bank for allocating project grants in BiH.
12 Interviews with Paolo Scialla, Delegation of the European Commission in BiH (March 24, 2004) and Boris Mrak, EU Cards Project.
13 Research conducted by Adam Fagan (Principal Investigator) as part of a project entitled "An Assessment of EU Capacity Assistance for Environmental NGOs in the Potential Candidate Countries of the Western Balkans," funded by the British Academy (SG 45257).
14 Ibid.
15 Interview with Anamaria Golemec Powell, Social Policy Co-ordinator, DFID, Sarajevo, November 2004.
16 Support Group Green (Grupa za podrska) was established in April 2004 with the aim of stopping the canyon road and other environmentally hazardous projects in the region. The coalition is an eclectic mix of organizations, including mountaineering organizations, the Ornithology Society of BiH, and caving clubs, all of whom feel affected by the canyon road construction.
17 The Rakitnica canyon, situated in the southwest of BiH, is one of the last unspoilt areas in Europe and has had protected status since 1966. The canyon, which is an 800-meter drop, contains magnificent rock formations and is home to numerous endangered species. Information on SGG was obtained from several interviews with Thierry Joubert and Tim Clancy (Green Visions, part of the SGG network) and Kenan Muftic (SGG co-ordinator) during the period March 2004–December 2005.

References

Andersson, M. (2002) "Poland," in H. Weidner and M. Jänicke (eds.) *Capacity Building in National Environmental Policy*, Berlin: Springer, 347–74.

Assetto, V. J., Hajba, E., and Mumme, S. (2003) "Democratization, Decentralization and Local Environmental Policy Capacity: Hungary and Mexico," *The Social Science Journal*, 40(2): 249–68.

Baker, S. and Jehlicka, P. (eds.) (1998) *Dilemmas of Transition: The Environment, Democracy and Economic Reform in East Central Europe*, London: Frank Cass.

Batt, J. (2005) "The Question of Serbia," Chaillot Paper no. 81, Paris: Institute for Security Studies.

Belloni, R. (2000) "Building Civil Society in Bosnia-Herzegovina," Human Rights Working Papers, no.12 (January): 2. Online. Available at www.du.edu/humanrights/ workingpapers/papers/02-belloni-0100.pdf (Accessed September 12, 2007).

Caddy, J. and Vari, A. (2002) "Hungary," in H. Weidner and M. Jänicke (eds.) *Capacity Building in National Environmental Policy*, Berlin: Springer, 219–38.

Caplan, R. (2007) "From Collapsing States to Neo-trusteeship: The Limits to Solving the Problem of 'Precarious Statehood' in the 21st Century," *Third World Quarterly*, 28(2): 236.

Carmin, J. and Jehlicka P. (2005) "By the Masses or for the Masses? The Transformation of Voluntary Action in the Czech Union for Nature Protection," *Voluntas*, 16(4): 397–416.

Caruthers, T. (2002) "The End of the Transition Paradigm," *Journal of Democracy*, 13(1): 9–10.

Cellarius, B. A. and Staddon, C. (2002) "Environmental Nongovernmental Organizations, Civil Society and Democratization in Bulgaria," *East European Politics and Societies*, 16(1): 182–222.

Chandler, D. (2005) "Introduction: Peace without Politics?" in D. Chandler (ed.) "Peace without Politics? Ten Years of International State-building in Bosnia," *International Peacekeeping*, 12(3): 308.

——(2005a) "From Dayton to Europe," in D. Chandler (ed.) "Peace without Politics? Ten Years of International State-Building in Bosnia," *International Peacekeeping*, 12(3): 336–49.

Clapham, C. (1996) *Africa and the International System: The Politics of State Survival*, Cambridge: Cambridge University Press.

Deacon, B. and Stubbs, P. (1998) "International Actors and Social Policy Development in Bosnia-Herzegovina: Globalism and the New Feudalism," *Journal of European Social Policy*, 8(2): 99–115.

Duffield, M. (2001) *Global Governance and the New Wars*, London: Zed Books.

Fagan, A. (2001) "Environmental Capacity-building in the Czech Republic," *Environment and Planning A*, 33(4): 589–606.

——(2005) "Taking Stock of Civil Society Development in post-Communist Europe: Evidence from the Czech Republic," *Democratization*, 12(5) (Autumn).

Grindle, M. S. (ed.) (1997) *Getting Good Government: Capacity-Building in the Public Sector of Developing Countries*, Cambridge, MA: Harvard University Press.

——(2004) "Good Enough Governance: Poverty Reduction and Reform in Developing Countries," *Governance*, 17(4): 526.

Hardt, M. and Negri, A. (2000) *Empire*, Cambridge, MA: Harvard University Press.

Harrison, G. (2004) *The World Bank and Africa: the Construction of Governance States*, London: Routledge.

Hilson, C. (2002) "New Social Movements: The Role of Legal Opportunity," *Journal of European Public Policy*, 9: 238–55

Ignatieff, M. (2003) *Empire Lite: Nation-Building in Bosnia, Kosovo and Afghanistan*, London: Vintage.

Jänicke, M. (1997) "The Political System's Capacity for Environmental Policy," in M. Jänicke and H. Weidner (eds.) *National Environmental Policies: A Comparative Study of Capacity-building*, Berlin: Springer.

Mandel, R. (2002) "Seeding Ccivil Society," in C. M. Hann (ed.) *Postsocialism: Ideals, Ideologies and Practices in Eurasia*, London: Routledge.

OECD (1992) *Market and Government Failures in Environmental Protection: The Case of Transport*, Paris: OECD.

——(1994) *Capacity Development in Environment*, Paris: OECD.

——(1995) *Developing Environmental Capacity: A Framework for Donor Involvement*, Paris: OECD.

Pugh, M. (2005) "Transformation in the Political Economy of Bosnia Since Dayton," in D. Chandler (ed.) *Peace Without Politics: Ten Years of International State-Building in Bosnia*, London: Routledge, 142–56.

Quigley, K. F. F. (2000) "Lofty Goals, Modest Results: Assisting Civil Society in Eastern Europe," in M. Ottaway and T. Carothers (eds.) *Funding Virtue: Civil Society Aid and Democracy Promotion*, Washington, DC: Carnegie Endowment for International Peace, 191–216.

Rhodes, R. A. W. (1996) "The New Governance: Governing without Government," *Political Studies*, 44(3): 652.

Sampson, S. (1996) "The Social Life of Projects: Importing Civil Society to Albania," in C. M. Hann and E. Dunn (eds.) *Civil Society: Challenging Western Models*, London: Routledge, 121–42.

VanDeveer, S. D. and Dabelko, G. D. (2001) "It's Capacity, Stupid: International Assistance and National Implementation," *Global Environmental Politics*, 1(2): 20.

VanDeveer, S. D. and Sagar, A. (2005) "Capacity Building for the Environment: North and South," in E. Corell, A. Churie Kallhauge, and G. Sjostedt (eds.) *Furthering Consensus: Meeting the Challenges of Sustainable Development Beyond 2002*, London: Green Leaf, 3.

Wedel, J. (2001) *Collision and Collusion: The Strange Case of Western Aid to Eastern Europe, 1989–1998*, New York: St. Martin's Press.

Weidner, H. and Jänicke, M. (2002) "Summary: Environmental Capacity Building in a Converging World," in H. Weidner and M. Jänicke (eds.) *Capacity Building in National Environmental Policy*, Berlin: Springer.

11 Conclusions

Environmental governance, power and knowledge in a local–global world

Ronnie D. Lipschutz and Gabriela Kütting

Each of the chapters in this volume interrogates, from a different perspective, the social relations of knowledge and power in a local–global world. These can be summarized as guided by space–place dichotomies and top-down versus bottom-up approaches, although this dichotomy conceals more than it reveals. As with capital, the extraction of knowledge from particular places, and its accumulation in certain spaces, tends to overlook the structures of social power through which this process takes place, and whose relations cannot simply be localized or globalized. "Resistance" to such extractive and accumulative tendencies, which is often regarded in terms of the "local," is also constituted through similar structures and relations that transcend place and extend through space. It is for this reason that we prefer to think in terms of *epistemes* (and not epistemic communities, which are quite different) which, although not organized in any strong institutional sense, nonetheless operate through the dissemination of both knowledge and practice.

The term "episteme" has been popularized in recent decades by, among others, John G. Ruggie, via Michel Foucault (1993: 157). As the latter put it (1980: 187),

> I would define the episteme retrospectively as the strategic apparatus which permits of separating out from among all the statements which are possible those that will be acceptable within, I won't say a scientific theory, but a field of scientificity, and which it is possible to say are true or false. The episteme is the "apparatus" which makes possible the separation, not of the true from the false, but of what may from what may not be characterised as scientific.

In other words, an episteme rests on scientific knowledge but is not, itself, what we would call "science." Thus, we could speak of a "climate episteme," which has become very widely wielded across a range of policy issues, possessing a "hard" kernel of science-based knowledge but surrounded by a "cloud" of inferences, claims, assumptions and arguments whose "truth" is subject to contestation. Indeed, we might go so far as to draw (somewhat dubious) parallels with the atom, whose nucleus consists of complex particles, surrounded by a cloud of electrons whose precise location is always uncertain (here Heisenberg is appropriate). The climate episteme has become, in some sense, what the broader public "knows" about climate change, and such knowledge seems to motivate some number of that public to action, much of which is patterned on similar actions elsewhere.

As we have discovered, however, and as the chapters in this volume illustrate, the particularity of place and people means that scientific knowledge cannot be applied indiscriminately in terms of cause and effect. Biodiversity may be threatened around the world, but *how* and *why* it is threatened in specific places is quite particular. Climate change may be a global phenomenon, but how it plays out here and there will depend on any number of factors that are not global. Moreover, given the unavoidable imbrication of the social with its bio-geophysical environment—indeed, in the *shaping* of that environment—it is almost impossible to act in general ways without encountering significant obstacles. Neither people nor nature respond willingly to force.

Such considerations raise a number of questions that are addressed, if not wholly answered, in this book's chapters. First, and most obvious: what is the role and place of knowledge and expertise in environmental governance? And how is knowledge, itself a product of social power (and relations), to be wielded in a way that does not simply reproduce those structures, hierarchies, and practices that are the source of damage in the first place? Second, where do we begin to understand the multilayered nature of social and political relations in order to reorganize them in ways that address and ameliorate environmental damage? Is "global governance" feasible without "local praxis?" Can the latter accomplish greater goals in the absence of political coordination at larger scales?[1] Third, what is required to move from episteme to practice? That is, and returning to the uncertainty conundrum discussed in the Introduction, can individuals and groups be motivated to effective action (what does "effective" mean?) and how can this happen? What should they know, and what are the limits to knowledge and knowing?

Although diverse in their approaches, the chapters in this book are very focused on these questions and what we might characterize as the schism between environmental necessity and institutional feasibility—in other words, the gulf between what is needed to prevent environmental degradation and what is feasible as a policy option in the face of conflict and contestation among various social groups, on the one hand, and predominant concepts of knowledge, on the other. Thus, the same conceptual problems are highlighted from a variety of perspectives and angles, illustrating the complexity of the relationship between power, knowledge and environmental governance while also showing that the same concerns and shortcomings exist in different spaces and at different levels of organization.

Question 1: knowledge, expertise, environment

The three conceptual chapters in Part I each offer a somewhat different approach to these issues. Timothy Luke is concerned primarily with the notion of the "green state" in a local–global world (Eckersley 2004) and its conditions of possibility. He argues that the multitude of spatial identities at the core of a person's life is the key characteristic of contemporary governance in a global free market economy. Global environmental problems tend to be analyzed and addressed via policy tools that are based on "one size fits all" technocratic solutions. The green state, based on a particular form of environmentally sensitive democracy, is one example of this approach. Luke critiques, in particular, Robyn Eckersley's view, arguing that it

> is completely muddied up with most of the same ethico-political worries that one would drag up to discuss a red (socialist) state, white (conservative), purple (aristocratic), or black (fascist) state. "Environment" as site, system, setting or structure appears only an epiphenomenal or, at best, ephemeral aspect of this political effort to describe a green (ecological) state.

In this frame, nature becomes a moral issue—the "green citizen" has ethical obligations to the state and polity—rather than the spatial one that it is. In the green society, citizens represent green issues through greater equality in their social relations with nature and each other, and greater democratic accountability leads to a greener state. As Luke points out, however, the connection between greater accountability and "greenness" is not at all clear, especially if the latter is understood as moving toward the "healing" of nature. Moreover, the green state, as conceptualized by Eckersley and others, maintains nature as commodity which, in Luke's view, is the crux of the problem. What, then, is to be done? Luke argues that the hegemonic project of constructing the environment as a technocratic sphere to be managed by universal expertise must be challenged through local knowledge and practice.

Luke's chapter sets the scene for further discussion of knowledge, expertise and the environment. Andrew Karvonen and Ralf Brand approach the issue of technocracy from another angle, in a more applied and optimistic setting yet arriving at conclusions similar to Luke's. They analyze the social relations of expertise and lay knowledge as expressed through sustainability discourses.[2] In modern society—what Ulrich Beck (1992) has called "risk" society—experts (engineers, natural scientists, town planners, etc.) are trained and regarded as highly qualified in their area of knowledge, yet so narrowly specialized that they are blind to or ignorant of the social framework in which their object of knowledge is situated and into which their actions feed. The more expertise is critically acclaimed, the less holistic it becomes: "knowing everything about nothing." Moreover, expertise is challenged— when it is—not from an epistemological or post-positivist angle but, rather, by "counter-experts" who share expertise but offer contrasting interpretations of methods and data. Under these circumstances, the public perception of the sanctity of science is undermined and comes to be regarded as a matter of conflicting interests.

One salutary result of the interpretive impasse is that "informal" knowledge—which is also likely to be more participatory—has gained greater credence. As Karvonen and Brand warn

> recognition of different forms of knowledge by post-positivists highlights the tension between democratic forms of governance and technical expertise. When discussing scientific and technical problems, holders of experiential, local, or tacit knowledge are generally not granted a seat at the decision making table due to an institutional bias toward formal knowledge. As such, the possession of technical expertise has significant political implications by marginalizing those who do not subscribe to a positivist worldview and the primacy of expert opinion.

Nonetheless, they are optimistic about the possibilities of harmonization of positivist expert science with the goals of sustainable development, and argue that there are several types of expert who can bring a more reflective view to the table while still engaging with the mainstream. Karvonen and Brand call them, respectively, the outreach expert, the multidisciplinary expert, the meta-expert and the civic expert, each of whom combines expertise from different sources and can bring them together, and offer several examples in which the cooperation of different types of experts and the merging of several approaches has led to very positive policy outcomes.

Peter Jacques breaks with critiques of expertise to examine how the world ocean has been conceptualized and constructed at different times and in different places, around particular structures of law, order and power. We are accustomed to thinking about the ocean in terms of national waters and international high seas and domination by great naval powers, as territory and property. Furthermore, the commodification of the ocean—as Philip Steinberg (2001) puts it, the change from "Davy Jones' Locker to the Foot Locker"—has overwritten more organic constructions of the relationships between land and sea, people and water. This was not always so and, perhaps in response to new forms of knowledge, at least some of the world ocean has come to be seen as global common property (as articulated in the UN Convention on the Law of the Sea). This chapter contributes the importance of the historical in generating knowledge for environmental governance, and argues that power relations can be understood only if their socio-historical context is known and considered.

Thus, both Luke and Karvonen and Brand critique the positivist nature of most knowledge utilized in environmental governance. While Karvonen and Brand see hope through the rise of new types of experts who can work with old style experts, Luke's critical approach argues that only a system of governance which gives equal voice to nature *and* expert policy makers can successfully transcend existing problems. Jacques, by contrast, alerts us to the ways in which particular constructions of "problems" tend to shape both epistemology and knowledge, and the role of "histories" in these constructions.

As seen in the case studies that follow, certain threads—the radical, the reformist, the historical—form the backbone of the empirical chapters, and are reproduced throughout the book.

Question 2: space, place, relations

The second part of this book moves between the "local" and the "global," and deals with moving among "levels-of-analysis," from local to global. Indeed, in light of the complexity of social relations and structures of production and reproduction, the very notion of "levels" tends to simplify what are, in reality, intricate and tangled networks of material and ideational flows, of global epistemes, on the one hand, and physical landscapes and concrete practices, on the other. Here, the very meaning of "governance" comes into question—and reminds us of Foucault's notions of "governmentality" and "biopolitics," both of which are being applied with new interest to what has been called "global governance." Some have argued that "governance," focused as it is on institutions and control through them, elides the role of social power in global environmental politics; hence, governmentality is more appropriate, especially to the extent that it emphasizes not only rule but also rules and "self-rule" as it were.

The controversy—if there is one—has to do with the institutionalization of global governmentality. Within the state, of course, there is government, with all its appurtenances, laws, legislatures, agencies and so on, to manage the population. Outside of the states, the situation is not quite so clear. More positivist approaches try to measure power, numbers, flows, and so on, and argue that this constitutes governance; others bemoan the "legitimacy gap" arising from the lack of institutionalization. Neither has much use for social theory, whatever its provenance.

Ulrich Brand, consequently, posits an "internationalized state" to explain the global governance of biodiversity, applying a neo-Poulantzian historical-materialist state theory to analyze its role in relation to societal developments, norms and identities—but also to see the state as a contradictory unit of various apparatuses, policies and discourses. As Brand writes,

> Poulantzas argues ... that social forces and their strategies, political and social struggles as well as the relations of social forces are constitutive for capitalist societies and therefore necessary to consider for an adequate understanding of the state. ... [It] is not just the condensation of societal power relations but the *material* condensation of it. This means that it has its own materiality (i.e. apparatuses), and changes in the relations between forces need to fit into the materiality of the different apparatuses.

What this suggests is that the internationalized state is not an entity unto itself, as many have imagined a world state might be, nor is it divorced from national governments—"which are themselves material condensations"—as some theorists of global governance have suggested. Rather, it is a site of struggle, action and effect among the myriad social forces that constitute human society. This site—or space—is not, however, anarchic. It is rule-governed and a site in which hegemony is at work.

But what does this mean for global environmental governance? Brand sees the internationalized state and its power relations as they relate to the question of knowledge and hegemony as the root cause of disturbed nature–society relations. As Brand shows in his discussion of biodiversity policy, the struggle for the intellectual products of nature takes place through an intricate architecture of property rights. These are, on the one hand, "part of a comprehensive and hegemonic state project" that is, on the other hand, effectuated though a system of international "material condensations" (or what others might call regimes or international institutions), such as the Convention on Biological Diversity, the World Trade Organization, and the Trade-Related Aspects of Intellectual Property Rights (TRIPS). These are not uncontested, but in embedding a market-based approach to nature–society relations, they simply perpetuate the root causes of environmental degradation. And it is exactly this internationalized state that Luke sees as the root of the structural problem, namely the commodification of nature or, in post-Fordist terms, the appropriation of nature. Brand's chapter thus takes up and develops the historical and radical perspectives offered in the conceptual part of the book, by identifying the role of the internationalized state as one of the major structural sources of unequal knowledge access and decision making power.

Christoph Görg and Felix Rauschmayer argue that the question of scale and its underlying social relations of power and hierarchy, have been under-represented in the literature. Multi-level governance (MLG) approaches normally take as given different levels of interacting governance—the European Union offers such an example—but are silent on how these levels are produced as well as on their historical significance. Analyses therefore underestimate or often simply neglect processes of scaling up and scaling down decision making, especially through the strengthening or weakening of existing levels and/or the construction of new levels. Consequently, MLG approaches often miss the associated impacts on policy making. This is exactly where a critical politics of scale becomes important.

Based on the example of the Millennium Assessment, Görg and Rauschmayer show that governance approaches, by focusing on social relations, tend to ignore nature–society relations and miss the ecological dimension in social relations. This is particularly the case where asymmetric power relations are in play. Although at first sight, this chapter does not seem to fit directly the theme of the volume, it nonetheless presents yet another critique of the absence of ecological considerations in environmental governance and in the production of knowledge in governance processes. Brand targets the internationalized state as the unit of analysis that is structurally problematic, while Görg and Rauschmayer complement his approach by highlighting the difficulties with governance processes in which the internationalized state, among others, is engaged. Both chapters provide persuasive arguments for what is addressed throughout the book: the disconnect between political decision making and ecological requirements. Political institutions are always social networks primarily concerned with their own representation and reproduction. The environment is represented through these institutions and, lacking agency, standing and social power, becomes a pawn in the power relations of the main actors. Only a system of governance, or a state, that could overcome this "representation deficit" would be able to engage with the assorted problems meaningfully and successfully.

Karen Litfin's chapter on the ecovillage movement moves us from the social relations of governance processes to the praxis of sustainable living at the local level. While most of the chapters in this book are about top-down power structures and how the local gets co-opted into larger, hegemonic structures, the ecovillage movement is different. The ecovillage movement can be understood as a form of constructive postmodernism, a conscious and pragmatic response to the material and ideational crisis of modernity and the failure to incorporate nature into social relations. It does not aim to change the social relations of power but still opens up possibilities for empowerment through community and innovative living practices. The main commitment of the ecovillage movement is to holism, which is exactly where it differs from mainstream nature–society relations. Its main contribution to knowledge and governance is that the ecovillagers aim to lead by example on the assumption that a successful strategy will be copied and thus spread. Ecovillage residents understand that global environmental governance is disconnected from—or intentionally disregards—ecological principles; they respond with conviction by living sustainably. Yet, the ecovillage movement is not a social movement, as commonly understood, seeking political change; rather, ecovillages are "condensations" of a particular episteme that leads by example. Thus, although Litfin's chapter, and the ecovillage movement, do not directly challenge the relationship between power, knowledge and governance, or engage in political struggles that do not/cannot resolve the tension between society and ecological considerations, they do speak quietly to the human mind as a rational alternative to the existing problematic state of affairs, offering an opportunity to live with a lifestyle that quietly demonstrates alternatives.

The three chapters of Part II approach the problem of universal knowledge use and unequal power relations in global environmental governance from a variety of angles and critical perspectives, yet manage to speak with one voice about disempowerment of alternative approaches to environment–society relations. Litfin's ecovillage chapter is, however, unique here, presenting an actually existing example of a lived challenge to orthodoxy in a framework that deliberately sidesteps both activism and any other efforts to contest mainstream thinking and practice. Indeed, it is worth considering what might be the linkages or relationship between the ecovillage and Brand's

"internationalized state" or Görg and Rauschmayer's "multi-level governance." Can the kind of "local ecological sovereignty" proposed by the ecovillage example replace or trump the global governmentality that seeks to
squeeze all shapes into round holes?

Question 3: theory, policy, practice

The third (and final) part of this book examines the relationship between
global governance (or governmentality) and local outcomes, through a set of
situated case studies. Here, we see three instances in which international
regimes, deploying expert knowledge and working on behalf of the internationalized state, attempt to shape social structures and behavior so as to
generate outcomes favorable, in these instances, to global capital. It would be
too generous to argue that the state's management efforts have been, historically, directed toward the interests of people rather than profit (Scott 1998). The
broad move, however, in recent decades, toward enclosure of public commons,
privatization of public goods and services, and creation of new forms of
property rights—sometimes called "neoliberalism"—reflects a search for new
commodity frontiers and accumulation opportunities, often at cost to those
who held prior forms of "property rights" to said resources.

Recent cases of water privatization programs are exemplary in this respect,
seeming to trade off lower-quality public utilities providing water at low cost
for more "reliable" service at much higher prices. Water privatization is the
result of neoliberal policies that favor the creation of markets, even in the
utilities sector in developing countries, and has been described consensually
as the "best policy option for the South" at the 2002 World Summit on
Sustainable Development in Johannesburg. Privatization is nothing new:
During the nineteenth century, urban waterworks were often developed by
private parties, with supply directed only toward those who could afford it.
Industrial interests and public health advocates lobbied and organized to
extend water provision more widely, establishing municipal agencies whose
sole responsibility was meeting the water needs of a city's residents. A century
later, the public resources required to maintain water supply infrastructure is
lacking, and private ownership is widely regarded as the only way to repair
and maintain antiquated systems. Yet, there is a trade-off: capital is not free
and repayment can come only from users. When the latter are poor, there are
limits to the costs they can bear.

Michael Goldman analyzes this dilemma, with reference, in particular, to
the involvement of the World Bank, and the consequences for the world's
poor. He argues that neoliberal principles are not the progeny of Margaret
Thatcher or Ronald Reagan, but appeared first in early policies of the World
Bank, as prescriptive tools for poverty alleviation. Today, the panacea of privatization is accepted even by many nongovernmental organizations, such as
WaterAid and Environmenal Defense. As a "solution," water privatization is
usually formulated by a diverse group of actors that includes government

officials, civil society networks, global governance actors and industry representatives. The composition of such "expert" networks makes a difference, inasmuch as they tend to be guided by efficiency (and accumulation) considerations rather than effective plans to overcome poverty. Often, projects utilize "public–private partnerships" to raise capital—governments will authorize bonds, corporations will receive the proceeds and pay the (usually wealthy) bondholders—but this is done to allay the latter's concerns rather than to address the interests of the local poor. Because private entities seek to make profits as well as to pay bondholders—bond redemption is off in the distant future—there is always a risk that the poor will refuse to pay new, often extortionate rates for what was, previously, almost free if only intermittently available. Water privatization offers yet another example of how power relations favor expedient solutions over the needs of affected social groups. The disempowered poor in developing countries thus fare no better than the environment—both are bereft of representation.

Tim Forsyth takes issue with the global "deforestation regime" and the growing trend of planting of trees in developing countries in exchange for carbon emission offsets and credits. He demonstrates that the expertise underlying such policy tools is highly contested—once again, how certain can we be that trees will mature and remain in place for their 60–100-year lifetime, and be replaced?—and suffers, too, from a democratic deficit—who in the target countries are asked what they want? Instead of this, forest expertise in relation to the field of global climate change seems to be based not on a diversity of norms but, rather, on a fixed set of agreed principles and practices to be applied everywhere. Forsyth finds this problematic because it involves more than just reconciliation of different or conflicting claims to expertise. Rather, what is required is a deeper and more historically rooted societal understanding of forests, one that reflects existential relations between society and forest. He proposes a "coproduction" approach as the best vehicle to understanding and evaluating democratic environmental expertise. This would ask which social norms a global society desires to govern human relations with forests, and which social forces or groups are to be empowered (or disempowered) through this approach. Coproduction would involve simultaneous evaluation of facts and norms, in acknowledgment of their connection. Forsyth's paper illustrates the contrasting expert-based and sociological approaches to the environment very clearly, and connects to Luke's and Jacques' chapters as a further illustration of their arguments.

Finally, Adam Fagan takes issue with the policy tool of "capacity building" for the environment, focusing on the ways in which civil society, in this case in Bosnia, is coopted into wider multilateral strategies such as those addressed by Ulrich Brand's and Christoph Görg and Felix Rauschmayer's chapters earlier in this book. International aid directed at empowering local environmental organizations and helping them build deeper relations with the communities they aim to represent, is targeted primarily toward the strengthening of environmental governance as it links to the concerns of powerful states and interests. As Fagan puts it,

> the core assumption on which the provision of such assistance is based is that NGOs require the transfer of organizational management know-how to make a more effective input within policy processes, professionalize their operations, obtain donor revenue and successfully manage project grants.

The core argument of the chapter is that such a manifestation of global–local linkage has less to do with "new" governance and the empowerment of environmental actors and communities, and more to do with external governance and, in particular, the conditionality governing the accession of the former socialist states into the EU.

Capacity-building thus becomes an exercise in environmental streamlining and modeling state–civil society relations along Western lines, rather than developing locally appropriate and robust environment–society relations. Indeed, this is yet another example of Luke's point that a more accountable and democratic society is not necessarily a greener society, and also demonstrates that, by itself, local empowerment is not enough to mainstream green knowledge and green forms of governance.

Does anyone have any answers?

The lessons and conclusions to be drawn from this collection on power and knowledge in environmental governance are, we would argue, twofold. First, despite widespread assumptions that the increasingly transnational nature of global environmental politics will lead to a more inclusive power base, decision making and agenda setting policies and processes remain driven by a top-down governmentality perspective. The forms of knowledge used and applied in global environmental governance very much reflect this form of management. Several chapters offer possible ways to overcome this top-down dimension, notably Karvonen and Brand's alternative experts and Litfin's ecovillages, which attempt to bypass such governance altogether. Other chapters have critiqued this power inequity, and attempted to account for it. Second, regardless of debates on the democratization of society and a resulting greening of society, the chapters in this volume have made clear that more inclusive social relations do not, by themselves, improve nature–society relations, nor do they necessarily foster greater ecological consciousness in global environmental governance.

In reaching these conclusions, the authors and this book present a powerful case for bringing to the forefront of a global environmental politics of the twenty-first century two dimensions: first, serious and sustained attention to power and inequality; second, a focus on environmentally effective rather than institutionally successful forms of knowledge. Whether incorporation of these two elements would constitute reform or radical change, we cannot say; that their incorporation would begin to make real differences in protecting both nature and society, we do not doubt.

Notes

1 The anarchistic approach to local politics tends to look a lot like the idealized market: coordination without regulation. Even the simplest, most local markets, however, are the product of social regulation.
2 Over the past decade, "sustainability" has become both an episteme and a discourse that encompasses a number of more narrowly construed frameworks, including energy, resources, climate change, biodiversity, and oceans. In some sense, it represents a return to holistic thinking, although not in a coherent systems analysis fashion.

References

Beck, Ulrich (1992) *Risk Society*, London: Sage.

Eckersley, Robin (2004) *The Green State: Rethinking Democracy and Sovereignty*, Cambridge, MA: MIT Press.

Foucault, Michel (1980) *Power/Knowledge: Selected Interviews and Other Writings 1972–1977*, edited by Colin Gordon, London: Harvester.

Ruggie, John Gerard (1993) "Territoriality and Beyond: Problematizing Modernity in International Relations," *International Organization*, 47(1): 139–74.

Scott, James C. (1998) *Seeing Like a State: How Certain Schemes to Improve the Human Condition Have Failed*, New Haven, CT: Yale University Press.

Steinberg, Philip (2001) *The Social Construction of the Ocean*, Cambridge: Cambridge University Press.

Stone, Christopher D. (1972) *Should Trees Have Standing? Toward Legal Rights For Natural Objects*, Oxford: Oxford University Press.

———(1996) *Should Trees Have Standing? And Other Essays on Law, Morals, and the Environment*, Dobbs Ferry, NY: Oceana Publications.

Index